Scottish Mountaineering Club
District Guide Books

THE NORTHERN HIGHLANDS

General Editor: MALCOLM SLESSER

SCOTTISH MOUNTAINEERING CLUB
DISTRICT GUIDE BOOKS

THE
Northern Highlands

by Tom Strang

THE SCOTTISH MOUNTAINEERING TRUST
EDINBURGH

First published in Great Britain in 1970 by
THE SCOTTISH MOUNTAINEERING TRUST
369 High Street, Edinburgh, 1

First Edition   1924
Second Edition   1936
Third Edition   1953
First Edition New Series 1970
reprinting history excluded

Designed for the Scottish Mountaineering Trust by
West Col Productions

WHOLSESALE DISTRIBUTORS
West Col Productions
1 Meadow Close
Goring on Thames
Reading Berks RG8 OAP

SBN 901516 42 2

Set in Monotype Plantin Series 110 and Grotesque 215
and printed in Great Britain by Cox & Wyman Ltd,
London, Reading & Fakenham

CONTENTS

ILLUSTRATIONS

LINE DIAGRAMS

8

FOREWORD

THIS Guide to the NORTHERN HIGHLANDS is not only new, it is comprehensive in a way that earlier editions could not have hoped to achieve. Readers of all sorts will find here detail and advice on a level and with an authority that has never hitherto been applied to this region. Tom Strang's clear delight in the Northern Highlands emerges from every page. His understanding of background and the social history makes it possible for the reader not just to see the area in present day terms but as it once was – and could be.

It is a pleasure to take this opportunity to record the Scottish Mountaineering Club's thanks to the author for the enormous effort and care he has put into this publication.

Malcolm Slesser, *Glasgow, March 1970.*

ACKNOWLEDGEMENTS

I wish to acknowledge my indebtedness to the Editors of the earlier editions of this guide-book, and to the many others who contributed towards their making; also to all those who have so willingly given assistance with information, and in many other ways, to make this new edition possible. Special thanks are due to I. G. Rowe, North Rock Guide Editor, and to Dr T. W. Patey, both of whom have provided a wealth of detail on climbing routes throughout the Northern Highlands and have given invaluable advice on many points.

I am particularly grateful to all who made available their photographs to help illustrate the text, and to J. Lunday, for his painstaking work in producing line drawings; also to those officials of the Red Deer Commission and of the Nature Conservancy who provided so much specialized information.

The Cambridge University Mountaineering Club and the Corriemulzie Mountaineering Club published interim guides in 1958 and 1966 respectively, both of which provide a rich source of information on the districts covered. To the editors, M. J. O'Hara (C.U.M.C.), and the late P. N. L. Tranter and the late A. R. M. Park (C.M.C.), I am deeply indebted.

Finally, I would like to express my gratitude to Dr Malcolm Slesser, General Guide Books Editor, for his help, encouragement and forbearance throughout.

INTRODUCTION

Area

The area covered by this guide to the Northern Highlands of Scotland includes the mountains of the northern half of Ross-shire, the whole of Sutherland and the south-west corner of Caithness.

The southern boundary follows for its greater part the line of the Dingwall – Kyle of Lochalsh Railway, that is from Dingwall at the head of the Cromarty Firth by way of Garve and Strath Ban to Achnasheen and westwards by Glen Carron to the Atlantic seaboard.

The Mountains

The Northern Highlands contain some of the most spectacular mountain scenery on the Scottish Mainland, characterised by the comparative remoteness of the area as a whole and by the isolation of the individual peaks.

It is worth noting that of the twenty-one regions of outstanding beauty described by Mr W. H. Murray in his survey for the National Trust for Scotland – *Highland Landscape* – six are located in the area of the guide. These are – Applecross, Ben Damph and Coulin Forests, Torridon, Loch Maree, Strathnasheallag and Fisherfield Forests, Inverpolly and Glen Canisp Forests.

The area is covered by Sections 10, 11, 12 and 13 of Munro's Tables, which list 32 separate mountains over 3000 ft. – marked by asterisk in the chapter headings – and 32 subsidiary tops.

In addition, sections 10, 11, 12 and 13 of J. Rooke Corbett's Tables lists 41 mountains over 2500 ft. and under 3000 ft. Where it is appropriate, these also are included in the chapter headings.

Those lesser mountains, unlisted by either Munro or Corbett, but which are nevertheless of special interest, are also covered in the text of the Guide.

Maps

Six-inch O.S. – Although most Scottish Sheets still belong to the old 'County' edition dating from the beginning of the century, post-Second War sheets based on the National Grid are gradually being completed. Except for some of the coastal sheets, these are square, with sides representing 5 kilometres. Sheets are available for most of the area of the guide. They have little value, however, to hill-walkers.

Two-and-a-Half-inch O.S. – (1:25,000) – There is limited coverage in the North of Sutherland and part of central Ross-shire and it is advisable to check from time to time which new sheets have been published.

One-inch O.S. (Seventh Series) – These are essential. The following sheets apply to the Guide: No. 25 (Portree), No. 26 (Loch Carron), No. 27 (Strathpeffer), No. 22 (Dornoch), No. 21 (Bonar Bridge), No. 20 (Ullapool), No. 19 (Gairloch), No. 15 (Helmsdale), No. 14 (Lairg), No. 13 (Lochinver/Loch Assynt), No. 10 (Tongue), No. 9 (Cape Wrath).

Quarter-inch O.S. – (1:250,000) – The whole of the Northern Highlands is covered by sheet No. 3 of the Quarter-inch to the Mile Series. It is very convenient for gaining an overall impression of the area.

Bartholomew – Half-inch to the Mile – Contoured. – These provide a useful supplement to the more essential One-inch Map, and are especially useful for general planning of expeditions. The contours are shown by colour code at 250 ft. intervals. The area of the Northern Highlands is covered by the following sheets: Sheet 54 – Torridon; Sheet 55 – Moray Firth; Sheet 58 – Cape Wrath; Sheet 59 – Dornoch Firth; Sheet 60 – Caithness.

In the text, the location of places is often given as a National Grid reference, relating to the One-inch O.S. Maps. These are marked as (for example) NG.276206.

Transport

Rail travel is limited to the east and south border of the area and once one leaves the more populated eastern strip, public road services are very infrequent.

The road system in the area is now a good one, with improvements all the time, and does not at all justify the fearful travellers' tales which one often hears in connection with Highland roads. Private car is still the most convenient method of travel to and between suitable centres and for those who prefer cycling, some of the better kept cross-country paths are possible short-cuts.

For those without their own form of transport, it is possible, but less convenient, to use the system of local transport to travel between centres and the new publications by the Highland and Island Development Board – *Getting around in the Highlands and Islands* – give fully comprehensive and up-to-date information on all forms of travel within the region. These include ferries, buses, local hirers, and planes and trains where applicable. The volumes covering this region are No. 3 – Inverness-shire and Easter Ross; No. 2 – Caithness and Sutherland; No. 4 – Skye and Approaches. They are obtainable, price 6d., from the H.I.D.B., Castle Wynd, Inverness, or from the County Tourist Associations of Ross-shire, Sutherland and Caithness. Highly Recommended.

Accommodation

Accommodation throughout the area has increased considerably with the growth of the tourist trade and will continue to improve.

Hotels

On the whole, the most conveniently located hotels from the climber's point of view have become firmly established favourites with the fishing fraternity, and are usually well booked up over the summer months. They tend to be seasonal, being closed during the winter. It is safer to check beforehand to save disappointment.

With few exceptions the hospitality is first class and the food excellent.

A comprehensive register of Hotels and Boarding-houses is to be found in the Scottish Tourist Board Publication – 'Where to Stay in Scotland', obtainable from the S.T.B., 2 Rutland Place, Edinburgh, 1, or 2 Academy Street, Inverness.

Bed and Breakfast

Bed and Breakfast accommodation can usually be found close to most of the mountain areas and generally the prices are reasonable and the standard good. Even where no sign is displayed advertising it, it is worth while enquiring as most of the local population are now prepared to accommodate the overnight visitor.

The most useful sources of information are the excellent and up-to-date lists published by the various local Tourist Associations. These can be obtained from the Local County Development Officers at the following addresses:

County Offices, Wick, Caithness.
County Offices, Dornoch, Sutherland.
County Offices, Dingwall, Ross-shire.

These lists cover Guest-houses, Bed and Breakfast and Caravan Hires. Caravan and Camp-site information will also be supplied on demand.

Hostels

The Scottish Youth Hostels Association have two useful publications giving full details of Hostel provision in the North. These are: *The Northern Highlands* and the *S.Y.H.A. Annual Handbook*. Hostels tend to be concentrated along the North and West Coastline. Many of them are fairly small and require prior booking and it is necessary to check each season on winter closing dates.

Bothies

The area abounds in disused steadings and croft houses in various degrees of repair, which are often well situated from the mountaineer's point of view. Some of those are already recognised climbing bothies and their use has been authorised by the estate-owner with few restrictions. Others have been used on dubious authority and consequently local relationships have suffered.

Where bothies are mentioned in the text, this does not imply permission to use, and in the interests of good local relationship it is emphasised that permission should be obtained in advance.

The Mountain Bothy Association have done good work here as in other regions in acquiring permission and reconditioning where possible many old buildings of this type and have a fairly comprehensive location list obtainable by members only. All information concerning this growing Association can be obtained from The Secretary, Mountain Bothies' Association, (Bernard J. Heath), 7 Jim Lane, Marsh, Huddersfield, Yorks.

Camp-sites

The Northern Highlands still abound in pleasant uncluttered

camp-sites, a fast disappearing phenomenon. Where these are near habitations, it is diplomatic to seek permission – this is seldom withheld. On certain estates, care should be taken in the choice of sites during the stalking season. Camping by the roadside is becoming steadily more difficult.

Shelter-stones

In many areas there is a wide choice of natural shelter-stones to be found among the great boulder fields of Torridon Sandstones. In many cases these are both roomy, dry and comfortable and once familiarity with particular areas is gained the use of a tent becomes unnecessary.

Hill Tracks and Drove Roads

The intricate network of hill-tracks which covers the area of the Northern Highlands provides the mountain traveller with the key to a vast unspoiled wonderland of rolling moorland, lonely glens, dark hill lochans, and isolated peaks.

The development of lines of communication in a wild mountainous region is greatly influenced by natural physical obstacles and consequently every hill-track had a sound reason for its existence. The Highland population in the distant past can hardly be said to have been road-minded. The frequency of inter-clan foray and cattle reiving often made inaccessibility desirable, and their own clandestine routes would hardly have been advertised.

According to a local minister, writing the Statistical Account of his parish at the end of the eighteenth century – 'Travelling it must be owned is difficult and disagreeable, there being no roads, but such as the feet of men and cattle have made' – and of the country as a whole – 'The most inland parts are nothing but a vast group of dreadful mountains, with their summits piercing the clouds, and divided only by deep and narrow valleys, whose declivities are so rugged and steep, as to be dangerous to travellers not furnished with guides.'

As in all mountainous country, the tracks followed the most natural line along the driest ground of the straths, avoiding peaks and crossing watersheds by the lower bealachs at the head of glens. In this country of a thousand lochs, water supplies were of great importance and chosen with care especially along those routes which were to become established as drove-roads.

Droving and the subsequent development of the main drove roads which were to form the basis of the present day main communication system of the area were a natural outcome of the Highland way of life. By its physical formation and climatic pattern, the area, like other parts of the Highlands is a vast natural grazing land, and in the days before the advent of 'The Great Sheep', cattle was the main tangible form of wealth. The system of Land Tenure led to a great proportion of the population having grazing rights with resultant over-stocking. The primitive and limited form of agriculture practised made it essential that stocks should be drastically reduced annually since it was impossible to produce enough winter feeding for the whole of the summer herds. There was always a demand for cattle in the south; cattle provided their own transport to the marts; consequently droving was a natural economic outcome and remained so for nearly 400 years until the latter part of the nineteenth century.

Droving seemed to suit the nature of the Highlander with his background of clan forays and reiving; the ability to endure hardship over great distance was bred into them. A Memorandum covering the Highlands in 1746 speaks of cattle thieving among the people as – 'the Principal source of their barbarity, cruelty, cunning and revenge [which] trains them to the use of arms, love of plunder, thirst for revenge'.

Scott's assessment of the Highlander's aptitude to the craft of droving is more sympathetic – 'the Highlanders in particular are masters of this difficult trade of droving, which seems to suit them as well as the trade of War. It affords exercises for all their habits of patient endurance and active exertion. They are required to know perfectly the drove roads which lie over the wildest tracks of the country, and to avoid as much as possible the highways which distress the feet of the bullocks and the turnpikes which annoy the spirit of the drover; whereas on the broad grey or green track which leads across the pathless moor, the herd not only may move at ease and without taxation, but, if they mind their business, may pick up a mouthful of food on the way.'

These 'broad grey or green tracks' were the economic links from the North and West to the East and South. Beauly Tryst – Faill na Manachaim – was the greatest market for cattle from Caithness, Sutherland and Ross-shire, and remained so until 1820 when the mart was moved to the neighbouring township of Muir of Ord.

Here too converged the cattle herds from the Outer Island which were brought by sea then often thrown overboard to swim ashore at Poolewe, Aultbea, Gruinard and Ullapool on the western seaboard of Ross-shire.

Droving has long passed from the economic life of the area, but many of the present roads still follow the line of the old drovers' routes through the glens, in part if not in whole. The present road from Poolewe to Kinlochewe takes the south shore of Loch Maree while the old drove road followed the north shore and can still be traced. From Gruinard, the drovers' route by way of Strath na Sheallag and the Fannichs to Achnasheen can still be followed by well-marked tracks. But the road which marks the southern boundary of the guide from Loch Carron to Dingwall follows exactly the line taken by the drove road as does the present road to Ullapool and the west and from Bonar Bridge on the A9 to both Lochinver and Laxford Bridge in the north-west of Sutherland.

Those tracks which provided lateral communication between Strath and Strath from west to east across the line of glen and mountain were never developed to the same extent as the drove routes. With local needs and habits continually changing, many no longer serve their original purpose but although no longer used to the same extent as before, they can still be followed, and provide for the walker both access to mountains and worthwhile expeditions in themselves.

Many of the more remote tracks are partially grown over and neglected but those which lie in the sporting estates are usually well-maintained for stalking purposes, frequently marked by cairns and in some cases cyclable for part of their way. This is especially true in the north of Sutherland and in Wester Ross.

To list in detail the numerous cross-country tracks still in use would detract from the pleasure of exploration. The walker may choose a combination to suit conditions and personal ability. It will be the policy in the text to indicate tracks of particular use and cross-country routes of special interest and beauty.

Rock, Snow and Ice Climbing

The potential of the Northern Highlands as a climbing area has long been realised but until comparatively recently serious exploration has been limited and many promising crags were virtually untouched. The remoteness of the area as a whole was one of the biggest drawbacks and with little information filtering out, few climbers were tempted to explore. Those who did were amply rewarded, and the increase in activity throughout the region over the past twenty years has produced a wealth of new routes of all grades. Perhaps the most fruitful 'finds' in this new era have been Foinaven in the Reay Forest in the north of Sutherland, Ben Dearg in the Inverlael Forest and the Fannichs both in Ross-shire. While there is still scope for further exploration the chances of finding any major new crag have rapidly diminished.

The new series of Northern Highlands Rock-Climbing Guide Books being published by the Scottish Mountaineering Trust now cover the area in great detail and include descriptions of the extensive list of new routes as well as of the original climbs from the earlier editions of this guide and various Club Journals. These include and expand upon the information contained in the interim Rock, Snow and Ice Guides published by the Cambridge University Mountaineering Club (1958) and the Corriemulzie Mountaineering Club (1966).

Within the text of this guide a selection of routes has been included, chosen both for their individual worth and to cater for varied abilities. Grading has been kept as uniform as possible and 'left' and 'right' refer to the climber facing the rock.

The separate winter classification is as follows:

Grade I. Straightforward, averaged-angled snow gullies, generally showing no pitches when given adequate snow cover. They may, however, present cornice difficulty.

Grade II. Pitches encountered in gullies, or gullies with high-angled or difficult cornice exits. The easier buttresses which under snow present more continuous difficulty.

Grade III. Serious climbs which should only be undertaken by parties with good experience. Reaches a technical standard of Severe.

Grade IV. Routes which are either of sustained Severe standard or climbs of higher difficulty which are too short to be classed as Grade V.

Grade V. Routes which give major expeditions and are only to be climbed when conditions are favourable. Technical standard Very Severe.

Ski-ing

There is no organised ski-ing of the 'downhill only' variety such as has developed in the older established Scottish winter sports centres, but for the ski-tourer many areas within the Northern Highlands offer excellent sport during most winters.

Ski-ing is often possible from the beginning of December to the end of March and even April, suitable slopes being reasonably sheltered from wind and weather. Snow conditions can be surprisingly good but the comparatively low level increases the chance of a quick break-up of fields following a thaw.

The most likely areas are: Ben Klibreck, Seana Bhraigh and Corriemulzie, Beinn Dearg (Ross-shire) especially from the Inverlael side, the Fannichs, the area around Forsinard north of Kinbrace on the rail line to Thurso, many of the eastern glens which stretch inland from Helmsdale down to Golspie and Ben Wyvis, which is about to be developed with ski-lift facilities.

Ben Wyvis has probably the greatest potential for proper development. The two big corries on the south-east side hold substantial snow-fields offering first-class ski-ing and detailed survey has already begun. There is reasonable access for tracked vehicles from Garbat, near Aultguish Inn on the Garve–Ullapool road and skiers can be taken to the top of the pass between Wyvis and Little Wyvis.

It is often practicable and desirable to combine ski-touring of a modest nature with winter climbing.

Cave Exploration

Opportunities in this field occur in three main areas, all in Sutherland.

Around Durness on the north coast of the county, the Smoo Cave is the largest and best known, figuring not unnaturally in several local legends concerned with the supernatural. Other exploration has been done in the sea caves at Balnakeil and further inland at Ach a'Chorrain.

At the east end of Loch Assynt near Inchnadamph, the strip of Cambrian dolomite over which has been thrust the older rocks which form the Assynt mountains, offer greater scope for investigation. The main area is along the course of the Traligill River and its tributaries with easy access from Inchnadamph hotel by track along Gleann Dubh. The main system – Cnoch nan Uamh NG.276206 – has three entrances and 1600 ft. of recorded passages and is the largest cave known in Scotland.

Slightly south, the course of the Allt nan Uamh has also been the

site of worthwhile investigation further complexes having been un-
covered. Here too occurs the famous Bone Cave – NG.269170 –
excavated in 1889 by Doctors Peach and Horne and later in 1927 by
Messrs Callender, Cree and Ritchie. These have been established as
the most northerly habitation of Palaeolithic Man in Scotland.

This area is now part of the Inchnadamph Nature Reserve and
comes under its regulations. The honorary warden can be contacted
at Stronechrubie for further information.

The most southerly of the three main cave areas occurs at Knockan
near the Sutherland border with Ross-shire. The limestone area to
the east of the villages of Elphin and Knockan is largely drained by
the Amhainn a'Chnochain which passes underground at Uamh an
Tartair – NG.217092 – above a dry waterfall. Two other pots – Uamh
Poll Eoghainn – NG.205094 and Uamh Cul Eoghainn – NG.210105
– have also been investigated and recent work in the area by members
of the Grampian Speleological group from Edinburgh anticipates the
penetration of a 'master cave' leading to a widespread underground
network.

Wild Life and Conservation

The area of the Northern Highlands provides a wide variety of
natural habitats still containing a wealth of specimens covering the
whole range of indigenous flora and fauna despite centuries of man's
misuse and depredation. They form an invaluable part of our national
heritage and have begun to receive more serious attention than
previously. Many of those areas have now become national nature
reserves under the control of the Nature Conservancy. Here preservation and ecological studies, the basis of conservation, are carried
on, and while the reserves are by no means the only areas where the
natural life of the country can be observed at close quarters, they are
usually the location of a particularly wide cross-section of species or
of some special interest.

In the area of the Guide, most of the reserves are located in the
more mountainous regions, a fact which should increase their
interest to the mountain traveller.

These reserves are located as follows:

Rasaal Reserve covers 202 acres near the head of Loch Kishorn on
the road from Loch Carron to Sheildaig, and here can be found one
of the few natural types of Ashwoods in Scotland and the most

northerly in Great Britain. The floor of the wood which is growing on limestone pavement is remarkable in that it has a peculiar hummocky surface, rich in mosses.

Beinn Eighe Reserve in the Torridon area of Wester Ross was declared in 1951 and became the first National Nature Reserve in Britain. Comprising 10,507 acres it contains one of the few remaining remnants of the old Caledonian Forest which once covered large areas of the North of Scotland. The preservation and study of this Caledonian Pinewood is one of the main projects of research carried out at Anancaun Field Station just north of Kinlochewe.

The Coille na Glas Leitire nature trail on the south shore of Loch Maree gives an opportunity to see many of the reserves features and wild-life. As well as otter, wild cat and fox, the animals of the reserve include the rarer pine marten. Deer management is carried on in liaison with neighbouring estate proprietors.

In 1967, the 14,100 acres of Torridon Estate, including some of Scotland's finest mountain scenery, was accepted in lieu of death duties by the Inland Revenue and placed under the care of the National Trust for Scotland. To this was added a few months later the 2000 acres of Alligin Shuas adjoining its western boundary.

Between them the National Trust and the Nature Conservancy control an area some 12 miles E.W. and 4 miles N.S. including Beinn Alligin, Liathach, Beinn Dearg and Beinn Eighe.

Information about the Reserve can be obtained from the warden at Anancaun Field Station and the National Trust have a caravan in Glen Torridon during the summer months.

Inverpolly Reserve on Ross-shire's northern border with Sutherland, covers 26,827 acres including 816 acres of woodland and three summits over 2000 ft. – Cul Mor, Cul Beag and Stack Polly. There is a diversity of habitats; loch, stream, bog, moorland, woodland, scree, cliffs and summits. Pine martens can be found here among the animals of the area and golden eagles can be seen. On the islands of Loch Sionascaig are untouched relics of primitive birch-hazel woodland. The reserve is rich in plant life and on the east boundary at Knockan cliff the now classical exposure of the Moine Thrust is of special attraction to the geologist. The Reserve is the second largest in size in Britain and is managed jointly by the Conservancy and the landowners. There are two wardens – one at Strathpolly and one at

Knockan Point – and while visits to the reserve are not normally restricted, contact should be made beforehand, especially in the case of parties of more than six, going on to the Drumrunie part during the stalking season – 15 July–15 October.

Inchnadamph Reserve covers 3200 acres between the east end of Loch Assynt and Ben More Assynt, the highest mountain in Sutherland. It is of great geological and botanical interest, lying as it does at the western front of an area of disturbed Durness Limestone and ringed round by outcrops of the Glencoul, Ben More and Moine thrusts.

Work on the reserve is aimed at preserving the interest of the limestone formations and at a study of the varied plant life. Peculiar to the reserve is a type of willow scrub common in Scandinavia but rare in Scotland. On the driest limestone areas Mountain Aven (Dryas Octapetala) is abundant.

The effects of traditional land-use practices – sheep grazing and rotational heather burning – are also the subject of research on the reserve.

The famous Allt nan Uamh bone caves lie within the reserve boundaries and permission to carry on any scientific work here or elsewhere on the reserve is required from the Nature Conservancy, 12 Hope Terrace, Edinburgh, 9.

Visitors to the reserve should contact the part-time warden at Stronchrubie, by Inchnadamph.

Invernaver Reserve covers 1363 acres near the mouth of the River Naver in the North of Sutherland. It is remarkable for the variety of habitats it contains within its relatively small area, including those of blown sand, and for its boreal plant communities, the finest in the North of Scotland. The mingling of species of montane and oceanic affinities is an added attraction. There is also an unusual development of Juniper scrub on peat which is within reach of the blown sand. Greenshank, Red-throated Diver, Ring Ouzel and Twites all breed within the reserve.

Handa Bird Reserve famous as a sea-bird sanctuary, is a 766 acre island lying close inshore off the N.W. coast of Sutherland, one and a half miles by sea from Tarbet and three miles N.W. of Scourie. It was established as a reserve by the Royal Society for the Protection of Birds in 1962 by agreement with the proprietors. It is renowned for its magnificent sandstone sea-cliffs rising sheer for 400 ft. while the Great Stack of Handa covered with nesting seabirds in summer poses its own peculiar problem to the rock-climber.

The island was inhabited until 1848 when potato famine influenced the seven families to emigrate to America. The ruined crofts can still be seen but the only inhabitable house is a reconditioned bothy which accommodates six.

The Warden, Mr Munro, Tarbet, conveys parties to the island by motorboat. There are no restrictions on day visits but permission to camp or to book the bothy must be made through the R.S.P.B. Office, 21 Regent Terrace, Edinburgh, 7. Only members of the society or of the Young Ornithologists Club can use the bothy, but camping is free. No dogs are allowed on the island in the interest of nesting birds.

The survey of breeding birds on the island is extensive and many others either breed or can be seen in the vicinity. A six-inch to the mile map extract of the island and detailed information sheet can be obtained from the warden by post – price 6d. – or from the Edinburgh Office.

Warden's Address – Mr A. Munro, Tarbet, Foindle, by Lairg, Sutherland. Telephone No. Scourie 26.

The classic text on the wild-life of the Northern Highlands is *The Highlands and Islands* by F. Fraser Darling and J. Morton Boyd, now published in the New Naturalist series by Collins (1964), and the following bodies also produce interesting publications on the subject.

The Nature Conservancy, 12 Hope Terrace, Edinburgh, 9.

The National Trust for Scotland, The Secretary, 5 Charlotte Square, Edinburgh, 2.

The Red Deer Commission, Elm Park, Island Bank Road, Inverness.

The Red Deer Commission

The Commission was set up under the Deer (Scotland) Act 1959 with the general functions of furthering deer conservation and control and of keeping under review all matters relating to red deer.

Of its twelve members, five represent sporting and landowning interests, five represent farming, forestry and crofting, and two represent the Nature Conservancy.

A well-equipped field staff of six works under the Field Officer on the practical work – taking census counts, calf marking and helping estates with their annual culls and the all-important work of investigating and dealing with complaints of marauding deer.

The Commission meets regularly to receive reports on the work of the field staff and to discuss all aspects of deer conservation and control. The broad problems of land use, the effects of forestry planting programmes, legislation and scientific research on red deer in Scotland all feature in its discussion. Its interests are wide and the Commission has long been aware that the sport of deer stalking often conflicts with that of mountaineering and that the addicts of each sometimes get irritated. The view of the Red Deer Commission is that, given reasonable courtesy and consideration by both sides, there is no need for such conflicts.

In an attempt to improve the situation they have published the following list of suggestions with relative background information.

First, to the hill walker, it is pointed out that shooting deer is not merely an expensive sport. The red deer is one of the finest wild animals in our island. When the last wolf in Scotland was killed, deer were left without a natural predator. But their numbers must be kept under control, otherwise the animals themselves suffer from insufficient food and are more likely to cause loss and damage on agricultural land. Hill stags are at their best for shooting only for a comparatively short period. They carry little fat until the growth of their antlers is complete, usually about mid-August; after this they rapidly gain weight until the onset of the rutting season, which reaches its climax in mid-October when most of the big stags have lost condition and their meat is of poor quality. Consequently every effort has to be made to kill the proper numbers between mid-August and mid-October.

The Commission feels, therefore, it would be in the general interest if all organisations connected with the tourist industry, and in particular those which provide information for climbers and hill walkers, would stress that those who wish to go to the hills from mid-August to mid-October should first, if possible, ascertain if stalking is being carried out in the area, and if so, whom they should contact – stalker, factor, owner or tenant – to enquire where they can go without interfering with stalking. It is hoped that most hotels, boarding houses, youth hostels and local information offices will be able to provide information on this.

On most estates no attempt is made to restrict access by walkers and climbers, except when stalking is in progress. Visitors are able to make use of the paths which saves them fatigue and enables them to cover greater distances than they could otherwise. Often these paths were made for deer-stalking, so it is not considered unreasonable to ask visitors to make enquiries before using them during the stalking season.

Owners and Tenants of deer forests and other shootings and their employees are urged by the Commission so far as is possible to meet all enquiries and requests that are courteously made. Where they cannot agree to the route which the party enquiring wishes to take they should suggest an alternative. It cannot be expected that those visitors whose requests meet a blank refusal to allow them to walk anywhere in the forest, will continue to seek permission: they can hardly be blamed if they do not consider that it is worth while. Good will is lost; they give up asking and go as they please.

Even the widest publicity in tourist pamphlets, Youth Hostels' notices and Club Journals does not reach all visitors who go to walk or climb on the hills, and in some places roadside notices could be helpful. These should be worded to seek the co-operation of the visitor by making it clear that while they are welcome to reasonable access, they are requested to call at the stalker's house before going to the hill between the dates when stalking normally starts and finishes on that estate.

Notices that are worded solely with intention of intimidating and deterring visitors seldom achieve their object.

The presence of a Youth Hostel or Climbing Club Hut on or close to a deer forest is apt to be regarded as a serious disadvantage by stalking interests. This need not, and should not, be the case: it has been found in several places that where relations are good between the local stalkers, hostel wardens, and members of climbing clubs, there is seldom any cause for complaint.

Geology

The Mountains of the Northern Highlands fall naturally into three main groups, according to the nature of the rocks of which they are composed:

(1) Unaltered or Slightly Altered Sedimentary Rocks – Old Red Sandstone, Cambrian Quartzite, Torridonian Sandstone.

(2) Metamorphic Rocks – Archaean Gneiss, Schists, Slates, Quartzites, etc., of the Central Highlands.
(3) Igneous Rocks – Granite and Porphyry.

SEDIMENTARY ROCKS

1. *Old Red Sandstone* – This formation rarely attains any considerable height above sea-level. Morven (2313 ft.) in Caithness is one of the few exceptions. It is composed of conglomerate arranged in regular and nearly horizontal layers, is smooth and conical in outline, and offers few if any features of interest to the climber.

More remarkable are the deep and narrow gorges, with vertical walls rising in some cases to a height of nearly 200 ft., that have been cut by streams along the parallel joints of Old Red Conglomerate. The best known of these is the Black Rock of Novar on the way to Ben Wyvis.

Caithness: Morven and Maiden Pap.
Sutherland: Ben Griam.

2. *Cambrian Quartzite* – This rock is slightly altered and hardened siliceous sandstone and follows the same line of country as the Torridonian Sandstone. It usually occurs as a thin capping on the mountains of the latter formation stealing up the slopes to the summits, or in isolated patches crowning the warm red-browns and purples of the underlying sandstone. In only a few cases does the quartzite compose the whole or greater part of a mountain. The notable examples of this are Foinaven and Arkle in the Reay Forest of Sutherland, the eastern peaks and ridges of Beinn Eighe in Torridon, and in some of the hills of the Coulin and Achnashellach Forests.

The rock is hard, splintery and full of joints, and consequently breaks up readily into sharp angular fragments of all sizes which stream down the hillsides in long scree slopes. Where the angle is especially steep, the instability of these screes can make traverse or ascent a slow, awkward operation and care has to be taken not to send the whole slope in motion. Where the angle is too steep to retain the debris, precipitous escarpments such as those that surround the northern corries of Beinn Eighe are formed and these are usually shattered and untrustworthy. Instability is the prevailing character of the quartzite mountains of the west, a fact which should be borne well in mind when climbing on them.

Sutherland:	Meall Sgribhinn	Beinn Spionnaidh
	Foinaven	Arkle
	Glas Bheinn	Braebag
Ross-shire:	Beinn Eighe	Sgurr Dubh
	Hills of Coulin and Achnashellach Forests	

3. *Torridonian* – There are no mountain forms in Scotland more striking in appearance than those found in the belt of Torridonian Sandstone that stretches along the western coasts of Sutherland and Ross-shire from Cape Wrath to Applecross and Loch Carron.

The regular parallelism of the beds, and the steady dip of the gently inclined and often horizontal strata, combine to produce that architectural character for which they are so remarkable: long lines of mural precipice which sometimes, as on Suilven, almost encircle the mountain; rounded and terraced bastions, and pinnacled ridges, are constant features of these mountains. The summits vary greatly in character, from the flat top of Beinn Bhan in Applecross, to the spiry cones of An Teallach or the sharp serrated ridges of An Fasarinen on Liathach and the smaller Stack Polly.

The terraced cliffs are cut at frequent intervals by vertical joints which give rise to steep gullies. These often form channels for the streams that rise in the higher corries and pour down the face of the mountain in a succession of waterfalls. When dry, the gullies form chimneys of excessive steepness, usually terminating in long stone shoots. The climbing, where it is not impossible, is good. The rock is firm and reliable and rarely slippery, while holds and ledges are plentiful, though the latter may be encumbered with loose rocks fallen from above. Suitable belay points, however, tend to be scarce.

The pinnacles afford plenty of good rock-scrambling, and chimneys, presenting every degree of steepness and difficulty, abound.

Sutherland:	Quinag (two peaks capped with Cambrian Quartzite)	
	Canisp (capped with Cambrian Quartzite)	
	Suilven	
Ross-shire:	Cul Mor (peaks capped with Cambrian Quartzite)	
	Cul Beag	Ben More Coigach group

Ross-shire:	Stack Polly	
	An Teallach (three eastern	
	spurs capped with Cambrian	
	Quartzite)	
	Sail Mhor	Beinn a'Chlaidheimh
	Beinn Tarsuinn	Beinn Dearg Mhor
	Slioch	Mullach Coire Mhic
		Fhearchair
	Sgurr Ban	Beinn Eighe
	Liathach	Beinn Dearg
	Beinn Alligin	Baosbheinn
	Beinn Damph	Beinn Bhan (Apple-cross)
	Sgorr Ruadh	Maol Chean-Dearg
	Beinn Liath Mhor	Fuar Tholl

METAMORPHIC ROCKS

The great majority of the Scottish mountains belong to this group. The Archaean or Lewisian Gneiss occupies a considerable area in the west of Sutherland and Ross-shire and forms the whole of the Outer Hebrides. On the mainland it seldom rises to any great height. Ben More Assynt and Ben Stack in Sutherland and the fine group of mountains on the north side of Loch Maree are the most noteworthy belonging to this formation.

The gnarled and corrugated nature of this ancient rock, and the absence of drift from the lower slopes, give a peculiarly rugged character to its hills. Their sides are usually broken up into a succession of rounded bosses and craggy steeps; but occasionally fine vertical precipices are developed such as those that fall from Beinn Lair to the Fionn Loch. The exceeding toughness and uneven surface of the gneiss make the climbing everywhere reasonably safe.

LEWISIAN OR ARCHAEAN GNEISS

Sutherland:	Ben Stack	Ben More Assynt
Ross-shire:	A'Mhaighdean	Beinn Airidh Charr
	Beinn Lair	Beinn A'Chaisgein Mor
	Glasbheinn	Sgurr a'Gharaidgh
Highland Schists:	(Flaggy gneisses, Mica schists, Quartz schists, etc. – of indeterminate age)	

Sutherland:	Ben Hope (Mica and Hornblende Schists)	
	Ben Hee	Klibreck
	Ben Armine	Meall Horn
Ross-shire:	Fionn Bheinn	Moruisg
	Beinn Dearg	Hills of Freevater Forest
	Ben Wyvis	

The Fannichs

Sgurr Mor ⎫
A'Chailleach ⎬ Mica Schist
Sgurr Breac ⎭

Beinn Liath Mhor ⎫
Sgurr nan Clach Geala ⎬ Mica and Quartz Schists
Meall A'Chrasgaidh ⎭

IGNEOUS ROCKS

The only Igneous rock in the district is the granite of Ben Loyal and Strath Halladale.

| *Sutherland*: | Ben Loyal |
| | Beinn Stumanadh |

Mountain Rescue Provision

The Ross and Sutherland Police Mountain Rescue Team, based at the Police Headquarters in Dingwall should be contacted in the event of any mountain accident in the area of the guide. Telephone No. – Dingwall 2222.

They maintain a fully-equipped rescue vehicle and will, if necessary take the responsibility of calling in the Mountain Rescue Team from R.A.F. Kinloss who also operate in this area.

In addition, a civilian volunteer team operate from Dounreay, by Thurso, and they too are on call by the Police.

Help is always obtained from local sources in the case of emergency and it is expected that any climbers in the vicinity will accept the traditional obligation to offer their services to the person in charge of the operation.

Mountain Rescue Posts in the area where equipment is held:

KINLOCHEWE   Police Station   Kinlochewe 222

ULLAPOOL	Police Station	Ullapool 17
GARVE	Police Station	Garve 222
ELPHIN SCHOOL	Unattended (key available from Suilven Guest House)	Elphin 239

First Aid Posts – Where the British Red Cross Society hold their normal first-aid equipment:

AULTGUISH INN by Garve	POLICE STATION, GAIRLOCH
KINLOCHEWE HOTEL	AULTBEA HOTEL
ACHNASHEEN HOTEL	DUNDONNEL HOTEL
DISTRICT NURSE'S HOUSE, LOCHCARRON	AULTNAMAIN HOTEL

N.B. – *Check locally, the location of a post is sometimes changed.*

Public Telephones – It is sensible to locate their position from your map before setting out. They are not too frequent, and if you find none accessible to the area you intend to climb in, there may be a private phone more readily available.

Doctors – Nearly all of the medical practitioners in the area are involved in extensive country practices and are not always immediately available. In an emergency contact is best made through the police to save time.

The Mountain Rescue Committee Handbook – *Mountain Rescue and Cave Rescue* is published annually and contains much valuable information.

For queries or difficulties over organisation of Mountain Rescue in Scotland, contact the Mountain Rescue Committee of Scotland. Hon. Secretary, Mr Hamish MacInnes, B.E.M., Allt-na-Righ, Glencoe, Argyll (Kingshouse 305).

1

Applecross

(1) **Beinn Bhan** (2936 ft.). 2½ miles N.W. from Tornapress Junction, at head of Loch Kishorn.

(2) **Sgurr a'Chaorachain** (2600 ft.). 2 miles S. of 1.

(3) **Meall Gorm** (2325 ft.). 1¼ miles S.W. of 2.

MAP: O.S. One Inch to the Mile (7th Series). Sheet No. 25 – Portree and Sheet No. 26 – Loch Carron.

The Applecross Peninsula forms the extreme south-west corner of the Northern Highlands area. Fish-tailed in shape, it is bounded on the north by Loch Torridon and on the south by Loch Carron and Loch Kishorn. The 16 mile long western seaboard faces across the Inner Sound to the Islands of Rona, Raasay and Scalpa, beyond which rise the mountains of Skye. The eastern boundary is formed by Glen Shieldaig through which passes the main road from Loch Carron to Shieldaig. On some maps the road is marked as the B857 and is seen to stop at the village of Shieldaig but in recent years the long-needed 7-mile road link with Torridon has been completed and the approach to Applecross can now be made from either Kinlochewe via Glen Torridon or from Achnasheen via Loch Carron. From Loch Carron the main road rises westwards to a height of 450 ft., then passes down through the attractive deep gorge of the Amhainn Cumhang a'Glinne into Kishorn village – a distance of 4 miles. This attractive little community, scattered around the head of the bay, is marked on most maps as Sanachen, and can be reached by footpath from the Loch Carron–Strome Ferry road which passes the youth hostel at Achentraid 1 mile south of Kishorn.

Tornapress stands at the tidal head of the Loch and the flat green sward along the west side of the road from Kishorn to the junction has many pleasant camp-sites.

The motor road to Applecross is one of the highest in the British Isles. From Tornapress it swings southwards along the west side of the Loch then rises relentlessly around the lower slopes of Beinn

C

Bhan, crossing the Russel Burn at the mouth of Coire Lair which separates Beinn Bhan from Sgurr a'Chaorachain. Still rising steadily it continues to traverse upwards between Sgurr a'Chaorachain and Meall Gorm passing above the north side of the Allt a'Chumhaing and giving magnificent views of the great terraced faces on either side of the glen. The final section on to the summit of the plateau is accomplished in a spectacular series of 4 hairpin bends up the head wall of the glen which gives the road a distinctly Alpine character. The pass at the head of the glen is known as the Bealach na Bà – the pass of the Cattle 2053 ft.

From the plateau, the road drops less steeply down to the bay at the head of the Applecross River giving a sweeping view westwards of the mountains of Skye across the dead crater, Dun Ca'an on the island of Raasay.

Beyond Applecross Village the road passes southwards through several small communities ending at Toscaig. A daily steamer service from Kyle of Lochalsh runs from Toscaig and in winter this is often the only link with the mainland, for the road over the Bealach is quickly blocked by snow and can be impassable for days.

At present there is no motor road from Applecross around the north of the peninsula to Shieldaig, though the track is passable for motor-cycles. This is in the process of being reconstructed and eventually will provide an alternative motor route into the area.

Another footpath following the valley of the Applecross River to its head, crosses the pass below Croic-bhenn (1213 ft.) from where the right branch leads down to the head of Loch Shieldaig. It is too far from the mountains to be of much use however. It is rugged terrain, and the words of the minister who wrote the statistical account of the area in 1792 are still largely true – 'neither public road or footbridge from one extremity of it to the other. ... The foot traveller is guided according to the season of the year, what course to take, over rugged hills, rapid waters, and deep marshy burns. Besides here, as in all the adjoining parishes and Western Isles, the computation of miles is merely arbitrary, always terminated by a burn, cairn, well, or some such accidental mark, which renders them so remarkably unequal that it is impossible to reduce any given number of these imaginary miles to a regular computation.'

Applecross village is the centre of activity. Small crofting communities are dotted along the coastal fringe occupied by an ageing population. This pattern of inhabited coastline and deserted interior

34

becomes only too common as one travels through the north. The villages of Applecross were the last footholds of the native inhabitants who were evicted from their croft holdings inland to make way for the sheep and the deer. Crofting still forms the basis of life here but now even the coastal crofts are fast falling empty and there are no young people to take them over. The area is almost entirely within the Wills' estate which along with tourism and fishing provides the only alternative employment. The Dockland Settlement London administer the West Highland School of Adventure at Hartfield House near the village. Courses are run for youths in a variety of Outdoor Pursuits throughout part of the year.

The charm and isolation of Applecross attracts an ever increasing number of visitors each year and one can understand that the Gaelic name is A'Comaraich, meaning Sanctuary. In ancient times it was a famous place of refuge for fugitives recognised as such by the Church. In the old churchyard at Cruarg on the north side of the river lies buried Saint Maelrubha who gave his name to Loch Maree further inland. He ruled as Abbot here for almost fifty years in the seventh century and his influence extended over a wide part of the inland area of Ross-shire. The sandstone Celtic cross which stands at the gate of the churchyard is probably the one which previously marked his grave.

Local legend has it that if you take a handful of earth from the grave of Saint Maelrubha you will always return again safely to the Sanctuary of Applecross.

The mountains of Applecross form an elevated plateau of Torridonian Sandstone rising more or less gradually from the north-west and falling to the east in a series of deep corries with steep, terraced cliffs and fine buttresses. The main tops lie to either side of the Bealach na Bà (2053 ft.) and the summits can easily be reached from here without dropping lower than 1900 ft. The plateau is relatively flat, but the boulder strewn surface gives remarkably rough walking throughout. From all points the view westwards of Skye is by far the most exhilarating, although in all directions the view is extensive and spectacular.

Meall Gorm (2325 ft.)

Meall Gorm lies to the south of the Bealach and its summit is quickly reached from the road in just under half a mile. The ridge extends for a mile south-eastwards towards Loch Kishorn falling in imposing cliffs to the north and east above the Allt a'Chumhaing.

35

These are frequently split by deep gullies and wide stone-shoots and are well-terraced and vegetated. The prominent buttress near the hair-pin bends gives a moderate route first climbed in 1953 by J. M. Taylor, C. D. Thomson and R. P. U. Tait but a better route *Blue Pillar*, 500 ft., Very Difficult (A. G. Nicol and T. W. Patey, 1953) is

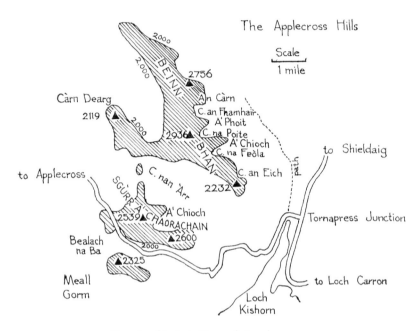

Fig. 1 Sketch Map of Applecross.

found on the slender ridge to the left of the Buttress. The route follows the narrow crest throughout. At mid-height there is a vertical step where a steep crack to the right is used. This has a precarious jammed flake at its top. The final tower is surmounted by a deep chimney on the right.

A harder route is *Blaeberry Corner*, 350 ft., Severe (W. D. Brooker and A. J. D. Norton, 1955). The route lies on the broad buttress to the left of the Blue Pillar and is separated from it by a broken-up buttress. It is in three vertical tiers, the route being on the left side. The climb has four steep, continuously difficult pitches on clean, sound rock.

Sgurr a'Chaorachain (2600 ft.)

Sgurr a'Chaorachain lies on the north side of the Bealach na Bà. The summit is flat and curves south-eastwards to Loch Kishorn sending broken slopes down towards the roadside on its south and south-eastern flanks. On the east side are two fine spurs of terraced sandstone cliffs. The main summit of the mountain stands at the base of the south spur and a subsidiary top of 2539 ft., stands $\frac{3}{4}$ mile north-west along the main ridge at the base of the north spur. Both tops can be climbed without difficulty from the road at the top of the Bealach $\frac{1}{2}$ mile south-west.

The north spur terminates in the mountain's finest and best known feature – A'Chioch of Sgurr a'Chaorachain. This is reached from the road at the mouth of the glen by following the Russel Burn into Coire nan Arr to Loch Coire nan Arr from where a slanting line leads upwards to the foot of the buttress. For walkers a pathless way leads onwards along the Allt Coire nan Arr over the Bealach nan Arr into Coire Attadale between Beinn Bhan and Carn Dearg and thence to the valley of the Applecross River.

The first climb on A'Chioch was made by Dr Collie whose route began at 1100 ft. on steep grass and rounded rocks up the shallow chimney which splits the south wall of A'Chioch and is clearly apparent when approaching from the road along the Russel Burn. Several other parties followed the same general line but the more recently climbed route on the Nose of A'Chioch has been described as 'the finest of its category in Scotland and certainly the best on Torridonian Sandstone'.

The Cioch Nose – 600 ft., Very Difficult (T. W. Patey and C. J. S. Bonnington, August 1961). Start from the Midway Terrace on A'Chioch at the first obvious break (some 60 ft. or more) to the left of the true nose of the buttress. Here for 100 ft. upwards there are several disjointed grass ledges the topmost of which is below a considerable line of overhangs.

(1) Climb 100 ft. to terrace below the overhangs. Then traverse the terrace rightwards towards the Nose.

(2) 90 ft. – A conspicuous chimney is now reached (Hard Difficult) climbed using a small jammed stone. From its top break out to the right and follow easy rocks to a ledge on the very nose of the Buttress; block belay and superb situation.

(3) 60 ft. from 10 ft. right of the block belay climb the steep frontal

slab on magnificent holds tending diagonally left. A remarkable pitch.
(4) 100 ft. – Climb up to left of overhang above and then back to the
right keeping to the Nose. Small Rowan Sapling on large ledge.
Move right to huge block.
(5) Climb the true right edge in 3 pitches each of 100 ft. on fine rock
to the top of the Cioch.
Throughout it maintains the same standard of difficulty and
exposure.

The *North Wall* of A'Chioch has yielded another fine route 800 ft.,
Hard Severe (T. W. Patey, G. B. Leslie, J. M. Taylor, J. Morgan).
This gives a great climb on perfect rough rock, with hardly any
terraces. The lower tier has numerous grass ledges up to the narrow
midway terrace girdling the Cioch; but the upper part is almost
unbroken and very steep. The upper 400 ft. above the midway
terrace are on clean rough rock throughout.

Beyond this face in a recessed corrie, T. W. Patey investigated
five great buttresses in June 1952, four of which have given routes
ranging from 450 ft., to 1000 ft. in length, varying in standard from
Difficult to Mild Severe. Number 3 Buttress has an apparently
impregnable centre but the right grassy flank has been descended.

The south face of Sgurr a'Chaorachain gives two fine routes –
Sword Stick and *Sword of Gideon* – both on the rock pillars immediately above the road on the right looking up the Bealach na Bà
(nearly opposite the waterfalls). These give the best climbing in
Applecross outwith a'Chioch and together with the latter, the best
routes anywhere on Torridonian sandstone.

Sword of Gideon – 350 ft., Very Severe – starts a mere 100 ft. above
the road on the left-most of the series of rocky ribs. Easy climbing
of 150 ft. leads to a wide ledge below the big wall which is the feature
of the route. Climb the right edge of the frontal face for 50 ft., till
the holds give out then traverse 12 ft. to the left, step down and tread
delicately (crux) across to good footholds in the centre of the face
immediately below. A prominent discontinuous crack is climbed for
20 ft. to good ledge then continue up the crack after an awkward
start. Difficulties diminish after a further 20 ft. and the logical line
is continued to the top of the rib in another 100 ft. The Crux may
require 120 ft. lead.

Beinn Bhan (2936 ft.)

Beinn Bhan is the highest point of the great plateau of Applecross and lies on its north-eastern side. The summit is flat and is easily reached from the Bealach na Bà along the north-west flank of Sgurr a'Chaorachain and the intervening Bealach nan Arr (2000 ft.). Alternatively the long south-east ridge from Loch Kishorn can be climbed without difficulty in any conditions. The western slopes fall gradually into the basin of Coire nan Arr which separates Beinn Bhan from Sgurr a'Chaorachain, but on the east the mountain presents four magnificent corries separated by precipitous sandstone spurs. From north to south these are: Corrie nan Fhamair (the giant's corrie). Coire na Poite (corrie of the Pot), Coire nan Feola (Corrie of the Flesh), and Coir 'Each (Horse Corrie). Terraced cliffs fall sheer into the middle two corries and there is no easy way down into them. Even in winter conditions, however, the head of Coire nan Fhamhair can be descended.

A good track leads into the corries from the west side of the bridge over the Kishorn River towards Loch Gaineamhach. This can be left at any convenient point and a direct line taken upwards into the corries.

The obvious short cut on to this track from the Shieldaig road through the grounds of Couldoran Lodge should not be taken. It leaves the road one and a half miles north of Tornapress and saves more than half a mile of walking, but the lodge tenants have indicated that they desire their privacy to be respected. Lochan na Poite lies at a height of 1232 ft., at the foot of Coire na Poite but several hundred feet higher two tiny lochans lie on top of a rock barrier which forms the lip of the inner corrie. Immediately behind these rises the 1200 ft. wall of Beinn Bhan, its steep slabs broken by occasional vertical rifts and narrow terraces. The corrie is enclosed by a narrow ridge with precipitous sides, their outer ends forming the great castellated buttresses which are prominent features of the mountain. The right-hand buttress is A'Phoit and the left is A'Chioch (of Beinn Bhan). The ridges can be gained by scree slopes behind the terminal buttresses but there are difficulties in getting from there on to the summit. The general angle of the back wall of the corrie is at least 60 degrees and the individual slabs are steeper.

The corrie face of A'Chioch is a grand wall of overlapping rock. Its North Buttress which falls towards the lower lochan was climbed by S. Paterson and D. J. Bennet, starting near the foot of a prominent chockstone gully forming the left boundary of the Buttress. It gave 500 ft. of Mild Severe climbing, trending to the right.

A'Phoite presents an unclimbable face to the corrie, but The Lochan na Poite face gives 500 ft. of climbing graded Very Difficult starting from a cairn up at the foot of a short severe wall leading to a fine 60 ft. slab. The route then trends left and finishes back to the right and can hardly be called a genuine climb as the face is broken by ledges but with good pitches. This was first climbed in 1948 by Messrs Parker and Young.

The North Gully of A'Chioch was climbed by J. Wood and I. Rettie. There is a big pile of rubble at the entrance, and one climbs on loose scree broken by five chockstones, each of moderate difficulty. A pinnacle divides the gully, and the route goes left up a grassy wall. The final 120 ft. pitch is a difficult, steep scramble.

The left hand wall of Coire nan Fhamair is perhaps the most continuously steep cliff of its height on the Scottish mainland and as yet is unclimbed, summer or winter.

Much recent winter exploration in the three northerly corries of Beinn Bhan has already yielded several outstanding 1000 ft. gully climbs, with many more still unvisited. Scope here is reported as comparable to Coire Ardair of Creag Meaghaidh although good snow and ice conditions are much less frequent.

Details of all routes in Applecross appear in the appropriate volume of the new series of North Climbing Guides and in the case of the most recent routes in the *S.M.C. Journal, 1970*.

3. *Above:* The Cioch of Sgurr a'Chaorachain, Applecross.

Overleaf
1. At the summit of Bealach na Ba, Applecross.
2. The approach to A'Chioch of Sgurr a'Chaorachain along
the Russel Burn.

4. Terraced sandstone cliffs of Meall Gorm, near the head of the Bealach na Ba.

5. Coire nan Fhamhair of Beinn Bhan, Applecross.

2

The Ben Damph and Coulin Forests

(1) **Beinn Damph** (2957 ft.). 3 miles S. of the head of Loch Torridon.

(2) *****Maol Chean-Dearg** (3063 ft.). $3\frac{1}{2}$ miles S.E. of the head of Loch Torridon.

(3) **An Ruadh Stac** (2919 ft.). 1 mile S. of 2.

(4) *****Sgorr Ruadh** (3141 ft.). 3 miles N.W. of Achnashellach.

(5) **Fuar Tholl** (2968 ft.). $1\frac{3}{4}$ miles W. of Achnashellach.

(6) *****Beinn Liath Mhor** (3034 ft.). $3\frac{1}{2}$ miles N.W. of Achnashellach.

(7) **Sgorr nan Lochan** (2840 ft.). $\frac{3}{4}$ mile N. of 6.

(8) **Sgurr Dubh** (2566 ft.). $1\frac{3}{4}$ miles N.N.E. of 7.

MAP: O.S. One Inch to the Mile (7th Series). Sheet No. 26 – Loch Carron.

The mountains of the Beinn Damph and Coulin Forests lie between Glen Torridon and Glen Carron along the southern boundary of the area of the Northern Highlands. On the west side they are separated from the Applecross Peninsula by Glen Sheildaig and on the east side they reach the line of Loch a'Chroisg and Glen Docherty, bordering on the area of the Fannichs.

Since the completion of 7 miles of new road between Shieldaig and the head of Loch Torridon – known locally as the Balgie Gap road – the area is conveniently ringed by good motor roads which greatly facilitate the approach to the mountains. In addition, the four main villages are located on each of the corners and provide good facilities for accommodation, provisions, garages and other service.

Achnasheen is the main road junction from the east and here the road from Dingwall divides for Kyle of Lochalsh and Gairloch. It is also the railhead for the latter and for Torridon. The south fork of the road leading by way of Achnasheen to Loch Carron has been mainly reconstructed and now gives a fast passage by car to the mountains of the Coulin Range. The road passes the recently opened Achnashellach Hostel (NH.037493) which offers accommodation to climbers throughout the year at a reasonable charge.

Past Loch Carron village it links with the south by Strome Ferry but it should be remembered that this does not operate on Sundays. A road link along the head of Loch Carron from the south side of the ferry is under construction which will greatly improve the position.

Loch Carron is an attractive village on the north shore of the loch is a good centre for the mountains. The main road passes south-westwards along the loch-side to the North Strome Ferry and from here it is possible to reach the Youth Hostel at Achintraid, $2\frac{1}{2}$ miles north-west on the shore of Loch Kishorn by either of two good hill tracks.

The road from Loch Carron north to Shieldaig has been described in the previous chapter with its superb views into the great corries of Beinn Bhan on the Applecross Peninsula and eastwards across the summit of the principal mountains dealt with in this chapter. As one approaches Shieldaig the giants of Torridon fill the landscape across the Loch.

The new stretch of road east from Shieldaig to the head of Loch Torridon gives increasingly splendid views of the whole Torridon Range. It skirts the tops of numerous little bays and inlets whose names are characteristically Gaelic in origin. Further north along the coastline, the Gaelic word 'Ob' for a bay or inlet gives way to the Norse 'Geo', showing the extent of the Viking influence here along the western seaboard of the Highlands.

Just before the tiny clachan of Annat at the head of Loch Torridon the road passes Ben Damph House which is now a large, modern Hotel. The 26,000 acre Ben Damph deer forest is run in conjunction with the Hotel and enquiries concerning access can be directed here. Past Annat, the road joins with the branch from the north side of Inner Loch Torridon – the Diabeg road. There are fine camp-sites in Pine trees beside the river, less than half a mile from the junction, and bunkhouse accommodation is now available to climbers at a moderate charge in Glen Cottage, a mile further east.

The Scottish Mountaineering Club's Ling Hut lies on the south shore of Loch Bharranch, reached by a track which leaves the road $1\frac{1}{4}$ miles east of Glen Cottage, opposite the entrance to Coire Dubh of Liathach and Beinn Eighe. The key is available to club members on application to the Honorary Hut Custodian (1970), C. S. Rose, Heathercliff, Alligin, by Achnasheen, Ross-shire.

From here on to Kinlochewe, the road passes the south boundary of the Beinn Eighe Nature Reserve and no camping is allowed on that side of the road.

The village of Kinlochewe marks the north corner of the area and is an excellent centre for all the mountain groups surrounding it. There is a caravan and camp-site at the road-junction in the Centre of the village and another maintained by the Nature Conservancy by Taagan Farm close to the main road at the head of Loch Maree. This is intended for overnight stays only, however. Beinn Eighe towers above the village to the west and the view along Loch Maree and of Slioch standing on its north-east shore are superb.

The main mountain tops of the area lie within three great estates – Ben Damph, Coulin and Achnashellach – the latter is now governed mainly by Forestry Commission. The area immediately behind Loch Carron in the south-west corner is further split amongst other smaller estates but contains few mountains of note.

Estate and Forestry work subsidised by crofting and the passing tourist trade form the main means of livelihood, a pattern too familiar throughout the north. Loch Carron was established as a fishing community at the end of the eighteenth century and its importance in this capacity lasted into the nineteenth century. It has now declined, and boats generally operate from the Kyle of Lochalsh.

The completion of the Dingwall–Kyle of Lochalsh railway in 1865 brought a period of revitalisation to the area for a time, and it is interesting to note that this even was included in the prophesies of the Brahan Seer (cf. Appendix III) in the early seventeenth century.

'Every stream shall have its bridge, balls of fire will pass rapidly up and down Strath Peffer and carriages without horses shall leave Dingwall to cross the country from sea to sea.'
– a fair description of what came to pass.

The land is now mainly under deer and sheep and the interior is uninhabited.

An exceptionally fine system of cross-country tracks cover the area making for relatively easy access to the principal mountains from all directions and providing the hill-walker with a variety of rewarding routes. The general line of the tracks is from north to south, connecting Glen Carron with Glen Torridon, but most of these interconnect in their middle stretches providing lateral communication as well.

43

Beinn Damph (2957 ft.)

Beinn Damph is the most westerly of the mountains of this group, and can be climbed without difficulty from Ben Damph Hotel. The summit lies 3 miles south of the head of Loch Torridon and is the highest point on the 2-mile ridge, whose western flanks rise steeply from the shores of Loch Damph. An estate road is seen to follow the foot of the slopes along the loch-side for almost $2\frac{1}{2}$ miles, but the gate at the main road $\frac{1}{2}$ mile east of Balgie Bridge is locked for private cars and the best approach to the mountain is by the track from Ben Damph Hotel.

The track leaves the road by a wicket gate beside the bridge over the Allt Coire Roill and rises through a magnificent pinewood along the steep sides of the gorge through which the river drops in a series of fine waterfalls. Once above the tree line, the rounded dome of An Ruadh Stac looms up beyond the far end of Coire Roill, framed by the precipitous north-eastern ridge of Beinn Damph and the southern slopes of Beinn na H'Eaglaise (2410 ft.). The main track continues for $2\frac{1}{2}$ miles over the Bealach Coire Roill then swings round the foot of the south slopes of Beinn Damph for another 4 miles to the south end of Loch Damph. The bothy here is locked and the track leading back north along the lochside connects with the motor track to Balgie. A branch leads westwards on to the road through Glen Shieldaig.

The way on to Beinn Damph is by way of the right fork of the main track which leaves just after the treeline and winds up steeply on to the saddle between Sgurr na Bana Mhoraire (2251 ft.), and the main top. This is cairned for part of the way but these are hardly necessary. To the left of the saddle is a wide scalloped corrie, between the main ridge and Creag na H'Iolhaire; this is broken and stony but has no great continuous rock face.

The ridge steepens considerably on to the summit from where a steep, craggy, shoulder drops north-eastwards into the Bealach Coire Roill. It is possible, with care, to descend the shoulder on to the bealach, but if need be an alternative descent can be made down the high corrie enclosed by the shoulder and the east face of the main ridge. This is distinctly awkward and unpleasant, involving negotiating a way through unpleasant scree slopes in the upper part of the corrie and descending a series of steepish sandstone walls in the lower part. The east face of Beinn Damph has some interesting sandstone faces, broken by deep chimneys and gullies, which could well be worth further exploration.

Maol Chean-Dearg (3060 ft.), An Ruadh Stac (2919 ft.), and Meall nan Ceapairean (2150 ft.)

The compact group of tops formed by Maol Chean-Dearg, An Ruadh Stac, and Meall nan Ceapairean can be reached equally well from Annat at the head of Loch Torridon or from the road bridge at Coulags, 5 miles north-east of Loch Carron.

The track from the cottage at Coulags is a right of way to Torridon and eventually joins with the Annat track on the north side of the Bealach na Lice between Maol Chean-Dearg and Meall Dearg (2100 ft.). The main track follows the right hand side of the Fionn Amhainn from the road bridge at Coulags. There is another indistinct track from the prominent lay-by on the west side of the bridge but this should be ignored. It soon runs out and the river can only be forded with difficulty at the first big bend to join the main track.

The river drops in a series of rocky basins along the west side of the track and is crossed 1½ miles from the road by a wooden bridge or alternatively by the conveniently placed line of uniformly square stepping-stones just below. The track is well marked throughout and now rises steeply into the inner Coire Fionnaraich. There is a locked bothy ½ a mile from the bridge with an open, semi-derelict stable which could be used for shelter in emergency. Past the bothy, the curious forefinger of stone on the right hand side of the path is Clach nan Con Fionn – The stone of Fingal's Dogs – allegedly where the giant Fionn tethered his staghounds when hunting in the glen. Beyond this the track forks, the main track continuing over the head of the coirre and a branch climbing steeply to the west which can be easily followed on to the flat saddle at 1900 ft., which connects the three mountains on this side of the glen.

From the saddle the track is seen to continue downwards along the west side of Maol Chean-Dearg past Loch Coire and Ruadh Stac. From the floor of the U-shaped corrie which hold the Loch, it disappears round the northern side of Maol Chean-Dearg to reach its junction with the Bealach na Lice track at the north end of Loch an Eoin.

From the junction, the track continues north-westwards between Beinn na L'Eaglaise and Meall Dearg; to Annat at the head of Loch Torridon. The approach from the Annat side to the north face of An

Ruadh Stac probably requires less effort and provides equally fine views of the mountains.

The saddle is the junction of the summit ridges of all three tops and gives an easy means of ascent. The mountains are generally of Torridonian Sandstone interfolded with Cambrian Quartzite.

The summit of Meall nan Ceapairean rises a modest 200 ft. to the south-east of the saddle and though steep and rocky on its eastern side above the Coire Fionn path, is mainly of interest as another viewpoint for the mountains lying on the east side of the corrie and to the south across the Attadale forest.

From here Fuar Tholl and Sgurr Ruadh are seen as a continuous ridge which never drops below 2000 ft., sweeping round northwards into the Bealach Ban. Beyond them rises the summit of Beinn Liath Mhor more than 3 miles distant across the intervening Coire Lair.

The north-west ridge leads on to Maol Chean Dearg, with precipitous faces to the north and to the east above the head of Coire Fionn. The ridge is easily climbed to the summit and the western flanks above Loch an Ruadh Stac have no noteworthy rock faces, and provide reasonable access. The view from the summit on to the whole length of the Torridon Ridge is superb and beyond Loch Maree, the peaks of the Letterewe Forest can be identified in clear visibility.

An Ruadh Stac (2919 ft.)

The south-west ridge from the saddle leads on to An Ruadh Stac, which unlike the remainder of the mountains surrounding it is composed mainly of quartzite. The way to the foot of the summit ridge leads past one of those lovely deep-coloured lochans which one comes to expect in every mountain col in the north. From here the ascent looks forbiddingly steep, but at close quarters presents a scrambling route over large quartzite blocks which in winter require care. The south-east face is of long slopes of highly polished quartzite running at angles measured at between 40 and 46 degrees which give a more interesting scramble on to the summit.

The north face of the mountain is by far the most rewarding and rises in two tiers of 300 ft., giving excellent rock for climbing with an abundance of holds. C. J. S. Bonnington and T. W. Patey pioneered one route here in 1960 which gave 600 ft., of Very Difficult climbing. A prominent slabby rib just left of an obvious white scar on the lower tier gives 300 ft. of delightful climbing. Direct continuation on the upper tier by a long curving damp chimney looks unpleasant, so the climb continues about 100 ft., further left (cairn). 150 ft. diagonally leftwards leads to a big recess and a spike belay. The recess is left from the left side and the route continues straight up for 100 ft. to easier rocks and scrambling.

The descent from the mountains back to Coulags is best made by retracing the track. A line down the west side of the south face of An Ruadh Stac involves circumnavigating some awkward rock walls and the way is blocked by the deep ravine of the Allt Ruigh Sleigheich 1 mile south-east across the lower hill-side. It is best to follow the wire fence directly down the north side of the gap to the Fionn Amhainn in the Coulags glen. It is difficult to cross over to join the main track and one is forced to take a rather boggy line along the west bank of the river to the bridge.

Fuar Tholl (2968 ft.)

Fuar Tholl rises conspicuously above Achnashellach station at the head of Glen Lair and with Sgurr Ruadh (3142 ft.) forms a 3-mile ridge running north-westwards between Coire Fionnaraich and Coire Lair whose crest never drops below the 2000 ft. contour.

The climb on to the saddle between the two mountains can easily be made up the steep grassy western slopes rising from Coire Fionnaraich, but this holds little interest.

The best approach is from Achnashellach Station, 3 miles east of Coulag Bridge, by a side road leading past the keeper's house which crosses the railway line a few yards west of the station platform. The track into Glen Lair branches west through the young trees; an unsurfaced motor track branches right through a wooden gate. This will be described later.

The track leads up through the wild magnificent scenery of Coire Lair, following the course of the River Lair along its right hand side. The river follows a wild course down through a deep narrow gorge, broken frequently by waterfalls and bordered by distorted pine-trees. It is a formidable barrier to cross and one is well advised to keep to the well-surfaced tracks.

After 1½ miles of steady climbing, the path reaches a junction at the wide mouth of the upper corrie. A right hand fork leads up on to the saddle between Carn Eite and the main Beinn Liath Mhor ridge, and continues eastwards along the Easan Dorcha to meet with the motor track previously mentioned.

47

The main track continues for three miles. It covers the head of the corrie and traverses the north side of the ridge back into the head of Corrie Fionnaraich by the Bealach Ban. This joins with the track previously described leading through the Bealach Lice to Annat.

The west fork of the Lair track leads steeply upwards on to the 2200 ft. saddle between Fuar Tholl and Sgorr Ruadh and from here either summit is easily reached. Fuar Tholl radiates three spurs which hold its main rock features. The south-east ridge has a precipitous 'Nose' prominent from lower Coire Lair and climbed direct in 1961 by T. W. Patey giving a 500 ft. route of Very Severe standard. It was found to be exposed and vegetated throughout and offered no escape. High above this spur and between it and the south spur is a small corrie with continuous 500 ft. cliffs on its west flanks. These are the South Cliffs and were climbed first in 1933 by Messrs Ludwig and Maclennan, giving a climb of Severe standard. Between the north and south-east spurs lies the Mainreachan Buttress – a great buttress of terraced sandstone which hangs perpendicularly over a tiny lochan on the north face of Fuar Tholl. The *Enigma Route* on this buttress was climbed in 1952 by W. J. Cole, J. R. Marshall and I. Oliver.

The climb starts from the left end of the lowest terrace and goes to left skyline on easy rock to mossy stance. Now climb crack on right for 60 ft., to a ledge. Traverse left into steep grooves and up to a large grassy ledge. Go up 70 ft., rightwards to moss patch; then left up to east end of big ledge. Climb for 30 ft. up groove, and then to top of large flake. The crux 50 ft. Traverse right, and up steep wall on good holds to ledge, traverse left of cairn. Climb rib above for 30 ft. Scramble up to a bigger cairn below steep rib. Climb rib, 70 ft., on small holds and then trend leftwards. Short pitches and easier rock leads to top in about 200 ft. There are belays between pitches. The standard was found to be Severe.

For a long time this was the sole route but the buttress has recently attracted greater attention and there are now five new routes reported of high standard.

Sgorr Ruadh has an impressive north face which throws out several distinct buttresses separated by narrow couloirs which usually hold no snow into the summer. The most northerly of these, Raeburn's Buttress, is the highest and forms the skyline on the approach from Glen Lair. This is separated from the two more southerly buttresses by a wide couloir whose steep upper section is usually corniced in winter. The longest of the two southerly buttresses is named Academy Ridge, next to it Robertson's Buttress with a steep intervening gully named Robertson's Gully.

The last-named buttress gave the earliest route on the mountain and was ascended, partly by rocks and partly by the gully on the right by A. E. Robertson in 1898.

Academy Ridge (so called by the Inverness Royal Academy Climbing Club) gives 100 ft. of moderate climbing at the start on the projecting rock paw. A walk leads to buttress proper at 1700 ft. The upper section narrows and the climbing becomes difficult with an awkward section near the top where a detached mass resting on a ledge has to be negotiated.

Raeburn's Buttress (Difficult) was climbed in 1904 by H. Raeburn and A. E. Robertson in winter conditions. The lower rocks are extremely steep and can be avoided by the chimney on the left for 80 ft., then the ridge regained by a ledge traverse to the right. 300 ft of difficult climbing lead to a col from which easier rocks lead to the summit plateau. The top of the mountain lies $\frac{1}{2}$ mile north-west across a dip of several hundred feet.

Raeburn's Buttress occupies the angle between the north-east and north faces of Sgorr Ruadh and is seen in profile with a steep north-east wall, bounded on the right by a deep scree-filled gully. Beyond this is Upper Buttress, the last considerable rock face in the glen climbed in 1955 by I. H. Ogilvie and P. M. Francis.

Sgorr Ruadh North Face Upper Buttress (Very Difficult). On the left edge of the buttress is a series of overhangs and on the right are steep rocks and a prominent pinnacle. Between these is a face, rather less steep, and broken by a series of vertical cracks.

Climb a 10 ft. corner near the overhangs and traverse, 40 ft. to the cracks. The route goes now, more or less straight up the buttress, with slight traverses. The main difficulties end about 300 ft. up, where a through route goes behind a boulder, jammed in the right-hand crack (cairn). A further 400 ft. of scrambling leads to the top, near the col separating Raeburn's Buttress from Sgorr Ruadh.

The north wall of Raeburn's Buttress has also yielded a route, *Splintery Edge* – 400 ft., Very Difficult, T. W. Patey, 1961). A deep chasm separates it from Upper Buttress, but the wall of Raeburn's Buttress which hems in this chasm on the left is nearly

D

vertical for several hundred feet. The rock is very shattered and there is less scope than might be apparent.

200 ft. or so up the chasm a concealed left hand branch ends in a formidable cul-de-sac. The route follows the near vertical edge on its left. The lower 150 ft. of the ridge looks very severe and dangerous, and was by-passed up the crumbly bed of the branch gully for 50 ft., whence a shelf led leftwards out on to the edge via some loose blocks. The edge was climbed more or less directly for some 300 ft., the rock improving. The route comes out exactly at the subsidiary top of Sgorr Ruadh, the culminating point of Raeburn's Buttress proper.

Beinn Liath Mhor (3034 ft.)

Beinn Liath Mhor forms a two mile ridge along the north side of Coire Lair and can be easily climbed from the branch track to Easan Dorcha already mentioned. It is of more interest geologically than from a climbing point of view. Here, the Red Torridonian Sandstone and White Cambrian Quartzite have been folded together in a complex pattern which can be traced on the rather bare sides of the mountains.

The buttress west of the Long Gully trailing down into Coire Lair provides a moderate route of sorts but recent exploration of other ribs on this face has produced several good 300 ft. routes and the outcrops here are reported as providing good sport.

The ridge can be included in a circuit over the tops of Sgorr Ruadh and Fuar Tholl giving a long high-level walk of over 9 miles with a steep drop of 1500 ft. into the bealach at the head of the corrie. Here the small rock tower can be climbed or turned on the left at the discretion of the individual, but care should be taken in any choice of route down from the Beinn Liath ridge below the summit. Several parties have got into difficulties here.

An alternative expedition is to include the ridge in a traverse over the summits of Sgorr nan Lochan Uaine (2840 ft.) and Sgurr Dubh (2566 ft.). These form a 3-mile broken ridge running at right angles from Beinn Liath Mhor towards Loch Clair in Glen Torridon.

They can be traversed either in conjunction with the latter mountain or direct from the road in Glen Torridon from which they rise in a series of broken sandstone terraces. To the east, they enclose the three open corries which form the sanctuary of the deer forest and to the west a track from the Ling Hut follows their lower slopes up on to the bealach at the head of Coire Lair. This is shown as stopping some 1½ miles short of the bealach but in fact reappears intermittently further on.

There is one vehicle road crossing the area to the east of the principal mountains but this is private for the greatest part of the length. From Achnashellach Station it crosses the Coulin Pass and then follows the River Coulin down along the wooded shores of Loch Coulin and Loch Clair to reach the Glen Torridon road 3 miles west of Kinlochewe.

The Achnashellach Forest is now controlled by the Forestry Commission but the Coulin Forest is in private hands and through vehicle traffic is not normally permitted. There is a locked gate across the road on the Coulin Pass. The proprietors have agreed to allow a right of way for walkers and the path should on no account be omitted from any exploration of the area. The views through the trees from the lochs on to the white-quartzite capped peaks of Torridon are magnificent and provide one of the finest spectacles in the Northern Highlands.

The old right-of-way track to Kinlochewe continues along the north side of Loch Maree to Letterewe and Poolewe which was once a main port for the cattle trade from the Outer Isles. This is marked on Roy's famous Military Map of the middle eighteenth century which gives a wealth of detail on old tracks and rights of way. The map was never published but can be consulted in the British Museum.

3

Torridon

MAP: O.S. One Inch to the Mile (7th Series). Sheet No. 26 – Loch Carron.

This chapter deals with the mountains to the north side of Glen Torridon lying in the Torridon and Fisherfield Forests – an area which has been described by W. H. Murray as 'exhibiting more of mountain beauty than any other district of Scotland, including Skye'. Here the sculptured Red Sandstone first encountered in the eastern cliffs and corries of the Applecross Peninsula is on a greater and more majestic scale and is further enhanced by the distinctive quartzite capping which forms a jagged skyline along the length of the southern ridges.

The area is bounded on its east side by the length of Loch Maree and to the west and south-west by Loch Torridon. The northern boundary stretches from the west side of Loch Maree to the head of Loch Gairloch.

The main mountains of Torridon lie within the south-eastern corner of the area and are easily approached by the two main roads which pass north and west from their junction at Kinlochewe.

The road west through Glen Torridon to the head of the loch has already been described. From the road junction before Torridon village, it branches towards Loch Carron giving easy access from the south. Further west the north branch continues along the north shores of Loch Torridon as far as the crofting-cum-fishing village of

Diabeg, in its most wonderful setting on the bay formed by Loch Diabeg, an inlet of Loch Torridon. The road stops here but a path continues around the coast line for 7 miles to Red Point giving a worth-while walking route. The way goes past Craig where there is a Youth Hostel (an isolated cottage) ½ mile inland approached only by moorland path. Even cyclists would find this hostel difficult of access. From the crofting village of Red Point a motor road leads towards Gairloch.

The origin of the name Diabeg is obviously Norse – 'Djup-vik (or 'Deep-bay) and although the Vikings never really settled in this part of Wester Ross they certainly raided the coastline here. Shieldaig on the south side of Loch Torridon also shows the Norse influence – 'sild-vik' or 'herring bay'.

The road north from Kinlochewe follows the side of Loch Maree for more than 10 miles through some of the most picturesque terrain in an area renowned for its scenery. From either side of the loch, great mountain ridges rise upwards; to the west those of Torridon and to the east those of Slioch and Beinn Lair. The view is especially fine approaching Kinlochewe from the head of Glen Docherty on the way from Achnasheen, but it is unfortunate that this has been marred slightly in recent years by the rather ugly low slung electric cables which have been strung along the roadway.

The shore of Loch Maree was at one time entirely wooded but now only remnants of the Old Caledonian Pine Forest remain and the north shore which was once covered with oak trees was burned long ago to provide fuel for the old iron-smelting industry once carried on here around 1700. The track along the north shore from Letterewe was used by smelters to carry fuel, and is also a long established right of way. The pine forest along the south shore is preserved by the Nature Conservancy, and lies within the Beinn Eighe Nature Reserve where the study of regeneration of the existing forestland is one of the main projects.

Loch Maree itself is named after the Celtic Saint Maelrubha who lies buried in Applecross Churchyard. The Saint's influence here was very strong, and the Holy Isle Maree, one of the many lovely wooded islets along its northern reaches has a well which allegedly cures insanity. As late as 1858 the treatment was applied to a mad woman. She became a raging lunatic. In 1868 the same treatment cured a male lunatic. Coins were struck into a sacred tree beside the well as an offering to the spirits and even Queen Victoria observed the custom on her visit here in 1877. The rites carried out on the island until well into the seventeenth century were a strange mixture of christianity and paganism involving the sacrifice of bulls to Saint Maelrubha. The local smith killed the bull and was given the head in payment – an old druid rite. These practices caused great concern to the Church and feature frequently in the old records of the Presbytery of Dingwall.

Beinn Alligin

(1) *Meall an Laoigh* (2904 ft.). Unnamed on 1″ Map; 3½ miles W.N.W. of Torridon.

(2) *Tom na Gruagach* (3021 ft.). ⅜ mile N.N.E. of 1.

(3) *Sgurr Mor* (the highest peak also known as Sgurr na Tuaigh or Hatchet Peak) – (3232 ft.). 4 miles N.W. of Torridon and ¾ mile N.N.E. of 2.

(4) *The Rathains of Alligin* (2840 ft. aprox.). ¼ mile N. of E. from 3.

Beinn Alligin is the most westerly of the Torridon Mountains and though its proportions fall slightly short of those of Beinn Eighe and Liathach its splendid ridge contains several fine individual features which makes the traverse of this mountain a good introductory exercise for the longer and more varied expeditions provided by the former two.

The ridge of Beinn Alligin curves inland above the new road from Torridon to Diabeg to form the west side of Coire Mhic Nobuill. The new road to Diabeg climbs up above the old road to Torridon and continues westwards for a mile to cross the Amhainn Coire Mhic Nobuil by a stone bridge. This marks the start of the easiest approach to Beinn Alligin, Beinn Dearg, and the north side of Liathach.

A track leads up through the pines on the right-hand side of the river to a wooden bridge just above the junction of the Allt A'Bhealaich. The left hand fork now follows the right hand side of this stream north towards the Bealach a'Chomla between Beinn Alligin and Beinn Dearg crossing a second bridge higher up and continuing along the left hand side of the water into the pass on the 1250 ft. contour. The right hand fork from the first bridge leads eastwards between Beinn Dearg and the north corries of Liathach and connects eventually with the track through Coire Dubh from the Glen Torridon road. The track on to the pass gives good walking and the 2½ miles from the road is easily covered in an hour.

The traverse of the Alligin ridge from this north-east end is undoubtedly the most interesting expedition. The eastern spur can be climbed by its south-east corner to the skyline and involves some scrambling but alternative lines involving no rock-work can easily be found. The way along the ridge is now well marked and between here and the main top, Sgurr Mhor, passes over the three 'Horns of Alligin'.

These three rocky pinnacles offer a pleasant variation and give no great difficulty but if need be they can be by-passed at a lower level across the steep grass slope on the south side. It is possible to traverse it on its west side not much below the level of the ridge, but its east wall is unbroken. The floor of the Gash is slabby above 1600 ft., at an angle of something less than 45 degrees and has been used as a rather tiring way of descent but an easier escape is provided by the dip to the east of the main top.

South of the main top and below the Gash lies the great corrie of Toll a'Mhadaidh which contains a remarkable ½ mile long deposit of gigantic boulders. This reaches well up to the 1100 ft. contour with another branch up hill on the east side of the Gash. Some of the great blocks littered here reach fantastic proportions.

The traverse southwards over Tom na Gruagaich and Meall an Laoigh is straightforward and the views from here extend from Ardnamurchan to Cape Wrath and from Skye to the Outer Hebrides as fine as one can obtain from any point in the area. In contrast to its north and eastern aspects, Beinn Alligin falls down to the west towards Diabeg in a series of long grassy slopes which continue round on to the southern end of the ridge and if need be can be descended. The usual way down is by way of the slope between Tom na Gruadaich and Meall an Laoigh, following the stream which falls into Coire an Laoigh.

This bends to the east at its lower end and it is advisable to leave it at an appropriate point and take a direct line cross-country back down to the Diabeg Bridge. Beinn Alligin lies in what was formerly the estate of Alligan-Shuas now controlled by the National Trust for Scotland.

Beinn Dearg

(1) *Main Top* (2995 ft.). 3 miles N. of Torridon.
(2) *Stuc Loch na Cabhaig* (2500 ft. approx.). ½ mile N. of (1).
(3) *Carn na Feola* (2478 ft.). 1¼ miles E. of (1).

Beinn Dearg lies across the Bealach a Chomla east of Beinn Alligin and like that mountain tends to be overshadowed by the neighbouring ridges of Liathach and Beinn Eighe. It is easiest approached by the track leading from the Diabeg Bridge already described and from here the south and west sides rise in a continuous precipitous escarpment which at first glance seems impregnable. Fortunately the walls are breached in several places by rock gullies and these offer a way on to the summit ridge with varying degrees of difficulty but caution should be exercised at all times. The ridge leads eastwards over a rocky tower to its eastern end and the descent to the watershed at the head of Coire Dubh Mor is made by threading a way through the outcrops of the south-east slope to join the Coire Dubh track to Glen Torridon. An alternative descent can be made from the summit cairn on the south side by any of the three chimneys which cut the line of the escarpment at this point. The spurs between these offer a detour to the side when the gullies themselves become too perpendicular. From the ridge there are exceptionally fine views into the nearby northern corries of Liathach.

In poor visibility, Beinn Dearg should be approached with caution. Sound navigation is required to negotiate a route around the sandstone exposures and this is not a hill for an inexperienced party in adverse weather.

Baosbheinn (2869 ft.)

Baosbheinn, an equally fine mountain, lies in the Flowerdale deer forest $2\frac{1}{2}$ miles to the north of Beinn Alligin and Beinn Dearg and like the neighbouring peak, Beinn an Eoin (2801 ft.), loses much of its individuality by reason of its proximity to the greater ranges in the south part of Torridon. The approach is normally made from the road to Gairloch along Loch Maree leaving at a point 4 miles north from Loch Maree Hotel where a bridge crosses a neck of water between Feur-Loch and Loch Bad an Sgalaig. A track leads south-eastwards in towards Loch na h'Oidhche for some 4 miles and the climb on to the ridge of Baosbheinn on the west side or that of Beinn an Eoin on the east can easily be made from the north end of the loch. Both mountains reach their highest point at the south end of their respective ridges and fall down steeply in that direction. Baosbheinn has a prominent cliff-face on its southwest side under the top west of the summit but this appears too monolithic and steep to offer climbing routes.

Beinn a'Chearcaill (2376 ft.)

Beinn a'Chearcaill lies on the opposite side of Strath Lungard from Beinn an Eoin and the route on to both these can be made by path from the roadside opposite Loch Maree Hotel. This follows the west side of the River Talladale through forestry plantations for almost 2 miles before petering out. There a long slanting line on to either ridge gives a reasonable climb on to the summit. Beinn a'Chearcaill is probably best approached, however, by the well-known track from Grudie Bridge which leads towards the north corries of Beinn Eighe.

All three mountains provide fine view points for the surrounding area; the outlook from Beinn a'Chearcaill across on to the great rock buttresses of Coire Mhic Fhearachair on Beinn Eighe being especially noteworthy.

Liathach

(1) *Stuc a'Choire Dhuibh Bhig* (3000 ft. approx.).
(2) *Bidein Toll a'Mhuic* (3200 ft. approx.).
(3) **Spidean a'Choire Leith* (3456 ft.) and the highest point 7 miles W.S.W. of Kinlochewe. 2¼ miles E.N.E. of Torridon.
(4) *Am Fasarinen* (3050 ft. approx.). A range of pinnacles lying immediately S.W. of 3.
(5) *Mulloch an Rathain* (3358 ft.). 1 mile W. of (3).
(6) *Meall Dearg* (3150 ft. approx.), close N.E. of (5) but across the Northern Pinnacles.
(7) *Sgorr a'Chadail* (2297 ft.). 1½ miles W. of (5).

Liathach is the name given to the whole range of seven tops which stretches for five miles from west to east along the north side of Glen Torridon. Like Beinn Alligin, it is now under the control of the National Trust for Scotland. On its eastern flank it is separated from Beinn Eighe by Coire Dubh. Its western ridge drops down towards the head of upper Loch Torridon and on the north-west side it is separated from Beinn Alligin and Beinn Dearg by Coire Mhic Nobuil.

The steepness of the southern slopes is greatly accentuated by their proximity to the road from Kinlochewe through Glen Torridon which passes right along the foot of the ridge and consequently fore-shortens the view. From this side, the summit ridge can be reached by several routes of varying degrees of difficulty.

The north side of the ridge is undoubtedly the most magnificent. Here the ridge drops down into three fine corries; Coire Dubh Beag to the north-east above Coire Dubh, the north-east Corrie from the main top, and Coire na Caime (The Crooked Corrie). This is the finest feature on the range. It is bounded on the east by the north ridge leading from the main top, Spidean a Choire Leith. To the west it is encircled by the northern pinnacles along the ridge from Mullach an Rathain on to Meall Dearg. Its headwall is backed by the jagged skyline of the Fasarinen Pinnacles.

The main mass of the mountain is composed of highly sculptured Red Torridonian Sandstone which gives the ridge a rosy-coloured tint in certain light conditions, but the four highest peaks are capped with white Cambrian Quartzite which on the main summit, rises in a sharp symmetrical cone of loose angular blocks which require careful negotiation.

The eastern top, Stuc a'Choire Dubh Bhig, has a bold terminal buttress but easier slopes on the south side. South-west of the main summit, the ridge narrows for almost half a mile over the Fasarinen Pinnacles which in summer are of no real difficulty requiring only a good head. There is a certain amount of exposure on the north of the pinnacles, but there are plenty of good holds to compensate. If need be this section can be avoided in good conditions by a path on the south side at a lower level, but in winter they usually have to be taken direct.

From Mullach an Rathain a north-east spur leads over the jagged northern pinnacles to Meall Dearg (unnamed on the 1″ Map).

The pinnacles require a certain amount of rock-climbing technique and should be left strictly alone by parties with no such experience. The spur can be misleading to ridge-walking parties in the event of poor visibility and should be kept well in mind. The main ridge westwards from Mullach an Rathain is now uniformly broad and grassy and gives no further difficulty. There is an easy descent by the north-west slope from Sguorr a'Chadail to the Coire Mhic Nobuil path and thence to the Diabeg Bridge.

Suggested Routes on to the Liathach Ridge:

(1) The most used route starts from the Torridon road, between the bridge over the Allt a'Choire Dubh Mhoir and Glen Cottage, and makes more or less directly to a point just west of (1).

There are no difficulties between here and the main summit – No. 3.
(2) Up the east side of the stream which descends due south of the main top.

(3) Via Coire Leith, south-east of the main top (3). The rock terraces are skirted on the left and the route requires some degree of judgment. (4) By the course of the Allt an Tuill Bhain due south of (5). The approach from the road past the camp-site in the pine-trees leads up over sloping sandstone pavements into a wide grassy corrie. Grass tongues penetrate the upper screes and lead on to the ridge.

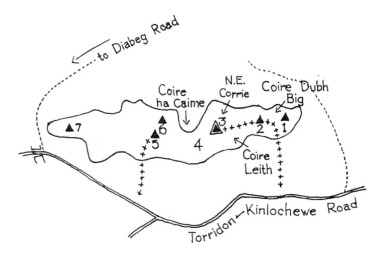

++++ Tourist Route

〰〰 2,000' contour

-------- track

Scale 1 inch : 1 mile

Fig. 2   Sketch Map of Liathach (the numbers relate to text).

(5) By the prominent stone-shoot leading up on to the summit ridge to a point ¼ mile west by south of (5). This and the previous route are also useful means of descent. The upper portion of the stone-shoot is now greatly loosened and requires care if used by a party. (6) The south-east ridge of Mullach an Rathain (5) gives a fine slightly exposed scramble on to the ridge. The top 500 ft. is especially interesting and is broken by several small pinnacles. This upper section could be graded moderate and requires some care, but difficulties encountered can be avoided to the east.

(7) Up the scree slope at the head of Coire Dubh Beag to the main ridge between (1) and (2).
This is reached by the track through Coire Dubh from the road bridge.
(8) By a continuous scree-slope to the north-west of (3) which runs up from Coire na Caime. This can be approached by either the Coire Dubh track or the track from Coire Mhic Nobuil.
(9) The north-west slope on to Sgorr a'Chadail from the Coire Mhic Nobuil track.

The north and east faces of Liathach offer the best prospects of rock-climbing. The North ridge of Spidean a'Choire Leith gives a moderate route on to the summit if the difficulties in the middle section are taken direct.

The ascent of Mullach an Rathain via Meall Dearg and the northern pinnacles gives a fine though somewhat indirect ascent on to the mountains. This gives a route of Difficult standard. The approach from the road to Coire na Caime and the foot of the Meall Dearg Ridge takes about two hours. The northern pinnacles are extremely shattered and are covered with large, unstable blocks.

The east face of Liathach has a number of routes, all with awkwardly sloping rock. The upper third of the face consists of a steep, double-tier wall and except on the extreme left there is no real climbing on the lower portions.

On the north face of Liathach the back of Coire na Caime offers further possibilities. The 500 ft. Buttress which faces across to the Northern Pinnacles at the entrance to the inner corrie is known as Bell's Buttress and gives a route of Severe Standard.

The stepped Buttress immediately west of the Fasarinen Pinnacles is known as P.C.'s Buttress and has a Difficult route up its centre. The lower terraces are found to be easy, but the buttress narrows in its upper part and the route goes up a precipitous tower on the right centre, with some loose rock.

The winter traverse of Liathach should only be tackled by an experienced and well-equipped party. This is an especially fine expedition and the account by W. H. Murray in *Undiscovered Scotland* (Dent) 1950, is hard to improve upon and is recommended reading.

Details of all climbs on Liathach appear in the appropriate volume of the *S.M.C. Northern Highlands Climbing Guides*.

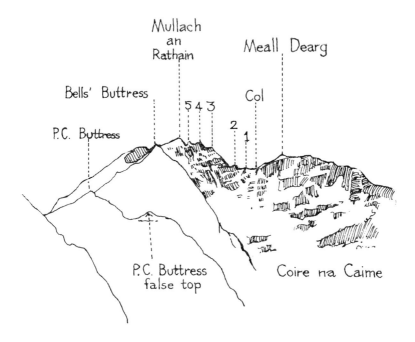

Liathach: Mullach an Rathain from Fasarinen
1, 2, 3, 4, 5 are the Northern Pinnacles

Fig. 3 North Face of Liathach.

Beinn Eighe

(1) *Ruadh-Stac Mor* (3309 ft.). N.W. Spur of Beinn Eighe.

(2) *Sail Mhor* (3217 ft.). West end of Beinn Eighe.

(3) *Coinneach Mhor* (3170 ft.). $\frac{5}{8}$ mile S. of (1).

(4) *Spidean Coire nan Clach* (3220 ft. approx.).

(5) *Sgurr Ban* (3188 ft.).

(6) *Sgurr an Fhir Duibhe* (3160 ft.). $\frac{1}{2}$ mile E. of (5).

(7) *Creag Dubh* (3050 ft.).

(8) *Rhuad-stac Beag* (2850 ft. contour). $1\frac{1}{4}$ miles N.N.E. of (4) over a dip to 2100 ft.

(9) *Meall a'Ghiubhais* (2882 ft.). N. of (8) over a dip to 1200 ft.

Beinn Eighe is the collective name given to the whole of the magnificent mountain range lying just south-west of Kinlochewe and Loch Maree, which with its equally fine neighbour, Liathach, rises up to fill the entire length of the north side of Glen Torridon. It is separated from the latter mountain by Coire Dubh and on the north-west its boundary is marked by Glen Grudie and the line of the Allt Coire Mhic Fhearchair.

From any direction Beinn Eighe is seen to be uniformly steep and imposing, its peaks linked in graceful curves of stony ridges are further accentuated by the distinctive white covering of quartzite which almost entirely blankets the summit.

This is one of the main points of difference between the mountain and Liathach. The steady but gentle eastward dip of the strata which allows the Torridonian Sandstone to form nearly all of Liathach only brings it to ridge level on Beinn Eighe at the col between Sail Mhor and Coinneach Mhor at its western end and takes it almost completely out of sight before the east end of the ridge is reached even more so on the south than on the north. Consequently, most of the slopes on Beinn Eighe are of quartzite scree although on the wider and flatter parts towards the west a mossy covering makes for easier walking.

The south side of Beinn Eighe is in full view from the Glen Torridon road and from the summit ridge of Sail Mhor at its western end to Spidean Coire nan Clach above Loch Bharranch this part of the range comes under the National Trust for Scotland. The remainder of the mountain lying to the east forms part of the Beinn Eighe Nature Reserve and consequently parties climbing here should observe the restrictions laid down by the Nature Conservancy. The resident warden can be contacted at Anancaun Research Station $\frac{1}{2}$ mile north of Kinlochewe for any information governing the area of the Reserve. The north side of the mountain is of more complex pattern than the south, and includes the mountain's finest rock features. The main ridge drops in this direction in three great corries enclosed by spurs. The most easterly is Coire Toll a'Ghiubhais (Firtree hole); separated by Ruadh-stac Beag and Meall a' Ghiubhais from the central corrie – Coire Ruadh-Stac of which the uppermost section of Coire nan Clach. Finally, at the western end, enclosed by Ruadh Stac Mhor and Sail Mhor is the great Coire Mhic Fhearchair. This contains in its inner recess the magnificent Triple-Buttress which provides one of the finest climbing grounds in the Northern Highlands.

This north-west corner of the mountain is easily the finest part and the view from Loch Coire Mhic Fhearchair or from the summit of Beinn a'Chearchaill should not be missed. The magnificent upper

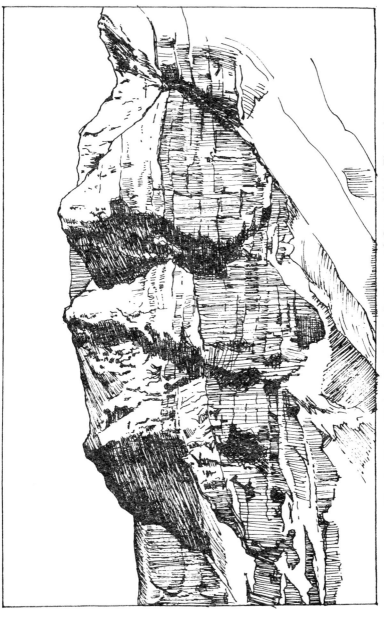

Fig. 4   Beinn Eighe: the Triple Buttress of Coire Mhic Fhearchair.

buttresses of quartzite stand on a plinth of sandstone rising to almost half the total height of 1000 ft., the two strata being separated by a 'Broad Terrace', lower and more continuous in its eastern extent, so that the East Buttress is two-thirds composed of quartzite while the West Buttress is almost half Torridonian sandstone.

The terrace is an easy scramble and is used as an approach to climbs on the upper parts of the East and Central Buttresses.

On the main buttresses the quartzite is divided into two layers, the lower half having a more pronounced bedding plane than the upper, and at their junction is a less pronounced terrace which marks the line of the Upper Girdle Traverse – a major climbing expedition which was first accomplished in 1960 by T. W. Patey and C. J. S. Bonnington.

The Upper Girdle at the intersection of the two distinct layers of quartzite gives a first-rate expedition with minimum scrambling, at least half a dozen pitches of severe standard and some remarkable exposure.

The fault line is obvious all the way across the face and for most of the way is the only practicable one. The climb starts near the foot of Far East Gully. The first segment of the traverse across the Eastern Ramparts is the most entertaining where for 600 ft. the traverse is continuously difficult and exposed. Then things go easily from East Buttress right along to West Central gully apart from a single awkward pitch on the east face of Central Buttress.

The east face of the West Buttress is perhaps the most impressive section of the circuit, and has three serious pitches on the last of which a security piton was left in place.

The right-hand aspect of each buttress is well-broken but the left-hand profiles rise sheer. That of the East Buttress merges with the Eastern Ramparts, a 500 ft. vertical face which stretches back for almost $\frac{1}{4}$ mile to Far East Gully. The cliffs continue slightly less formidable but equally steep – The Northern Ramparts – to merge on to the col on the true ridge leading to Ruadh Stac Mhor.

To the right of the West Buttress is Far West gully. This is strewn with the wreckage of an aircraft which crashed here in 1952. Beyond this lies Far West Buttress which is much shorter and less clearly defined. The three main buttresses are separated by East-Central and West-Central gullies.

The first attempts at climbing here were made by Dr Norman Collie and his party by the way of the West-Central Gully on to the

6. The summit of Maol Chean-dearg with the ridge of Liathach in the background.

7. Fuar Tholl from Achnashellach.

Central Buttress at the turn of the century. Since then the rock features of Coire Mhic Fhearchair have attracted an ever-increasing influx of climbing parties resulting in a wide variety of routes.

Far East Gully – 200 ft., Difficult, gives a straightforward climb on good holds. A traverse in the upper portion of the gully is necessary to avoid an overhang and a series of great blocks to the right are surmounted to the top.

The Eastern Ramparts have three recorded routes. *Boggle* – 400 ft., Very Severe (R. Smith and A. Wightman, October 1961); *The Gash* – 200 ft., Severe (T. W. Patey, A. G. Nicol, K. A. Grassick, and J. M. Taylor, June 1962); and *Gnome Wall* – 500 ft., Severe (T. W. Patey, August 1959).

The Gash follows a deeply cut chimney in the lowest tier of quartzite below the level of the Eastern Ramparts proper. It can be seen from the lochside to start up left to end in a terrace some one hundred feet right of the start of *Gnome Wall*. The route contains some dangerous loose blocks but is worth a visit for the rock scenery and as a preamble to *Gnome Wall*. There are three pitches: the first leads up to a large dry cave, the second uses a long through shaft behind chock-stones and the third goes up the clean rib on the left of the chimney.

Gnome Wall is the one obvious line of weakness near the right end of the Upper Ramparts. The route escapes from the Wall on to the East Buttress some hundred feet below the top near a projecting gargoyle. The start can be reached from the foot of Far East Gully and the route starts at the extreme right end of the screes below the Upper Ramparts. Starting directly below the gargoyle there is a choice of hard lines. It is doubtful if any two parties would take the same line throughout, however, on most pitches the correct solution is not the obvious one.

In 1954 Lovat and Weir attempted a line somewhat further to the right, starting from the main corrie floor. They retreated after six hours of Very Severe climbing when 100 ft. below the gargoyle.

The *Original Route* on the *Eastern Buttress* – Very Difficult (G. B. Gibbs, E. Backhouse and W. A. Moimsey, 1907) starts near the left side of the track, moving leftwards by ledges to reach the terrace near the east corner of the Buttress. The terrace is followed back to East Central Gully which is climbed for two pitches before gaining the Buttress by an easy terrace to the left. The route keeps right of centre on the quartzite and turns a tooth semi-detached from the cliff by an open chimney on the right, after which the climbing eases to a pleasant scramble.

The Direct Start to the *Eastern Buttress* is graded Severe, and begins by a prominent chimney 30 yards east of East-Central Gully.

East-Central Gully (Severe) is better as a winter route but was climbed in June 1963 by W. Proudfoot, D. Mackenzie, D. Williamson and R. Acock. The route stays close to the Gully dead throughout, and is extremely wet. The Second Pitch is the crux and this lies on the upper part of the sandstone 130 ft. and is climbed on small holds followed by bridging (Severe). Above the terrace the angle eases with the Gully gradually growing shallow and disappearing. The route then joins the original route of East Buttress.

The Central Buttress has five recorded routes. *East-Central Ribs* – 350 ft., Severe (L. S. Lovat and T. Weir, June 1954) follows the crest of three prominent quartzite ribs just west of East-Central Gully. They are bordered on the left by East-Central Gully and on the right by a narrow cleft. The Ribs are steep, narrow and exposed.

Left-Hand Face Direct – 350 ft. Mild Severe. (T. W. Patey, August 1957). At the terrace the East-Central Gully branches. The Climb follows the right fork which in 200 ft. peters out below a shallow depression in the vertical wall of Central Buttress. This becomes a watercourse in wet weather. The route on the vertical wall follows the next feasible line to the left of the watercourse. Climbing on the wall is continuously Mild Severe and exposed.

East Wall – 330 ft., Severe (L. S. Lovat and T. Weir, June 1954). There is a large rock tower level with the junction of the terrace and East-Central Gully. Above it easy ground leads to the start of the route which goes directly up the middle of the face. High above the starting cairn is another obvious tower.

Original (Piggot's) Route – 1000 ft., Mild Severe. Avoiding the lowest slabs, attack the sandstone wall (500 ft.) at the point where a large block is partly detached from the face, about one-third of the way from the West End of the Buttress.

On the sandstone, some traversing is inevitable. From the Terrace, aim at a prominent rock cannon. The final tower is at least 85 degrees and rickety. Attack by an open groove just right of a large block resting on the Upper Terrace. From the platform above, a crack seemed to lead to easier rocks, but a harder alternative was taken to the left, leading just below a nose and across an exposed spine.

Hamilton and Kerr's Route – Very Difficult. Takes the left branch of West-Central Gully for 150 ft., then traverses diagonally left across the sandstone to the Terrace. On the quartzite the route keeps to the corner near West-Central Gully on the right and is very steep. About the level of the Upper Terrace a traverse is made to the easiest slope at the centre of the Buttress. Some 200 ft. from the top where the Original Route is probably joined is another very steep slabby section on small holds.

West-Central Gully – Difficult (Dr N. Collie and party). This Gully is blocked 400 ft. from the top by an overhang and it has not been climbed in its entirety. The Gully is easy on the sandstone and difficult on the quartzite in the upper reaches. The winter ascent was done in Easter 1968 by W. Wallace and C. G. M. Slesser.

West Buttress Ordinary Route – Difficult. This route starts at the extreme right of the Buttress near Far West Gully and keeps to the right on the sandstone which is taken in four severe pitches. These may be avoided, however, by use of the Broad Terrace, and the climbing on the quartzite above is difficult only. The *Direct Finish* – 200 ft., Mild Severe (T. W. Patey and C. J. S. Bonington, May 1960) involves a strenuous climb on good holds up the clean 30 ft. wall below the final slab which the ordinary route skirts by means of a deep chimney. This leads up to a recess on the left of the final tower from where an easy move leftwards gives access to a flake crack slanting up to the top of the tower. *Fuselage Wall* – 300 ft., Mild Severe (T. W. Patey and J. M. Taylor, June 1962) is a short route on excellent rock on the upper tier of the quartzite overlooking the upper part of Far West Gully. It may be included in an ascent of West

Buttress, by walking round right below the steep upper section or maybe climbed from the bed of Far West Gully.

Far West Gully – Easy – provides a suitable means of descent to Corrie Mhic Fhearchair.

Far West Buttress – 200 ft., Mild Severe (L. S. Lovat and T. Weir, June 1954). The route starts at the obvious corner left of centre and goes up steep rock for 40 ft. before trending horizontally left for 15 ft. on large poor holds to Belay below right-angle corner. There is easy rock for 20 ft., then the Buttress steepens ahead with much variation possible.

The cliffs of Sail Mhor which is the southern containing spur of Coire Mhic Fhearchair are not as fine as the Triple Buttress and do not hold the same attraction. They are described as 'having all the worst features of Torridonian Sandstone – wet, occasionally over-hanging bands of cliff separated by steep grass ledges girdling the crag – all rock when seen from below and all grass from above.

The three deep-cut easy angled gullies were the scene of early pioneering. The most westerly is Morrison's Gully which gives an easy snow climb in winter. Number two Gully has no recorded winter ascent but was climbed in 1899 by Messrs Lawson, Ling and Glover. The lower half is easy angled and the original party diverged right at the upper steeper section on to the upper crest of the Buttress which narrows and swings left above multiple gullies in a fine tower to the summit buttress (Moderate). Number three gully is Easy in summer and was first climbed in winter by A. White and E. K. Edwards.

There are two possible approach routes to this North side of Beinn Eighe, both of which take the walker about two hours of steady going. The track from Grudie Bridge on Loch Maree Side, 5 miles north of Kinlochewe, leads up Glen Grudie for about half the way to a height of 900 ft. The more popular approach, sometimes said to be more laborious, is from Glen Torridon. Leave the road at the bridge over the Allt Coire Dubh Mhoir, 6 miles from Kinlochewe. There is a ruined building just off the roadside with pleasant camp-sites around it or alternatively the Ling Hut lies nearby on the side of Lochanan Iasgaich. A well-made stalker's track passes through Coire Dubh Mhor between Liathach and Beinn Eighe. Leave the main track shortly past its highest point and contour round Sail Mhor of

Beinn Eighe. A number of cairns mark the best line. An indefinite path is traced which improves as it enters the corrie but eventually disappears by the loch-side.

The track which leads directly south of Meall a'Ghiubhais from the Kinlochewe road opposite the entrance to the Anancaun Research Station can also be used but rough ground is encountered eventually and the approach by this route takes considerably longer.

The Traverse of the whole range is a long and strenuous expedition though there are plenty of escape routes and a convenient halfway approach by the stalker's track from the cottage by Loch Bharranch just over 5 miles along Glen Torridon from Kinlochewe.

This track leads northwards into Coire an Laoigh and an easy line can be taken to the crest of the conspicuous spur on the west side of the corrie. This is followed up on to the main ridge 200 yards west of Spidean Coire nan Clach. If used in the descent from the ridge, a cairn can be found marking the way from the spur in Coire nan Laoigh.

From Kinlochewe the traverse can be started from Cromsag, one mile south of the village. This is the popular approach route and follows the course of the Allt a'Chuirn to a height of almost 1500 ft. A steep grass slope continues on to the summit of Creag Dubh (3050 ft.) north-west of Coire Domhain and not named on the 1″ Map. Between this top and Sgurr an Fhir Duibhe (3160 ft.), also unnamed on the 1″ Map, it is necessary to cross a series of pinnacles – The Fhir Dubh or Bodach Dubh (Black old Men) – better known as the Black Carls of Beinn Eighe. To the inexperienced these can cause difficulty and can only be by-passed by a long descent and tiring traverse.

The north-west face of Sgurr an Fhir Dhuibe was explored by T. W. Patey in August 1957. The quartzite cliffs are 300–400 ft. high and take the form of a series of crazy pinnacles and arêtes. However, the ledges dip outwards and the long number of rickety, loose blocks would be a potential hazard to a roped party. The rock is very shattered. The climb was conveniently included in a traverse of the main ridge (west to east) by traversing horizontally along from the col between the above peak and Sgurr Ban. It is not recommended.

An alternative is to climb on to the ridge to Sgurr an Fhir Duibhe by the south-east spur along the south side to the Allt a'Chuirn. The ridge dips westwards for 400 ft. before rising over Sgurr Ban (3188 ft.) whence the going is relatively easy over Spidean Coire nan Clach (3220 ft.). This makes the halfway point mentioned earlier.

From Spidean Coire nan Clach to Coinneach Mhor (3170 ft.) the going remains good and from here the west top, Sail Mhor (3217 ft.) is reached after some easy scrambling to the intervening col. This is the Ceum Grannda or Ugly Step to the head of Easy Gully, an alternative start to the traverse from the west end leading from Coire Mhic Fhearchair.

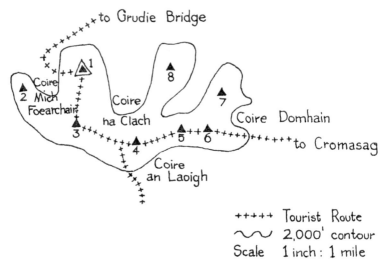

Fig. 5 Sketch Map of Beinn Eighe (the numbers relate to text).

From Coinneach Mhor the way on to Ruadh-stac Mhor (3309 ft.), the higher point on the range, involves a drop of 450 ft. – and a re-ascent of the same.The scree gully on the west side of Ruadh-stac Mhor gives another easy descent in Coire Mhich Fhearchair.

Ruadh-stac Beag (2850 ft. contour), is not usually included in the Traverse, it is separated from Spidean Coire nan Clach on the main ridge by a dip to 2110 ft. North again lies Meall a'Ghuibhais (2882 ft.) which involves a further dip to 1200 ft.

The main ridge with its 7 tops gives a superlative 7-mile ridge walk which in winter becomes a major expedition only for the experienced and well-equipped.

4

Loch Maree to Loch Broom

(1) ***Slioch** (3217 ft.).
(2) **Beinn a'Mhuinnidh** (2231 ft.).
(3) **Beinn Lair** (2817 ft.).
(4) **Beinn Airigh Charr** (2593 ft.).
(5) **Beinn a'Chaisgein Mor** (2802 ft.).
(6) ***A'Mhaighdean** (3061 ft.).
(7) **Ruadh Stac Mor** (2850 ft.).
(8) **Beinn Tarsuinn** (3050 ft.).
(9) ***Mullach Coire Mhic Fhearchair** (3326 ft.).
(10) ***Sgurr Ban** (3194 ft.).
(11) **Beinn a'Chlaidheimh** (just under 3000 ft.).
(12) **Beinn Dearg Mhor** (2974 ft.).
(13) **Beinn Dearg Beag** (2550 ft.).
(14) ***An Teallach** (3483 ft.).
(15) **Beinn Ghoblach** (2082 ft.).

MAP: O.S. One Inch to the Mile (7th Series). Sheet No. 19 – Gairloch and Sheet No. 20 – Ullapool.

The area between Loch Maree and Little Loch Broom contains the complex group of mountains of the Letterewe, Fisherfield and Strathnasheallag deer forests. To the north-west, the area is bounded by Loch Ewe and Gruinard Bay with the intervening peninsula of Rubha Mor. To the south-east lie the mountains of the Fannich group. The area is circled on three sides by motor road; from Dundonnell at the head of Little Loch Broom right round the coast line and along the west shore of Loch Maree to Kinlochewe; but the principal means of communication within the uninhabited maze of mountains in the central portion is by the numerous hill-tracks which lead into and across it.

The most populated centres are to be found around the western coastline. This part suffered little during the Clearances of the nineteenth century and from Gairloch right along through Poolewe to Aultbea, the surrounding lowland belt is the scene of thriving crofting and fishing industries. The Mackenzie lairds hereabouts subsidised early experiments in fishing in the early 1800's and Gairloch is now one of the busiest white-fish and herring ports in the west. The sheltered bay of Loch Ewe is climatically ideal for agriculture, and the surrounding croftland is probably one of the most favourable found anywhere in the Northern Highlands. The famous tropical gardens at Inverewe, created in the 1860's by Osgood Mackenzie, are an attraction which draws thousands of visitors each year. It is now under the National Trust for Scotland.

Accommodation in the interior is scant. This is estate country given over wholly to stalking and fishing, and even suitable bothies are in short supply. There are Youth Hostels at Carn Dearg, just west of Gairloch, Aultbea and Dundonnell, but only the last is of much use to the hill-walker or the climber.

The Junior Mountaineering Club of Scotland, Glasgow Section, have now established premises at Dundonnell. This is the Clarkson Memorial Hut, located at the Old Smiddy, some 200 yds south of the Youth Hostel on the An Teallach side of the road.

The most useful bothy accommodation can be found at Shenaval, in the north of the area at the end of Loch na Sealga, and at Carnmore, in the south, at the end of the Fionn Loch. Both lie on the main transverse track. The cottage at Shenaval is in fairly constant use and there now appears to be little restriction apart from during the recognised stalking season. The use of Carnmore is mentioned later in the text.

For the rest of the area it is best to set up a base camp within the mountains themselves and the choice of sites is fairly unrestricted except during the stalking season.

Shenaval is approached from the Dundonnel road, two miles before reaching Dundonnell Hotel at the head of Little Loch Broom. This is the famous 'Destitution Road' which was built during the potato famine in the 1840's to provide work for the local inhabitants. An obvious Land-Rover track leaves the south side of the road and follows the Allt Gleann Chaorachain through a birch wood before opening out on to the open moorland on the south-east lower slopes of An Teallach. The way rises steeply over the 1250 ft. contour then drops down into Strath na Sealga to join a narrower track bending north-westwards along the north bank of the Abhainn Strath na Sealga past the locked cottage of Achnegie. Shenaval lies less than one and a half miles along the track on this side. The river opens into Loch na Sealga one mile further on.

The rather tedious bend leading down to Achnegie can be cut out by leaving the main path just after it crosses its highest point and making across the rough shoulder down towards the river. This saves more than a mile. From Dundonnell the distance by following the track is seven miles.

It should be noted that the road seen marked as reaching the north end of Loch na Sealga from Gruinard Bay is strictly private and motor access is barred by a locked gate.

From Shenaval, the way across the end of the loch to meet the track to Carnmore, involves a rough pathless walk towards the Abhainn Glen na Muice. The building seen on the far side of the stream is Larachantivore and is kept locked. A wire bridge framework is found a short way upstream from here but the footplank is usually absent and the river has to be forded. The path continues for a mile along Gleann na Muice before rising westwards up Gleann na Muice Beag along the lower south slopes of Beinn Dearg Mhor. The prominent rock face at the junction of the glens is Junction Buttress which affords some rock-climbing. The head of Gleann na Muice Beag is exceptionally steep and this section requires steady going, but once over the top the way eases off and is straightforward for the next mile or so to Lochan Feith Mhic 'Illean. From here the path slants downwards along the south-eastern slopes of Beinn a'Chaisgein Mor to Carnmore. The total distance from Shenaval is almost seven miles. The Lodge at Carnmore lies above the south-east end of the Fionn Loch and bothy accommodation is usually obtainable in the barn when it is not required for Lodge use. The whole of the surrounding area lies in the Fisherfield Forest owned by Colonel Whitbread who does not encourage visitors, especially between August and October when stalking is in progress.

Carnmore can also be reached by track from Poolewe thus forming an important through route from north-east to south-west. The approach is by way of Kernsary, leaving the main road at the bridge over the Ewe near Poolewe Hotel. Permission to take a car up the private road to Kernsary can be obtained by communication with Mr C. Littlejohn, the estate factor at Letterewe, and there is usually a parking-cum-access fee of £1 charged at Kernsary. This saves almost 3 miles of walking leaving another 8 miles of rough going to Carnmore, much of which is over stalker's tracks but parts of which are indistinct. The track past the farm follows the left bank of the stream upwards on to the shoulder at its head and the small plateau is crossed pathless. Descend to pick up a broken track leading down to Loch na Doire Chrionnaich and this is followed on the north side until a good track is joined. After this the way is straightforward.

There is a direct path to Carnmore from Letterewe which is reached by private ferry from the road on the west side of Loch Maree but use of this cannot be guaranteed and is largely up to individual negotiation.

From Kinlochewe a useful track leads around the south-east end of Loch Maree which passes through Gleann Bianasdail to the South end of Loch Fada. This gives good access to both Slioch and Beinn a'Mhuinidh and by branching upwards over the shoulder of Meall Riabach just past the entrance to Gleann Bianasdail one can follow another main track to Letterewe.

The mountains can also be approached from the east by track along Loch a'Bhraoin to Lochivraon Bothy. From here a good track swings northwards by way of Loch an Nid to connect with the Shenaval track at Achnegie. Alternatively, the cross-country walker can reach the south end of Loch Fada over the Bealach na Croise.

Slioch (3217 ft.)

Slioch is the most impressive of the mountain ranges which stands immediately to the north of Loch Maree and its summit can easily be reached from the Gleann Bianasdail track from several points. The upper part of the mountain is of Torridonian Sandstone, the lower plinth being of Lewisian Gneiss. The summit lies on the western end above the steep cliffs which form the north-west face. Sgurr an Tuill Bhain (3058 ft.), the subsidiary summit, lies $\frac{3}{4}$ mile to the east and can be reached without much re-ascent along the connecting ridge. A south-east ridge from the summit terminates at Mheall Each and with the eastern ridge contains the big east-facing corrie of the mountain – Coire Tuill Bhain – which is the deer sanctuary.

The steep north-west face of Slioch is reached from the path over the shoulder of Meall Riabach to Letterewe. The path crosses a stream 1 mile beyond the end of the glen and this is followed to its source – marked by a cairned boulder.

The main Buttress of Slioch lies immediately above, and the Stepped Ridge is seen in profile on the left divided by a series of platforms which appear as towers from below.

Stepped Ridge – 800 ft., Very Difficult (*Direct*) (McDougall, Cram and Blackwood, 1933). The route is flanked on the right by a slabby forked gully but escapes as often as possible on the left. The Main Buttress gives a climb of 800 ft., Severe (A. Parker, 1952).

Beinn a'Mhuinidh (2231 ft.)

Beinn a'Mhuinidh lies on the east side of Gleann Bianasdail, and like Slioch, is most easily approached from Kinlochewe. The normal sequence of rock formation on Beinn a'Mhuinidh – Lewisian Torridonian and Cambrian – is further capped with Lewisian Gneiss marking the line of the Thrust Zone. The summit itself is unnoteworthy but the crags along the south-west and north-west sides are of interest to the rock-climber. The band of quartzite running for most of the length of these sides produces the most interesting features and at the corner of the glen has its best and largest exposure of rock in the Bonnaidh Dubh Buttress. The buttress on the south-west slope marked by the 300 ft. waterfall is Waterfall Buttress. This gave one of the original routes on the cliff, first climbed by G. T. Glover and Dr Inglis Clark in 1899. The original route, the West Climb, here starts 150 ft. left of the fall at a grassy chimney, at about 600 ft. above sea-level, and is steep and exposed throughout (Severe). It will give some indication of the continuous difficulty of this short route when it is remembered that the original party took six hours over it, though that time included much 'gardening'. The spray of the fall enables the vegetation to renew itself quickly, and the route is now of historical interest only.

When seen from Loch Maree, the mountains lying to the north-west of Slioch appear unremarkable, but on their north-eastern side they form an almost continuous line of steep cliffs of dark hornblende schist which offers a wealth of fine rock climbing. The summits can be reached with little difficulty from Poolewe by use of the Kernsary track already described and a choice of any of the cross-tracks leading from it to Letterewe.

Beinn Airigh Charr (2593 ft.)

Beinn Airigh Charr is the most accessible of the group and has extensive cliffs culminating in the north top, known as Martha's Peak. This rises as a huge rock tower above Lochan Doire Chrionach just over 2 miles along the track from Kernsary. Martha was a a legendary local lass who took her herds to graze on the mountains and is credited with the first and only traverse of the tower. Unfortunately she dropped her crook and fell to her death in an effort to recover it. Staircase Gully – basically a scree gully with occasional rock pitches – separates Martha's Peak from the rest of the crags, which diminish in height towards the east. East of the gully is a 400 ft. wall of overhanging rock rising from steep slabs, and further on, still, a lesser face containing Square Buttress.

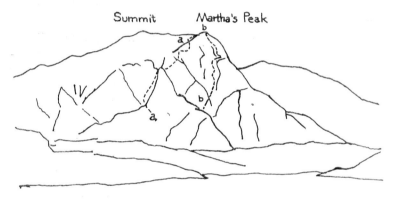

(a) original route South Buttress. (b) original route Main Tower.

Fig. 6   Beinn Airigh Charr: Martha's Peak.

The southern buttress of Martha's Peak was first climbed in 1909 by G. T. Glover and W. N. Ling and the *Original Route* (1100 ft. up to Difficult) on the Main Tower was made the following year by G. T. Glover, H. Walker, R. Corry and W. N. Ling. This route follows a line almost straight up from the broadest part of Lochan Doire Chrionach to the top of the tower, starting up the easy area between the two lower arms of rock, then threading ledges until directly below the steep, clean upper face which is climbed to the right of the steepest section. From the flat platform halfway up the upper crags there is a chance of routes to the top of the peak. The original party followed the well-defined chimney which is grassy and steep with not too many holds.

The lower part of Martha's Peak is split in two by a wide grassy scoop. The right branch does not seem to afford any great possibility for climbing but the left branch was explored by C. G. M. Slesser and party in 1951 and gives a Severe route of 500 ft. – *Lower Buttress Direct* – starting at the lowest rocks just above the east end of Lochan Doire Chrionach. The line trends leftwards up a gentle flake and the first 70 ft. are loose and flaky. It would seem possible to combine the climb with the Original Route to give over 1500 ft. of climbing.

Staircase Gully, which separates the main tower of Martha's Peak from the lower cliffs to the east gives a long route – 1200 ft., Severe (P. N. L. Tranter and N. Travers, 1964). The climb starts up the left wall from the bottom of the gully and has much easy scree between the pitches. The standard is about Very Difficult except for the crux pitch – an overhanging chimney in the upper thrust.

Square Buttress is contained in the last small face of Beinn Airigh Charr, to the east of a small unnamed lochan. It gives one route – Square Buttress, 400 ft., Difficult (J. C. Stewart, S. McPherson, W. D. Brooker and J. W. Morgan, 1951) – the difficulties here lie mainly in the lower half.

Meall Mheinnidh (2391 ft.)

Meall Mheinnidh stands south-east of Beinn Airigh Charr with an intervening dip to 1150 ft. – Strathan Buidhe – which carries one of the cross-tracks to Letterewe. On the south-east again a dip of 1600 ft. separates Meall Mheinnidh from Beinn Lair (2817 ft.). The Bealach Mheinnidh which lies between them carries the track from Letterewe Ferry to Carnmore Lodge.

There is one route here – *Glasgow Ridge* – 500 ft., Difficult (W. D. Blackwood, D. Parlane, B. Wright, 1947). This goes up the central rise. Skirting below an obvious slanting terrace the climbing being generally indefinite.

Beinn Lair (2817 ft.)

The cliffs on the north side of Beinn Lair overlooking Allt Gleann Tulacha, like those of Bein Airigh Charr, are comprised of hornblende schist. The rock slopes steeply into the hill giving a profusion of incut hold and is sounder and less vegetated than one might expect. Belays are scarce, however, and when wet, the rock needs special care. The face contains more than twenty buttresses, ridges or ribs each containing deep cut gullies, the height varying from 400 ft. to 1400 ft. The crags were first attempted in 1909 by G. T. Glover and N. Ling, but were neglected until 1951 from when there has been considerably more activity and there is a profusion of rock climbing routes of all degrees of difficulty. The gullies are largely untouched – partly because of their wetness and partly their general inaccessibility. The winter possibilities, however, could be worth exploring.

The cliffs of Bein Lair normally fall into two main subdivisions – The Fionn Loch cliffs at the north-west end of the escarpment and the Loch Fada cliffs at the south-east end.

The principal features and routes are described from north-west to south-east.

N. North Summit Buttress.	Ag. Angel Buttress.	E. Excalibur.
B. Butterfly Buttress.	Wi. Wisdom Buttress.	
A. Amphitheatre.	F. The Fang.	Creig na Gaorach.
M. Molar Buttress.	T. The Tooth.	G1. Zebra Slabs
Y. Y Buttress.	W. West Chimney.	G2. Jealousy

Fig. 7   Beinn Lair: the Fionn Loch Cliffs.

Fionn Loch Cliffs

Excalibur Buttress is the obvious clean looking mass of rock to the right of the crags. There is a deep cut gully on the left, and a buttress beset with overhangs on its right. The route, *Excalibur* – 400 ft., Very Difficult (E. A. Wrangham and A. Glegg, 1952) starts at the side of the gully and is moderate at first, becoming steeper.

West Chimney Route – 600 ft., Very Difficult (C. G. M. Slesser, G. Dutton, J. Wight, 1951) starts 100 ft. left of the most westerly of the large buttresses which lies west of the Tooth. A moist groove leads leftwards over steep discontinuous rock to a grass terrace at 400 ft. The steep wall above is climbed by a 70 ft. wet chimney in the left corner. Enter the gully leading to the cave above. Climb the steep rib of good rock up to the right or by back and foot from the cave. A scramble then follows to the top.

The Tooth – 650 ft., Difficult (D. C. Hutchison, B. S. Smith, Miss A. Hood and J. S. Orr, 1951). The climb starts towards the middle of the buttress to the right of Cavity Chimney and from mid height where the route joins the left hand edge of the buttress there is a delightful series of short, exposed pitches to the top.

Cavity Chimney and *Wisdom Wall* – 700 ft., Very Difficult (D. C. Hutchison and B. S. Smith, 1951). Starts at the base of the Chimney to the left of the Tooth.

Wisdom Buttress – 700 ft., Very Difficult (J. Smith, Miss A. Hood and J. S. Orr, 1951). A magnificent climb, exposed sustained and of continuous interest; maybe the best route on the cliff. Start at the bottom right corner of the buttress, which is a conspicuous object on account of its slender cigar-shaped aspect.

250 ft. Climb diagonally to the left, above a lower overhang, then up more to the right to a small platform, and an obvious line of weakness until it ends at a diminutive stance, and doubtful belay underneath a small overhang.

75 ft. Traverse left and evade the overhang by a slab on the left.

100 ft. Continue straight up slabs on the left, then traverse back by a ledge to the centre of the buttress, or go half right and climb an open chimney to reach the same point.

275 ft. Climb the nose above by an excursion on the right wall, steep and with sloping holds. Return to the crest, and belay (100 ft.). Continue up the steep nose above then follow the crest of the buttress to the top.

Between Wisdom Buttress and the next Buttress on the left, Angel Buttress, is a fine route, *Bat's Gash* – 700 ft., Very Difficult (B. S. Smith and D. C. Hutchison, 1951). The climb starts at the foot of the deep-cut chimney immediately left of Wisdom Buttress and the interest is maintained throughout, with magnificent cave scenery in the middle section.

About 100 feet up is a chimney pitch with a narrow exit, leading to a couch of blaeberries. At about 450 ft. there is a two-tiered chimney, followed by a four-tiered, the last of which overhangs. This is avoided by escaping on to the right-hand buttress, rejoining the chimney above the overhang and continuing in it to the top, only one pitch having any difficulty.

Angel Buttress – 800 ft., Moderate – lies to the left of Bat's Gash. In the upper half there is an obvious bar of overhangs, split towards the right by a deep chimney, which is continued below as a minor gully, splitting the lower part of the buttress into two separate noses.

There are four recorded climbs on the Buttress, of which *Pilgrim's Progress* – 800 ft., Severe (J. S. Orr and Miss A. Hood, 1951), is the best route. It starts from a scoop in the scree at the lowest point of the rocks, up a large triangle of slab which gives access to the main slabby face of the right-hand part of the buttress.

Molar Buttress is the broad buttress to the left of Angel Buttress, and right of the Amphitheatre. It has five routes on it and another runs up the right-hand gully, then up the minor buttress – Y-buttress – which lies between the upper parts of Molar and Angel Buttresses. The climbs from left to right are:

Y-buttress – 400 ft., Difficult (E. A. Wrangham and F. Adams, 1951). A messy and vegetatious climb. Between the branches of Y-gully and west of Molar Buttress.

Right-hand Route – 700 ft., Very Difficult (E. A. Wrangham and F. Adams, 1951). The climb starts up a stretch of easy angled usually wet slabs at the right-hand side of the buttress, and uses the most right-hand of the conspicuous breaks through the band of steep rock which crosses the whole buttress at two-thirds of its height.

Damocles Cracks – 700 ft. (Climbed by an Oxford party, pre-1953) starting at the lowest rocks and continuing straight up the middle of the Buttress.

Left-hand Route – 650 ft., Difficult (F. Adams and E. A. Wrangham, 1951). This starts at the foot of the buttress just left of a conspicuous short black chimney and follows the left hand edge of the buttress all the way.

Route 1 – 800 ft., Very Difficult (D. C. Hutchison and B. S. Smith, 1951). Starts up an obvious gully towards the left of the buttress.

Rose Route – 700 ft., Moderate (J. Smith and N. A. Todd, 1951). This starts well to the left of the Buttress and follows the left wall of

8. The Mainreachan Buttress of Fuar Tholl.

9. Raeburn's Buttress, Sgorr Ruadh, Lochcarron.

the Buttress not far from the gully on the left. This gully – The Amphitheatre – is suitable for descent.

The large mass of rock to the left of the Amphitheatre and right of the great bulk of the North Summit Buttress, is Butterfly Buttress. It is in fact composed of four separate buttresses, the two outside ones running the full height of the cliff, the two smaller ones, inserted between them at top and bottom.

There are two routes so far – *Right Wing* – 1000 ft., Very Difficult (E. A. Wrangham and D. St J. R. Wagstaff, 1953) and *Left Wing* – 1000 ft., Moderate (I. G. Rowe, 1967).

Immediately left of *Butterfly Buttress* the prominent cone-shaped buttress of enormous bulk which falls from the north summit of Beinn Lair to the upper reaches of Gleann Tulacha is North Summit Buttress which gives a 1400 ft. moderate route (Miss M. Langmuir and M. J. O'Hara, 1957). Starting at the bottom left-hand corner of the rocks, at the point where a stream emerges from the left-hand bounding gully. The route is recommended as a pleasant way on to the summit of the mountain from Glen Tulacha rather than as a rock climb.

Between the Fionn Loch and Loch Fada cliffs, rather nearer to the western end is *Marathon Ridge*. It is the first on the left of two very prominent buttresses to the south-east of the spur forming the highest part of the cliffs, and in a straight line between the summit of Beinn Lair and that of Beinn Tarsuinn Chaol. The route 1300 ft., Difficult (W. D. Brooker, S. McPherson, J. W. Morgan and J. C. Stewart, 1951), has probably an unavoidable pitch situated at about 800 ft. above the base, which is '. . . more than Difficult'.

Loch Fada Cliffs

The thin buttress on the immediate left of Marathon Ridge gives one route, *Olympus* – 500 ft., Difficult (E. A. Wrangham, D. St J. R. Wagstaff, 1953). The route is straightforward keeping as near to the left edge as possible.

The highest buttress visible from the head of the Loch distinguished by a large steep ridge in its upper section is *Stag Buttress*. This gives a route 800 ft., Severe (J. D. Foster and D. Leaver, 1951). The same party set up routes on the two clean looking buttresses which come low down near the head of Loch Fada. *Falstaff* – 400 ft., Very Severe, starts at the lowest points of the rocks on the right-hand buttress and

F   81

Sesame Buttress – 450 ft., Severe, on the left-hand buttress. Starting at the foot of a wall to the right of a prominent crack at the lowest point.

The highly distinctive rock tower high up on the slopes above the upper part of Lochan Fhada is known as The Keep. It appears as a very steep sided wedge of clean looking rock. The west face is smaller, but cleaner and continuous and contains *Rainbow Wall* – 400 ft., Severe. Starting at the lowest point of the buttress, *Central Route* – 650 ft., Severe, goes straight up the nose, with easier variations reported as being possible.

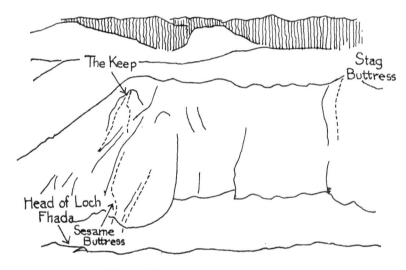

Fig. 8   Beinn Lair: the Fada Cliffs.

Enjoyable climbing on excellent rock is found on Creig na Gaorach below the Fionn Loch Cliff of Beinn Lair, which is reached by following the stream south-east from the junction of the paths at the south-west corner of the Fionn Loch. There are two obvious buttresses with a little buttress beyond them, just below the col, and another smaller buttress lies between them. Approaching from this direction the first buttress has one climb, *Jealousy* – 660 ft., Very Difficult (M. J. O'Hara and Miss M. Langmuir, 1957). The route starts at the lowest part of the rocks a few feet above the point where the stream washes against the foot of the rocks. The second buttress,

Nanny Goat Buttress – gives *Zebra Slabs* – 440 ft., Very Difficult (M. J. O'Hara and Miss M. Langmuir, 1957), starting from the centre of the buttress behind five large fallen blocks, just left of a small sapling, and just right of a water trickle.

Beinn a'Chaisgein Mor (2802 ft.)

Beinn a'Chaisgein Mor is a flat topped mountain lying on the east side of the Fionn Loch immediately above Carnmore Lodge. It falls away gradually towards the north and east and a roundabout route on to the summit is made by way of either the track north along the Fionn Loch or from the track to Shenaval. Its main importance is in the existence of the fine exposures of Carnmore Crag (NG.980773) and Torr na h'Iolaire (NG.984773) – both of which overlook the east end of the loch. Carnmore Crag, the most westerly of the two, lies above the barn at Carnmore and from here is seen to comprise of an Upper and Lower Wall with a Central Bay. The main features are described as follows:

The Lower Wall – This is the extensive mass of rock which forms the wall of the crag below the Central Bay, and below Grey Wall. It includes all the rock to the right of Fionn Buttress. The main features are:

(1) A curving red scar in the rocks on the left, isolating between it and Fionn Buttress route a scimitar-like sweep of very steep smooth slabs with minor ribs.

(2) The First Rib, a very prominent object in the morning light, which rises from the foot of the crag as a well-formed nose of rock, but merges back into the general angle at half height of the lower wall where the Red Scar swings across. To the right of this is a deep scoop, bounded on its right by the Second Rib.

(3) The Second Rib, which is also very obvious in the morning light. This rib also merges with the wall after 250 ft., but is topped by slabs in the Central Bay. At the right of its base is a conspicuous yellow scar.

(4) A broad area of steep vegetated slab, Botanist's Boulevard.

(5) A big overhanging mass with slabs to its right.

The Upper Wall. This is the very steep bar of rock above the Central Bay. On the left it is bounded by the out-thrust nose of Fionn Buttress.

To the right its height diminishes. The principal features from left to right are:
(1) An easy-angled grey slab at the bottom left, bounded by the wall of the Fionn Buttress on the left, and above by a bulging overhang topped by a 150 ft. vertical wall. In the top left-hand corner there is prospect of escape by a slanting crack.
(2) The top right-hand corner of the slab leads to the foot of a wall which is slightly less than vertical.
(3) Slanting from top left towards bottom right across this very steep wall is an overhang.
(4) Above this is another very steep wall whose height increases towards the right where it forms the left retaining wall of The Dièdre.
(5) The Dièdre, which is one of the most prominent features of the crag. This has twin cracks in the back and a vertical right wall coming out into a plumb vertical nose.
(6) To the right of this a steep ramp of slabs leads from the bay to the top of the cliffs.

The Crag has produced a wide variety of routes described as 'comparing favourably with any in Britain'. One of the finest is *Dragon* – 340 ft., Hard Very Severe (G. J. Fraser and M. J. O'Hara, April 1957). This is a very steep and in places overhanging route with great exposure. The rock is perfect throughout and security is good. The route is highly recommended. No particular crux. Start at the lower right corner of the relatively easy angled pale grey slab which forms the lowest part of the upper wall on its left. Spike belays in turf below a steep corner almost directly above the perched blocks.
60 ft. Move left on to the slab and climb it to turf patch. Rope sling thread.
50 ft. Continue up the slab to a narrow heather ledge on the right at the foot of the steeper wall. Peg belay in place, two doubtful spikes.
80 ft. Climb a groove for 15 ft., and pass the toit which fills it on the right. Traverse left out of the cracks a few feet above the toit to gain easier grooves, large spike belay.
30 ft. Up right to huge spike belay, good stance.
70 ft. Up and slightly to the left is a chimney in yellow rock, ending at the huge overhangs. Climb the chimney, escaping at the top on to a rib (little). Two leaf pegs in place, and a tiny ledge provides a sensational stance and belay.
50 ft. Traverse left to the skyline and up the rib.

The great central nose of the crag gives the best climb in the region, *Fionn Buttress* – 750 ft., Very Severe (M. J. O'Hara and W. D. Blackwood, 1957). The route is steep and exposed. The rock is perfect and the interest very sustained. The start is from a turf ledge at the foot of a great chimney at a prominent pale patch.

50 ft. Up slab, then traverse right into corner. Thread and spike belays below overhang.

50 ft. Up and over loose block on right wall to a ledge. Up crack on wall to right. Step right in 10 ft. and round on to a slab. Across and belay at chockstone in chimney beyond.

80 ft. Up the right wall, then up turf half right. Up a flake leaning against grey slabs. Belay at top.

50 ft. Crux. Up slab, left to a ledge, back as high as possible for 7 ft., then straight up to an overhung ledge.

80 ft. Cross left into a wet recess. Loose bollards. Up the wet corner to turf recess.

80 ft. Up corner or walls to left until below overhang. Traverse right, and climb the overhang 10 ft. from its right-hand end. Sensational. Move right above to stance and belays.

60 ft. Traverse right across the face to stance and belays on right edge of buttress.

70 ft. Gain a flake 20 ft. above on left. Above it move left a few feet then up right. Very inconspicuous thread belay.

70 ft. Up slabs above keeping to ridge crest. Belay at niche.

60 ft. Up crest to heather ledge, and perched blocks belay below overhanging slab.

60 ft. Over the blocks and up the slab on to a shelf. Move right to belay at top right-hand corner of this.

60 ft. Wall above, leftwards to the top.

Torr na h'Iolaire is the great rocky tower with falls south and west from the summit of Sgurr na Laocain directly above Carnmore Lodge. Seen from there the main features:

(1) Lower Wall, slanting down from left to right with two prominent red ribs at its left-hand end, below a huge perched block, and a small rib below a steep wall with overhangs along its base.

(2) Above a perched block is a bar of steep rock about 150 ft. high, composed of numerous coloured sections, Harlequin Wall. Above this is another terrace, with a prominent sharp-topped pinnacle, The Shark's Tooth.

(3) Above this terrace is a very steep wall divided by numerous ribs and corners. This is Carcase Wall. At the far end left is a lozenge of slab above the great gully.

(4) Above the Carcase Wall is a block of grey slabs, the Lower Summit Buttress.

(5) The summit of the hill is composed of a long wall of very steep and clean looking rock. Twin chimneys high on the left form a prominent land-mark. To the left of these is the west face. Well over to the right is a deep-set slab recess.

The longest climb is *Ipswich Rib* which gives 1200 ft. of very enjoyable climbing. First climbed by C. J. Fraser and P. R. Steele in March 1956 (1250 ft.), Very Difficult.

This is in effect a well-defined route on the lower wall, followed by a considerable length of easier ground to the foot of the Upper Summit Buttress, and a route on this:

Lower Wall – Start at the foot of the little rib below and at the right-hand end of the Lower Wall. This is the very lowest point of the rocks. 100 ft. – Follow crest of the rib to where it joins the steeper wall at the foot of a crack. 70 ft. – Ascend a few feet, traverse to the right and continue into a niche, beneath a bulging overhang. 60 ft. – Step down to another ledge below the right wall of the niche, then up for 15 feet and traverse a slab into an overhanging chimney. Exposed. Climb the chimney to easy ground. 50 ft. – Scrambling and a short chimney lead back left to the crest of an indefinite rib. 70 ft. – Easy scrambling up sheets of slabs, keeping near the rib aiming for the foot of the prominent slab recess of the Upper Summit Buttress.

Upper Summit Buttress – Start at the base which forms the left-hand boundary of the slab recess. 60 ft. – Climb a chimney just to the right of the rib, then up slabs to the foot of a very steep crack. 50 ft. – Traverse right to a platform below the dièdre in the slab recess. Mantelshelf, and make a return traverse to the top of the crack. 80 ft. – Up a chimney behind a flake and follow slabs to the top, keeping the crest of the rib. This combination forms a fairly natural line: an excellent introduction to the district. Climbing nowhere more than difficult after the first section, the rock is perfect and the route finishes at the summit of Sgurr na Laocain, one of the finest view-points of the area.

Details of all climbs on the crags are found in the Carnmore Section of the Scottish Mountaineering Club *Northern Highland Area Climbing Guide*, Vol. I, published in December 1969.

A'Mhaighdean (3061 ft.)

A'Mhaighdean is usually described as being the most remote of the Scottish mountains and lies almost 9 miles equidistant from Kinlochewe, Poolewe and Dundonnell. The mountain rises as a graceful, crested ridge from the Dubh Loch in a series of rocky steps leading up to its summit which lies at the south-eastern end some two miles from Carnmore. The north-west end of the ridge gives the most interesting climb on to the summit and this can be reached with little difficulty from the track leading up from Carnmore to Lochan Feith Mhic-Illean.

Alternatively, follow the track to the lochan and then take the branch track leading across the Allt Bruthach an Easain which leads upwards towards the Feur Loch between A'Mhaighdean and Ruadh Stac Mor (2850 ft.). The track is marked as stopping after a mile but in fact continues right up over the saddle between the two mountains and gives good walking throughout. The atmosphere in this corrie is one of utter seclusion and the scenery has a strange beauty. Fuar Loch Mor alternates in colour between deep blue and translucent green, accentuated by the stark contrast of the red cliffs of Ruadh Stac Mor on one side of the track and the light grey gneiss of A'Mhaighdean on the other. The summit of either mountain can easily be reached from the saddle.

The view from the summit is extremely fine. The mountain lies in the middle of three lochs – Loch Dubh, Gorm Loch Mor and Fuar Loch Mor – and to the north-west and south-east the longer waters of Fionn Loch and Fada stretch between the surrounding hills. The great crags on the north side of the mountains of Letterewe can be examined in detail, while to the north and east the ridges of Mullach Coire Mhic Fhearchair and Sgurr Bhan lead the eye towards the great range of An Teallach and its neighbour, Beinn Dearg Mhor.

Rock climbing on A'Mhaighdean is mainly to be found on the cliffs which fall south-westwards from the summit ridge. The mountain is of sandstone and gneiss. The four buttresses near the crest of the ridge on the south-west side are of sandstone, giving good, clean rock-climbing. The summit is of gneiss, the highest point to which this formation rises in Scotland, and so is the Pillar Buttress which falls 500 ft. from under the summit facing south. Below the west face of the Pillar Buttress is the West Gully.

The four sandstone buttresses (numbered from left to right) can best be approached by contouring round from the north-west ridge of the mountain. There is no climb on the First Buttress, but the Second, known as Breccia Buttress, gives one route starting from the bottom right-hand corner – *Conglomerate Arête* 300 ft., Very Difficult (M. J. O'Hara and Miss M. Langmuir, 1957).

The Third Buttress – The Red Slab – is identified by the single sheet of slab ending in a steep wall on the right. A huge pinnacle lying against the lower left-hand corner of the slab forms a small subsidiary buttress. *Red Slab Route*, 300 ft., Difficult (M. J. O'Hara and Miss M. Langmuir, 1957), begins from the corner between this subsidiary buttress and the slab at the furthest right accessible point to the slab. *Doe Crack*, 280 ft., Very Difficult (J. D. C. Peackock and A. Finlay, 1957) starts from the same point.

The Fourth Buttress – Gritstone Buttress – has three routes of Severe standard. The buttress has a central chimney which starts as a cave and narrows to a crack, opening out again at the top of the crag. The upper part is climbed by *Compensation*, 180 ft. (R. Isherwood and E. Birch, 1967).

Two longer routes are found to the right of the Four Buttresses on the left of the West Gully. *Whitbread's Aiguille* – 900 ft., Severe (M. J. O'Hara and G. J. Fraser, 1957), starts at the foot of the easy-angled buttress which forms the left-hand side of the West Gully using the pinnacle at the left-hand corner. To the left of this is *Vole Buttress* – 900 ft., Very Difficult (M. J. O'Hara and R. G. Hargreaves, 1957). The route starts at the foot of the prominent V-groove towards the left of the crag.

On the upper of the two bands of coarsely crystalline rock which slants across the Dubh Loch face under the sandstone cap of the mountains are the *Octave Ribs. Fahrenheit*, the 4th rib from the left next to an obvious red rib gives a sustained and exposed climb of 100 ft., Mild Severe (F. Green and G. McCallum, 1959). The fifth rib has a shorter route, *Soh What* – 110 ft., Very Difficult.

Access to the south-facing Pillar Buttress of A'Mhaidghdean from the west is awkward. The best approach from Carnmore is to traverse the summit and descend a big grassy gully near it which leads towards the mouth of Gorm Loch Mor, traversing right on the 2500-ft. contour line to the foot of the buttress. Alternatively, climb up to the crags from the shores of Gorm Loch Mor.

The true nose of the buttress gives 500 ft. of Difficult climbing, finishing at the summit cairn, a route pioneered by Dr and Mrs J. H. B. Bell. The first 80 ft. on easy rocks from the foot of the rib

10. The eastern section of the Coulin Forest, showing private motor road from Achnashellach to Glen Torridon, with Beinn Eighe in the background.

11. Liathach, main peak from east.

Overleaf
12. North Face of Liathach, showing Coire na Caime.

leads to a platform. From here the route continues up slabs and walls right of the true crest of the buttress, climbing on steep slab by parallel cracks. Easy rocks, a difficult crack, then 20 ft. of difficult slab lead to an impasse requiring an awkward traverse to a large chock-stone filled crack.

The parallel cracks pitch is also utilised by the *Alternative Route* – 175 ft., Very Difficult (J. D. Foster and D. Leaver, 1950), which starts to the right of a large crack up a short wall to the right of a cairn. *Baird, Croften and Lestlie's Route* – 500 ft., Severe (1953), lies close to and is partly the same as this latter one starting to the right of Pillar Buttress. *The Slot* – 485 ft., Mild Severe (R. G. Hargreave and M. J. O'Hara, 1957) follows a straight natural line which starts a few yards to the right of Pillar Buttress route at an obvious deep-cut chimney and continues to the left of the true crest of the buttress as a line of chimneys and cracks. The route is very similar to the earlier *Triple Cracks Route* – 400 ft., Very Difficult, climbed by J. Bennet's party in 1951.

The *West Face* of Pillar Buttress gives two routes, both of Severe standard. The *West Face Route* – 800 ft. (C. G. M. Slesser, G. Dutton and J. Wight, 1951) and *Eagle Grooves* – 360 ft. (M. J. O'Hara and R. G. Hargreaves, 1957).

Beinn Tarsuinn (3050 ft.)
This ridge lies 2 miles to the south-east of A'Mhaighdean on the south-eastern side of the head of Gleann na Muice and can be reached either by following the line of the glen from the bothy at Shenaval partly by way of the Carnmore track or from the direction of A'Mhaighdean. From the latter direction, the way is rather tedious, involving a considerable drop in height over some awkward sandstone ledges several of which attain a respectable height and force the walker westwards. The ridge seen from the south is uninteresting, but once on the crest it is remarkably narrow in places and in certain weather conditions requires good route-selection. To the north it falls in a series of terraced sandstone cliffs which can be reached from the floor of Gleann na Muice with little difficulty.

The mountain is seldom climbed for its own sake and is usually included in a circuit of the neighbouring tops which form a ridge along the east side of Gleann na Muice. To the east is a little pointed top of 2700 ft., and north of this rises **Mullach Coire Mhic Fhearchair** (3326 ft.), the highest point on this ridge. The western face is of red sandstone seamed with gullies, but above the 3000 ft. contour the summit cone is covered with quartzite blocks giving the usual unpleasant scrambling. The main feature of the mountain is the ridge of gneiss which extends for a mile east-south-east and terminates in some fine pinnacles. These are easier to climb over than try to by-pass. The mountain can be approached from this side from the bothy at Lochavroan but the intervening ground below the ridge gives difficult walking over peat bog and route finding is pretty much left to the individual.

Sgurr Ban (3220 ft.)

Sgurr Ban is similar in many respects to Mullach Coire Mhic Fhearchair. It is mainly of sandstone but if anything, its quartzite capping is even more unpleasant to walk over than the latter's. The summit lies $\frac{1}{2}$ mile to the north of the last. The quartzite on the eastern side of the summit is extremely unpleasant and in wet or icy conditions becomes dangerous. An unusual feature is the broad exposure of this formation which dips, completely unbroken, down towards Loch Nid. A descent to Achnegie from Sgurr Ban is a long and tedious business and necessitates negotiating the Amhain Loch an Nid by the best means possible. The track leading down the east side of the river is usually wet and dirty.

Beinn A'Chlaidheimh (just under 3000 ft.)

Beinn a'Chlaidheimh lies 2 miles north of Sgurr Ban and its ascent involves a drop to 2000 ft. Loch a'Bhrisidh nestling in the hollow of the intervening saddle is a good navigational guide in bad weather. The mountain lies at the northern extremity of the ridge and a way can easily be found down on that side towards the Shenaval track. From the bothy the summit is less than 2 miles almost due south.

A complete circuit of the ridge and the summits of A'Mhaighdean and Ruadh Stac Mor from Shenaval makes an excellent hill-walking circuit for a long summer's day.

Beinn Dearg Mhor (2974 ft.)

Beinn Dearg Mhor lies two miles to the west of Shenaval overlooking Loch na Sealga. Seen from Shenaval it is an extremely fine mountain, its two ridges curving inwards from north and south rise on to the cone-shaped summit enclosing on its north-east side Coire nan Clach with its fine rock buttresses. In winter the graceful outline of the ridges is even finer and are especially apparent from the ridges of the Fannichs. The summit itself can easily be reached, either by way of the Carnmore track which at the head of Gleann na Muice Beag gives a straightforward climb with very little ascent. Alternatively, by way of the north-east ridge or in conjunction with a climb over Beinn Dearg Beag (2550 ft.). This lies 1 mile north-west of Beinn Dearg Mhor and has a fine rocky ridge which gives a good winter traverse.

The cliffs of Coire nan Clach were first pioneered in 1899 by Messrs Sang and Morrison whose original route on the South Peak, the left-hand mass of the corrie wall, was of a Moderate scrambling nature. Fifty years were to elapse before any further recorded exploration took place and most of the climbing since has been done in winter conditions.

The narrow gully first on the left of Coire nan Clach finishing at a fierce-looking notch in the skyline, well below the South Peak is *Twisting Gully* which with a difficult unnamed gully further right were climbed in Easter, 1949. The whole of this East Face of the Coire is somewhat broken, and although impressive from below, the general angle is easy.

South of the East face are broken craggy slopes leading to a very slender buttress – *Flake Buttress* in the old edition of the guide but sometimes known as *Book-end Buttress*. This is cut off on both sides by deep gullies of which the left-hand one was climbed by D. Wilson and W. Beveridge in May 1966 giving a loose and vegetated route of Difficult standard. Both the east and west walls of the buttress are vertical and the buttress itself gives one of the best routes on the mountain. *Flake Buttress* – 350 ft., Severe (A. Parker and party, Easter, 1952). The route starts up the left corner and maintains its severity throughout. The crux of the climb is on the fourth pitch.

Start up the left corner for 10 ft., then traverse delicately right to the extreme edge. Up round corner on right to block. Then back left and up to a narrow ledge and piton belay (50 ft.). Thence to the right, round corner to side opposite G.B. Traverse 20 ft. on to this flank, then 5 ft. up steep awkward corner and back to face of buttress and belay (60 ft.). Up platform on left; difficult start up wall 8 ft. right by slanting ledge with crack, round ledge on right then across and up exposed slab to ledge then to right and back again to stance and belay below a steep wall (70 ft.). The crux follows. Traverse on left flank of buttress 20 ft., then 10 ft. up a short steep groove. A delicate traverse left and up leads to easier ground. Block belay in cave below chimney (40 ft.). Up chimney, then exit on right to a ledge. Up past the ledge to another (harder) and piton belay (50 ft.). Finally, round to the left at the next ledge, back and up to slab – rather artificial. Now scramble to top of the buttress, which is connected to the main hill by a narrow ridge with a perched block.

The *Central Buttress* of Beinn Dearg, lying to the right of Flake Buttress has been climbed direct giving an 800 ft. route of Severe standard. The left wall of the buttress comprises numerous snow fields in winter conditions separated by short vertical walls. This gives a winter route, *Left Flank* – 800 ft., Grade II (A. McKeith and I. G. Rowe, 20 November, 1966). The buttress is bounded on the right by *Trident Gully*, almost 1000 ft. long, the lower half being steep snow in winter and scree in summer. The gully forks 300 ft. up, the right fork being the main gully while the left fork is a chimney between the top of Trident Gully Wall and a prominent slender buttress – *Tower Buttress* – about 500 ft. up Trident Gully, above the first fork is the great triple fork which gives the gully its name. All three branches are about equal in size, the summit of the mountain lying between the Central and Right branches. The left branch has a pitch at the bottom but above that it is easy. The *Central Branch*, climbed by P. N. L. Tranter and N. Travers in December 1963, is similar in nature. The right branch appears to be harder.

The narrow buttress to the right of Central Buttress was climbed by D. Munro in 1950 but the broken buttress with a steep west face – *Wedge Buttress* – to the west of this is unexplored.

An Teallach

(1) *Glas Mheall Mor* (3176 ft.), lies at the north end of the range and is the only top visible from Dundonnell. $2\frac{3}{4}$ miles west-south-west of Dundonnell Hotel.

(2) *Unnamed Top* (3001 ft.).

(3) *Bidein a' Ghlas Thuill* (3483 ft.).

(4) *Glas Mheall Liath* (3150 ft. contour).

(5) *Sgurr Creag an Eich* (3350 ft.).

(6) *Sgurr Fiona* (3474 ft.).

(7) *Lord Berkeley's Seat* (3325 ft. approx.). A small pinnacle.

(8) *Corrag Buhidhe* (3425 ft.). North top followed by three slightly lower pinnacles.

(9) *Corrag Bhuidhe South Buttress* (3050 ft.).

(10) *Top above Cadha Ghobhlach* (3150 ft. contour).
(11) *Sail Liath* (3150 ft. contour).

An Teallach is the collective name given to the twisting pinnacled ridge of Torridonian Sandstone which is the most northerly of the mountains within the area of this chapter. From its position at the head of Little Loch Broom it is the dominating feature of the

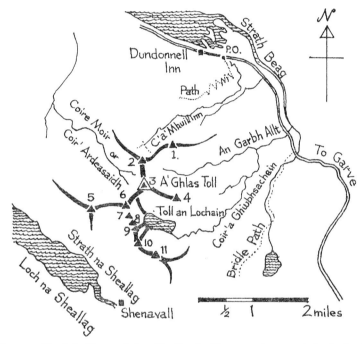

Fig. 9 Sketch Map of An Teallach (the numbers relate to text).

surrounding countryside and is clearly seen from most of the neighbouring mountain ridges. It is a magnificent example of Torridonian architecture and ranks amongst the finest mountain ridges in the Scottish Highlands.

It extends roughly north and south for upwards of 3 miles and forms a crescent-shaped backbone from which two branch ridges project for about half a mile on either side. The slopes to the north and to the west give relatively easy access to the main ridge, but to the east it drops steeply into the two great corries – A'Ghlas Thuill and Toll an Lochan – and access here is limited in normal conditions to some of the long scree slopes and gullies which lead down into them. In winter these become snow climbing routes and should be recognised as such.

The traverse of An Teallach is a stiff day's expedition and in winter one which requires no small amount of mountaineering experience. The approach for the circuit of the tops is usually made from Dundonnell. A well-marked path leaves the road just past the youth hostel and climbs steeply upwards towards the north-east lower slopes of Glas Mheall Mor (3176 ft.). The track disappears round about the 2000 ft. contour and here one has a choice. Either continue up the side of the burn for over 1½ miles on the north side of the Glas Mheal Mor ridge and then strike upwards to the main ridge of An Teallach or climb more or less straight up the north-east slope of the terminal ridge on to the first summit. This is direct but requires some route selection in the initial stages through broken rock and wet grassy ledges, which eventually open out on to easier walking leading on to the summit of Glas Mheal Mor. This top is one of the three found to be capped with quartzite.

Once on the ridge at this point the remainder of the tops can be climbed in order, with little difficulty in normal conditions. Route finding is fairly easy and the whole pattern of the ridge can be seen stretching out in front. In bad conditions a line along a lower level on the west side of the ridge by-passes the 'bad steps'.

The second top is unnamed (3001 ft.) and is reached along an easy stretch of ridge. Then follows a climb on to Bidean a'Ghlas Thuill (3483 ft.) the highest point on the range. From here a ridge to the east leads on to Glas Meall Liath (3150 ft.) separating the two great eastern corries. There are some fine buttresses on the south-west angle of A'Ghlas Thuill the most northerly of these, which culminates in two or three pinnacles on the branch ridge but these do not impede progress.

From Bidean a'Ghlas Thuill there is a drop of almost 500 ft., then a steep rise on to the other main top – Sgurr Fiona (3474 ft.) from which the north-west branch of the ridge ends after ½ mile in the top Sgurr Creag and Eich (3325 ft.). The main ridge now narrows over the spectacular rocky pinnacles which add so much to the fine silhouette. First Lord Berkeley's Seat (3325 ft.) a sharp-pointed peak which overhangs Corrie Toll an Lochan, followed by the four pinnacles of Corrag Bhuidhe which gradually decrease from a height of 3425 ft. to just under 3400 ft. In summer these give interesting

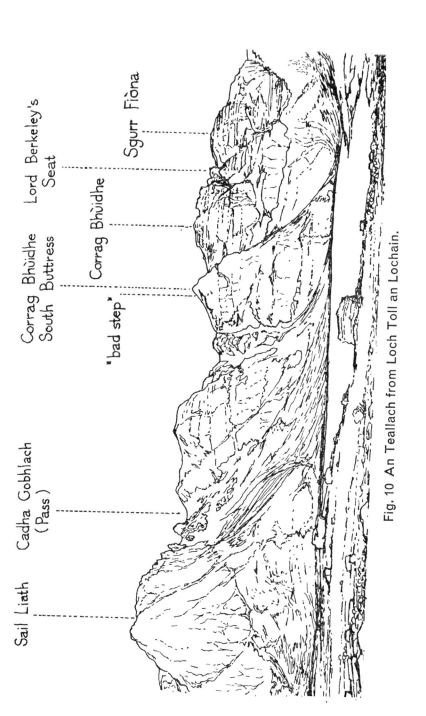

Sail Liath   Cadha Gobhlach (Pass)   Corrag Bhùidhe South Buttress   "bad step"   Corrag Bhùidhe   Lord Berkeley's Seat   Sgurr Fiòna

Fig. 10 An Teallach from Loch Toll an Lochain.

scrambling, in winter they become more difficult and all can be by-passed on the west at a lower level.

Slabs lead down to the dip before the Corrag Bhuidhe Buttress (3050 ft.) then follows the top above the Cadha Ghobhlach, a heather topped peak of 3150 ft. The way then leads up the steeper slope on to the final flat top of Sail Liath (3150 ft.) at the south end of the ridge. The 'bad step' on the south side of the Corrag Bhuidhe Buttress – 30 ft. of difficult rock – has already been the cause of two fatalities and should be kept well in mind in adverse weather conditions. It is only encountered if one intends to follow the true crest of the ridge and can be by-passed if desired by moving down to a lower level on the west side.

It is usual to return to the dip between the last two tops and descend into Corrie Toll an Lochan to view the cliffs from below, but it is possible to make a reasonable descent from the ridge of Sail Liath by the steep north-east side. A fairly obvious line lies down a big grassy gully some distance past the cairn where the slopes become less continuously rocky. This leads downwards over several small outcrops into Coire a'Ghiubhsachain whence the way towards the Dundonnell road lies along the sides of the Garbh Allt. The upper stretches of the corrie give enjoyable walking over great exposed pavements of sandstone which make for a quick passage to the road and more than make up for the lack of marked track.

Easy ways down into Toll an Lochan from the ridge can be found down the gully between the two main tops and down those of the Forked Pass or Cadha Ghoblach between the last two points on the ridge. Care should be taken by parties descending against dislodging loose boulders in the gullies.

Toll an Lochain, the southern of the twin corries of An Teallach is undoubtedly impressive but the tiered sandstone lacks continuity due to the liberal distribution of wide grass ledges. Its climbing potential is chiefly in winter in the long gullies which drop from the ridge. The long gully running up from a point below the summit of Sgurr Fiona to the base of the upper rocks of Lord Berkeley's Seat is known as Lord's Gully and has produced a fine route for both summer and winter conditions. It is dry even on rainy days and the rock here is clean and sound. The first summer ascent was in August 1958 by D. Robertson and F. Old. The first winter ascent was by J. H. B. Bell and E. E. Roberts (Easter, 1923).

The Summer Route in Lord's Gully follows the line of the watercourse over many pitches, one of which near the top is severe. From the base of the upper rocks go right up a steep slab. On the first ascent this was impossible after 150 ft., due to wet mud, so the party descended 60 ft. to poor belay and traversed 100 ft. across the slabby face below Sgurr Fiona to grass ledges, then up to the main ridge. In dry conditions the direct finish should be possible.

A more recent winter route – 1500 ft., Grade II (I. G. Rowe and A. McKeith, November 1966), starts directly below the summit of Sgurr Fiona. A narrow gully leads up to the left between the minor rib and the Summit buttress of Sgurr Fiona, towards Lord Berkeley's Seat. Early in the year there may be a few short pitches but later, they will probably be ironed out. Below Lord Berkeley's Seat, the gully opens out and forks. The direct finishes to both forks are fairly steep and as yet unclimbed, however, a diagonal traverse to the right for 300 ft., out on to the exposed summit buttress, leads to a horizontal ledge. It should be possible to reach the col fairly easily by a leftward slanting shelf from this point, however if the horizontal ledge is followed rightwards for 300 ft., a similar shelf leads to the ridge in a further 300 ft.

Glover and Ling's route on *Corrag Buidhe South Buttress*, the earliest climb in Toll an Lochan, is of an indeterminate nature whose difficulties can all be avoided. The *Sail Liath* cliff, though impressive, is too broken to give any worthwhile routes. The small pinnacle just right of *Sail Liath* and to the left of the left fork of the Cadha Goblach on the main ridge has been climbed (Mild Severe) but is dangerously loose and not recommended.

The *North Crag of Sgurr Fiona* – the crag near the bealach between Sgurr Fiona and Bidean a'Ghlas Thuill, has been climbed – Very Difficult – on its 200 ft. corner starting just left of the steepest line. Other hard routes of similar length would be possible here.

The south-east Corner of Corrie A'Ghlas Toll contains a number of buttresses separated by steep gullies. *Hayfork Gully*, dividing the largest of the buttresses (South Crag on its left and Central Buttress on its right) was the scene of the first climb in the corrie by Sang and Morrison in 1910. *Hayfork Gully – Fourth Prong* has been climbed in winter conditions. The gullies form a set of vertical prongs towards the left of the cliff. This is the fourth from the left, and seems to be the steepest. It is just left of Central Buttress.

The *South Crag* of *Sgurr Fiona* offers two routes. *Main Rib* – 350 ft., Difficult, on the left side starting immediately left of the lowest

G

crags. *Minor Rib* lies to the right of Main Rib and is separated from it by a narrow gully. This gives a climb of 1000 ft. which has been done in both summer and winter conditions.

The shoulder of Glas Mheall Mor has given a winter route – *Little Glass Monkey* – Grade III (Wilson and W. Beveridge, January 1967). The shoulder ends in a spur with two buttresses divided by a miniature corrie. The northernmost buttress which is easily reached from the Dundonnell path is cleft by a Y-shaped gully of which the left fork is taken.

The *Terminal Tower* of *Sgurr Ruadh*, the westmost bastion of An Teallach above the west end of Loch na Shealag also gives some climbing of a not too serious nature. Starting from the lowest points of the rocks which face north-west there is much scope for variation. *Coir a'Ghuibhsachain*, the west-facing scarp running parallel to and less than ½ mile west of the Shenaval track offers a continuous line of clean, steep quartzite of an average height of 200 ft. It provides an excellent practice crag readily accessible from the road. The rock is steep and smooth and the holds small but good, with a wide range of possible routes.

Beinn Ghoblach (2083 ft.). This is the fine bold mountain which is the terminating point of the peninsula between Little Loch Broom and Loch Broom. It is conspicuous from north and south and can be approached from either the east by way of the passenger ferry from Ullapool or from Dundonnell in the west. The road from Dundonnell is motorable for almost 5 miles as far as Badralloch. The mountain is worth visiting for the fine outlook in all directions.

5

The Fannich Forest

(1) *An Coileachen (3015 ft.). 2 miles N.E. of Fannich Lodge, Loch Fannich.

(2) Meall Gorm, east top (3030 ft. approx.). 1 mile N.W. of 1.

(3) *Meallan Rairigidh, west top of Meall Gorm (3109 ft.). Two-thirds of a mile W.N.W. of 2.

(4) Meall nam Peithirean (3175 ft. approx.). ¾ mile S. by E. of 5.

(5) *Sgurr Mor (3637 ft.). 3¾ miles N. by W. of Fannich Lodge and 3¼ miles N.W. of 1.

(6) Carn na Criche (3148 ft.). ½ mile N.W. of 5.

(7) *Meall a'Chrashaidh (3062 ft.). ¾ mile N.W. of 6; 2 miles S.E. of E. end of Loch a'Bhraoin.

(8) *Beinn Liath Mhor Fannaich (3120 ft. approx.). 1 mile E.N.E. of 5.

(9) Sgurr nan Clach Geala (3581 ft.). 1 mile S.W. of 6.

(10) *Sgurr nan Each (3026 ft.). 1 mile S. of 9.

(11) *Sgurr Breac (3240 ft. approx.). 2½ miles S. of E. end of Loch a'Bhraoin.

(12) Toman Coinich (3040 ft. approx.), unnamed on 1″ map, lies between 11 and 13.

(13) *A'Chailleach (3276 ft.). 1½ miles W. of 11.

(14) *Fionn Bheinn (3059 ft.). S. side of Loch Fannich, 28 miles N.N.W. of Achnasheen.

MAP: O.S. One Inch to the Mile (7th Series). Sheet No. 20 – Ullapool; 26 Strath Carron, 27 – Strathpeffer.

The area covered by the mountains of the Fannich group is roughly triangular in shape. The base is formed by the road from Garve to Kinlochewe which is part of the southern boundary of the area of the Northern Highlands, and the apex can be taken as the road junction at Braemore. The north-west side is formed firstly by the road from Braemore to Loch a'Bhraoin, and from the south-west end of the loch, a line across the Bealach na h'Imrich and through Gleann Tanagaidh to Kinlochewe.

Apart from some forestry commission plantations along the southern boundary, most of the area is deer forest and, once off in the main roads the only habitations are on the south side of Loch Fannich. This 7-mile stretch of water cuts across the centre of the area in a line approximately east-west and with one exception, the main mountain tops lie to the north side of it.

The Fannichs have usually been regarded as a fine high-level walking area with little to offer in the way of summer or winter climbing. This has been disproved by recent exploration of the individual mountains and their true worth is gradually being appreciated. It would be reasonable to claim that it now ranks as one of the finest all-round mountaineering areas in the country, offering fine high-level ridge walks of testing length, new climbing routes in both summer and winter, and like Beinn Dearg and Seana Bhraigh, the chance to combine climbing with ski-touring.

The main mountain group is divided naturally by the hill-pass running approximately due north-south from the east end of Loch a'Bhraoin to the west end of Loch Fannich. A good track follows the pass rising up to the 2100 ft. contour at the highest point of the bealach and forms the main through route in the area.

From the Braemore–Dundonnell road, the end of the loch is reached in less than a mile by a rough motor track. Several buildings stand at this end of the loch at the end of the motor track. These are in various states of repair and their use is limited. One outhouse is barely habitable and the boat-house is open at both ends. For a prolonged stay it is best to continue by track along the north side of the loch to the bothy at the west end – Lochivroan. This is in good repair, is frequently used by climbers and is well-appointed. It also forms a good base for the mountains to the west.

A path from the boat-house leads round the east end of the loch to cross the Abhainn Cuileig by a narrow raised footbridge and continues through the pass. The crossing of the burn $\frac{1}{2}$ mile from the end of the loch can be awkward and is largely a matter of personal choice. The south end of the path comes out at the empty house on the west end of Loch Fannich which is known as 'The Nest', then continues along the north shore of the loch to join the Hydro road at Fannich Lodge. The Nest is often used as a bothy and good camping sites can be found in the vicinity of Fannich Lodge which is usually occupied by one of the Estate shepherds. From the Lodge, a motor road leads past the dam and continues through the forestry plantations to the main road west from Garve at Grudie Bridge. The gate here is usually locked but the key can be obtained from the power station near by. In winter this road is often blocked and should be used with discretion.

A'Chailleach (3276 ft.), **Toman Coinich** (3040 ft.) and **Sgurr Breac** (3240 ft.)

The West Fannich group consists of three main tops – A'Chailleach, Toman Coinich, and Sgurr Breac, which run in a line west-north-west–east-south-east equidistant between Loch a'Bhraoin and Loch Fannich. The south-west slopes fall steeply down into the Nest of Fannich, the long U-shaped corrie which opens out on the west end of the Loch providing a natural deer sanctuary. A south-easterly curving ridge from the summit of A'Chailleach forms the south leg of the U, terminating at a height of 2411 ft. on the top of An Sguman overlooking Cabuie Lodge, on the loch-side.

On the north side of the main ridge, the walls of the corrie containing Loch an Toll Lochain are formed by the north spur of A'Chailleach which ends in the rocky bluff of Sron na Coibhre and the steep-sided, broad-topped ridge leading from the summit of Toman Coinich which slopes gradually towards the east end of Loch a'Bhraoin. This ridge provides the easiest route on to the summits of all three of the mountains of this western group. From the boat-house at the Loch's end the track into the Pass is followed for a short distance and then a steep grassy climb leads on to the broad flat lower slope of Druim Reidh. Easy walking leads upwards to Toman Coinich, and from there, the other two peaks can be climbed as desired.

In summer there is no difficulty, but in winter, the mountains take on a different aspect and the summit ridge should be treated with respect. The map does not indicate the true extent of the fall away of the slopes to the north and south of the main ridge and the edge of the crags can be heavily corniced. The view westward is dominated by Slioch and further to the north the whole splendour of the An Teallach range is unfolded. The eastern Fannichs appear as a rolling line of ridges dominated by the peak of Sgurr Mhor.

To the west, A'Chailleach drops down into the Bealach na h'Imrich which provides a cross-country link by way of Gleann Tanagaidh to Kinlochewe and the mountains of Torridon, and Loch Maree. A link track from the heights of Kinlochewe, 5 miles from the Belaach, leads to the south-east end of Loch Fada.

The East Fannich group consists of 10 tops of over 3000 ft., 7 of which form the spine of an 8-mile ridge running in a line north-west–south-east from the east end of Loch a'Bhraoin to the dam at the east end of Loch Fannich. From north to south these are in order: Meall a'Chrasgaidh (3062 ft.), Carn na Criche (3148 ft.), Sgurr Mor (3637 ft.), Meall nam Peithrean (3175 ft.), Meallan Rairigidh (3109 ft.), Meall Gorm (3030 ft.), and An Coileachan (3015 ft.).

A secondary ridge swings south from Carn na Criche for 3½ miles towards the north end of Loch Fannich over the tops of Sgurr nan Clach Geala (3581 ft.), and Sgurr nan Each (3026 ft.). The western slopes of this ridge which fall away into the bealach are steep but rich in grazing – the top of the broad basin enclosed by the broad saddle leading on to Sgurr nan Clach Geala from Carn na Criche is aptly named Am Biachdaich – the place of the fattening. The eastern slopes drop precipitously into Coire Mhoir and form the main climbing ground of the Fannichs to date.

From Sgurr Mor a second cross ridge cuts eastwards for 1 mile to Beinn Liath Mhor Fannaich (3120 ft.), from where it falls in broad rounded slopes towards the roadside by Loch Droma. The south slopes of this ridge terminate in Creag Dubh Fannaich (2500 ft.).

A great wedge-shaped glen pierces this eastern side of the Fannichs to the foot of Sgurr Mor, its side formed by the eastern and main ridges. The approach along this is pathless and although a way can be made along the Abhainn an Torrain Dubh from the road by Loch Glascarnoch, the going is heavy and involves steep climbs from the basins of Loch Li and Loch an Thuill Mhoir at the head of the glen.

The through-track along Loch Fannich is the key to the traverse of the ridges of this eastern group, giving easy straightforward ascents from three directions. Once on the ridge, the main tops can be climbed in any combination so desired with little difficulty, and escape is possible throughout down the grassy western slopes. Visibility in the Fannichs is often impaired by low-cloud and good navigation here is an essential skill. The east faces of Sgurr Mor, Sgurr nan Clach Geala and Sgurr Breac drop sharply from the summit cairns and at the south-east end of the ridge, the two steep, rocky corries of An Coileachan – Garbh Coire Mhor to the south-east and Coire nan Eun lying north-north-east – should be kept in mind.

It is worth noting that the track marked as leading from Fannich Lodge up the south ridge of Meall Gorm is practically non-existent and should not be depended upon.

From the north side, the ridge can be approached by three tracks which are worth attention, leading from the road angle around Braemore Junction.

(1) From the road to Dundonnell, $2\frac{1}{2}$ miles from the junction, a track leaves the road beside a stone bridge and winds upwards towards Meall a'Chrasgaidh over open moorland. In its upper reaches it tends to be difficult to follow but is useful in that it leads to the foot of the north-east ridge of the mountain.

(2) From the first big bend past the junction on the same road a straighter track leads in towards the same feature. On the map it is shown as stopping on the ridge north of Creag Rainich but a line of cairns can be traced and on the ridge south-west of Creag Rainich the path is clearer. A path now leads up on to the saddle between Meall a'Chraisgaidh and Carn na Criche to a cairn just below the level of the ridge.

(3) Leave the road from Garve at the north end of Loch Droma and follow the hydro road across the dam (unmarked on 1" Map so far) and along the pipe-line leading to the Allt a'Mhadaidh. A bridge over the burn connects with the stalker's track from the road which leaves the road a mile north of the dam beside a red roofed shed.

The track is now followed towards Loch a'Mhadaidh and can be left if desired to climb on to Beinn Liath Mhor Fannaich whose broad slopes and flat summit ridge leading to the boulder covered summit presents no difficulty. The map shows the track as crossing the main stream of the Allt a'Mhadaidh at a junction of the burns, but in fact here it disappears and the crossing is found another $\frac{3}{4}$ mile on. The path reappears and leads upwards over bad ground to Loch a'Mhadaidh. From here one can ascend the saddle between Sgurr Mor and Carn na Criche with little difficulty or, alternatively, skirt round the south side of the loch and make a direct ascent on to Sgurr Mor although this tends to be stiff going.

An alternative route into the great climbing area on the east side of Sgurr nan Clach Geala is to follow the Allt a'Choire Mhoir over pathless boggy ground from the track past Fannich Lodge to the head of Coire Mhoir.

The Geala Buttresses are not marked on the map but lie to the north of the summit of Sgurr nan Clach Geala rising 800 ft. above the more broken lower crags which abut on to the north ridge. The six narrow buttresses are of mica-schist and are numbered from 1–6 going northwards.

No. 4 Buttress – Skyscraper Buttress, and No. 5 – Sellar's Buttress,

have been climbed in summer conditions, giving excellent and compli-
cated routes.

Sellar's Buttress – 600 ft., Very Difficult (T. W. Patey and R. Harper,
1961).
This is the buttress to the right of the central spire and the start
of the climb is below a clean rock rib on the left. The route follows
the crest of a prominent shoulder and then a shattered rib for the
last 150 ft. in the direct line to the top.
It is thought that Buttresses 2 and 3 are too broken to be of worth
but Buttresses 1 and 6 should give summer routes. None have been
climbed in winter conditions to date.
The five deep gullies separating the buttresses offer superb winter
climbs. Named from left to right, Alpha, Beta, Gamma, Delta and
Epsilon, the approach in winter is awkward and has been described
in detail in the *C.M.C. Easter Ross Rock and Ice Guide* as follows:
'The approach to the foot of the main cliffs is guarded by a long
rock step, and in winter there is a steep Apron of snow between it
and the foot of the buttresses. The step is breached at only two
points. On the very left is a broken section giving access to Buttresses
1 to 4 and Gullies Alpha to Delta, but in any other than snowy
conditions this becomes a 60 ft. ice pitch and in any case care is
needed to locate it from above in event of a forced retreat. On the
right is a slanting rake climbing to the right below the feet of
Buttresses 5 and 6 and Epsilon Gully. This (Slanting Gully) links
with the Apron about 50 ft., above its only pitch, more or less with
the top of the Apron. As the pitch in Slanting Gully can be easily
avoided on the north, this approach to the Apron is always easy so
Slanting Gully is recommended as the approach to all climbs.'
Two of the gullies have been climbed to date – Alpha and Gamma.

Alpha Gully – 800 ft., Grade II, contained only snow when first
climbed by P. Baker and D. S. B. Wright in March 1965. The gully
itself is only 400 ft., but at the top, a continuation along the crest of
No. 2 Buttress is unavoidable and doubles the length of the climb.

Gamma Gully – 700 ft., Grade V (P. N. L. Tranter and I. G. Rowe,
6 and 7 March, 1965) gives a superb route and is described as follows:
'The first pitch is on the left of a shallow scoop on ice for 100 ft.,
followed by a very narrow, deep-set slot, 100 ft. also. Some 60 ft.
above the slot is the crux, a 30 ft., vertical ice wall with overhanging

13. Summit ridge of Liathach, looking south.

14. Beinn Eighe from the east.

15. Looking from Slioch to Beinn Tarsuinn and Mullach Coire Mhic Fhearchair, high above Lochan Fada, and to the roadless country which stretches to the Fannich mountains.

top, held in either side by holdless rock walls. A belay can be had above, followed immediately by a 40 ft. ice pitch. This can also be hard, as it may form a big mushroom growth of ice. The remainder of the gully is easier, steep snow with occasional rock steps, and it finally loses itself in the large scoop (often corniced) above Beta Gully.'

Fionn Bheinn (3059 ft.)

Fionn Bheinn lies within the area of the Fannichs but is entirely isolated from the main group of mountains. It must be one of the least inspiring 3000 ft. tops in Munro's Tables and can be climbed in just over an hour with no difficulty from the road junction at Achnasheen. The top is rounded and grassy and the two wide corries on the north-east side, Toll Mor and Toll Beag are steep but virtually unbroken. Local shepherds normally approach the mountain by a circuitous route from the south side of Loch Fannich by rough motor tract and hill path, but this is of little interest to the hill-walker. The one redeeming feature of Fionn Bheinn is the superb view it provides sweeping round from the Fannichs, westwards to Dundonnell, Loch Maree and Torridon.

6

Ben Wyvis and Easter Ross

MAP: O.S. One Inch to the Mile (7th Series). Sheets 21 Bonar Bridge, 27 Strathpeffer.

The mountains here described lie on the peninsula of Easter Ross, which is bounded on its north side by the Kyle of Sutherland and the Dornoch Firth and on its south side by the Cromarty Firth. The western boundary is the line formed by Strath Carron and Strath Vaich.

The eastern part of the area jutting out into the Moray Firth at Tarbet Ness is mainly low-lying farming land. The belt of Old Red Sandstone which occurs all along the north-east coast of the mainland produces rich soil and the inland moorlands provide good rough grazing for sheep. This part of Easter Ross holds the bulk of the population and is more like Caithness or the counties of Moray than the mountainous area to the west. The sheltered Cromarty Firth with its fine natural harbour at Invergordon is included in the development programme for the whole Moray Firth seaboard and the County town of Dingwall at the head of the Firth is one of the main road and rail junctions north of Inverness.

The main road to the north passes through Dingwall and continues around the coastline through Invergordon and Tain to Ardgay at the

head of the Dornoch Firth. A road over Struie Hill which leaves the
A9 2 miles past Evanton and joins the main road again 3 miles from
Ardgay is a useful shortcut. This saves about 10 miles of travel and
opens several approach routes on to the foothills of the Ben Wyvis
range. The road is often blocked in winter but adequate warning is
given at either end.

From Dingwall the main road to the west branches at Garve, the
right-hand fork passing onwards to Ullapool by way of the Dirrie
More and Loch Broom. At Garbat, 4 miles past Garve, the road
passes immediately below the main Wyvis ridge. There is no continuous road across the western boundary but it is possible to obtain
motor access from either end for the greater part of the way.

On the north side, a road from Ardgay goes up to Strath Carron
for 9 miles to the bridge at The Craigs. A Land-Rover track branches
past Amat Forest then up Gleann Mhor as far as Deannich Lodge.
There is a locked gate near Alladale Lodge and enquiries should be
made at the Benmore Estate office at Ardgay.

From the Garve–Ullapool road a side-road from the Black Bridge
1½ miles before Altguish Inn goes northwards up Strath Vaich
towards Loch Vaich. Just below Strath Vaich Lodge a hydro road,
not marked on the map, now continues up the east side of the loch
to the head of the glen and over the watershed to Gleann Mhor above
Deanich Lodge. It goes still further up Gleann Beag to finish at a
barrage about a mile below the bothy of Glenbeg. There is a locked
gate at the start, but the estate proprietor, Commander Williams of
Strathvaich, has courteously indicated his willingness to co-operate
if application is made to him for permission and sporting rights
recognised. The road is passable for cars and gives 11 miles of easy
access to the interior.

Ben Wyvis (3433 ft.)

The mountain mass of Ben Wyvis is made up of 7 tops over 3000
ft., which form a ridge running for more than 4 miles in a south-west–
north-east direction from Garbat to Loch Glass. Seen from most
directions it shows little indication of any great distinguishing feature.
The north-western slopes fall in steep, unbroken slopes to the road
by Garbat, and its south-eastern face is largely hidden by its own
foothills which stretch down towards the shores of the Cromarty
Firth. This eastern side, however, is split by two great corries, Coire
Mor and Coire na Feola, with impressive crags of folded Moine

Schist, on either side of the eastern spur of Ben Wyvis, An Socach (3295 ft.).

The easiest approach is undoubtedly from Garbat, on the road to Ullapool, 15 miles from Dingwall.

A rough track leads off from the road past the farm house to the Forestry Commission Fence. The gate here is usually unlocked. A boggy land-rover track, definitely unsuitable for any other vehicles, leads through the newly planted forestry ground upwards on to the pass between Ben Wyvis and Little Wyvis – The Bealach Mor. From the pass a steep heathery slope leads upwards to the summit of An Cabar. The distance from the road is only 2 miles by this route but involves one in 2600 ft. of steep ascent. Once on the main ridge the traverse of the plateau is easily accomplished and the views in all directions are extensive. On a clear day seven counties, the North Sea and the Atlantic Ocean can be seen from the summit.

The main top, Glas Leathad Mor (3433 ft.) lies $1\frac{1}{2}$ miles north-north-east of An Cabar along the broad flat plateau, and from here the remainder of the tops can be climbed in any convenient combination. The western slopes obviously take their name from the main top – the big grey one. These can easily be descended to the Garbat road at various points but care should be taken in adverse weather conditions when the walking can become treacherous. The circuit from Garbat along the ridge to Tom a'Choinnich and thence back to the start by way of the Carn Gorm shoulder gives a fine 9 mile hill-walk with very little intermediate ascent.

The mountain can also be approached from the Dingwall–Strathpeffer road by a side road leading to Achterneed which branches north 3 miles west of Dingwall, but the 10-mile route is of no great interest and is not recommended.

A longer, but much more rewarding approach from the south-east is from Evanton, 7 miles north of Dingwall on the A9. A road sign-posted 'Assynt' leaves the main road at the bridge in the centre of the village and leads north-westwards up Glen Glass for almost 5 miles to the bridge at Eileanach. From here the road continues along the west side of Loch Glass for another 5 miles or so to the Wyvis Lodge, but the gate at the bridge is locked and permission cannot be obtained to go further.

Between the main road and the Eileanach Bridge closer exploration of the glen itself is rewarding. The road passes along the north side of the River Glass through extensive forestry plantations of conifers.

Leave the road at Assynt house and make a way down through the trees towards the river bed. At first it seems as if the river has gone under ground but careful inspection will show that it is running along the foot of deep narrow gorge. This is the famous Black Rock of Novar which is not a solitary rock, but a mile long chasm cut through the Old Red Sandstone. The walls drop vertically throughout its length to depths varying from 60 ft. to 120 ft., and at places are undercut. The River Glass flows swiftly through the dark gorge taking with it most of drainage from the Ben Wyvis range.

A local man from Evanton, Donald Macdonald, once jumped across it at a point where it reaches a depth of 100 ft., and in more recent years a well-equipped party from the Ferranti Mountaineering Club, Messrs J. C. Cruickshank and D. Macdonald, traversed the gorge at water-level.

From Eileanach the way now lies cross-country to the junction of the Alt Coire Mistrich and the Alt nan Caorach. A track follows the Alt nan Caorach for 2 miles westwards and the choice of route is now open.

A good 13-mile circuit can be completed by ascending the south ridge of Coire na Feola to the summit then climbing in succession over Tom a'Choinnich and Glas Leathad Beac (West Top), and descending the broad south east shoulder of the ridge – Leacann Bhreac – to rejoin the track at Alt nan Caorach. If transport can be made available at the end, the complete traverse from Evanton to Garbat – 16 miles and 4200 ft. of ascent – is a fine expedition.

The approach from Eileanach also opens up the exploration of the two corries on this eastern side of Ben Wyvis. The rock in both of these tends to be vegetated and has not produced much worthwhile climbing. Four prominent spurs rise steeply above Coire Mor on its west side which in the previous edition of this guide were numbered from south to north. No. 2 consists of two buttresses divided by a narrow, easy gully named 'Fox Gully'. Both of these offer a climb of about Difficult standard. No. 3 has a vegetated cliff on its lower left and a very large slab on its right at middle height which offers some climbing. No. 4 consists of a series of short rock steps and grass ledges inconveniently sloping wrongly.

Ben Wyvis in winter garb is a much more impressive mountain and any expedition increases in difficulty. The snow fields on the eastern side have become increasingly popular with skiers and the development of a winter sports area for the north is a real possibility. Access from Garbat is often facilitated by the use of suitably tracked vehicles and snow conditions for ski-ing last for a considerable part of the winter. Snow can still be found in patches on the summit ridge even in mid-summer, which no doubt made it easy for the Mackenzie Earls of Cromarty who held this area in the past to pay their rent. Their estates were held from the crown on condition that they could produce a snowball from Ben Wyvis when called to do so throughout the year.

Beinn a'Chaisteall (2749 ft.) and Meall a'Ghrianan (2531 ft.)

Beinn a'Chaisteall and Meall a'Ghrianan are the highest points on the ridge which rises up from the east side of Loch Vaich, 8 miles north-west of Ben Wyvis. They are best approached from Aultguish Hotel by the road along Strath Vaich already described.

A track rises north-eastwards from the bridge past Lubriach over the saddle between Meall a'Ghrianan and Creag Bhreac Mhor into the neighbouring Strath Rannoch. From the saddle, the long south ridge of Meall a'Ghrianan is easily climbed to the summit. Beinn a'Chaisteall lies another $1\frac{1}{2}$ miles north-north-east along the ridge. This is a fine hill-walking area, but it lies in the heart of the deer forest and there are restrictions during the stalking season. Both Beinn an Chaisteall and Carn Chuinneag are listed in Corbett's Tables of 2500 ft. Tops.

Carn Chuinneag (2749 ft.)

Carn Chuinneag is the highest top on the south side of Glen Diebidale, 8 miles to the north of Ben Wyvis and the hills of this area are best approached from Ardgay. Following the road along Strath-carron for 10 miles by way of the crags to Glen Calvie Lodge. Diebidale Lodge lies $2\frac{1}{2}$ miles along Glen Calvie and a track rises steeply from the road past the lodge on to the 2500 ft. contour below the summit of the ridge. The ridge forms the south side of Glen Diebidale and on its east side is served by several long cross-country tracks stretching towards the road over Struie Hill some 12 miles distant. Their usefulness, however, is limited and permission to approach from this direction is somewhat restricted.

The road from Ardgay along Strath Carron also provides access to two relatively new rock faces – The Alladale Wall and the Gleann Beag Crags. These could equally well be included in the area of the next chapter as they lie north of Strath Vaich and Strath Carron.

Both have produced a number of worthwhile rock-routes, largely pioneered by the members of the Corriemulzie Climbing Club and the ever-active T. W. Patey. Details of the climb are to be found in the *C.M.C. Easter Ross Rock Guide.*

The Alladale Wall is an 800 ft. cliff on An Socach at the head of Glen Alladale. The approach is by way of Strath Carron to the Craigs, then past Amat Lodge to Alladale Lodge; 11 miles from Ardgay. The surfaced road stops at the turning to Glen Calvie and beyond this, roads generally become rough and require care. The locked gate before Alladale has already been mentioned. Just before the lodge a rough track goes westwards to Alladale, and there is an excellent bothy past the woods which can be used with the permission of the Factor at Ardgay. This gives an open view up the glen through which a track leads to the Alladale Wall.

Gleann Beag lies at the head of Gleann Mhor, and is approached by way of Deannich as already described or perhaps more easily, from Strath Vaich. The main crag lies south of Loch Sruban Mora on the north side of the glen. Also on this side but a mile to the east lies Niagra Slab and on the south side of the glen beyond the bothy is the only other rock explored, Cottage Slab. The bothy at Glenbeg has frequently been used by parties but is private property and it is advisable to enquire at Ardgay for permission to use it. It has been noted that the boulders below the Main Crag are suitable for bivouac purposes.

7

Inverlael and Strath Mulzie

(1) *Beinn Dearg (3547 ft.). 5 miles E.S.E. of Loch Broom.
(2) *Conamheall (3200 ft.). 1 mile N. of E. of 1.
(3) *Meall nan Ceapraichean (3192 ft.). ¾ mile N. of 1.
(4) *Eididh nan Clach Geala (3039 ft.). 2 miles N. of 1.
(5)   Beinn Enaiglair (2915 ft.). 2½ miles W. of 1.
(6)   Iorguill (2862 ft.). 2½ miles W. of 1.
(7) *Am Faochagach (3120 ft.). 3½ miles E.S.E. of 1.
(8)   Carn Gorm Loch (2980 ft.). 1 mile N.E. of 7.
(9) *Seana Bhraigh (3040 ft.). 10 miles S.W. of Oykel Bridge, 4½ miles N.N.W. of 1.
(10) Carn Ban (2762 ft.). 4 miles E. of 9.

MAPS: O.S. One Inch to the Mile (7th Series). Sheet No. 20 – Ullapool, and Sheet No. 21 – Bonar Bridge.

This exceptionally fine group of mountains lies in the area between Loch Broom and Strath Oykel to the north-west of Strath Vaich and Strath Carron. In the north, the area is divided from Coigach and Assynt by the road from Ullapool to Ledmore Junction.

The main road from Dingwall to Ullapool passes along its west border by way of Garve and Braemore Junction. This is completely reconditioned and gives a fast passage from the south. The eastern side can be approached by the road from Ardgay to Lochinver which follows the Oykel Valley.

The road from Ullapool to Ledmore Junction is too distant from the main tops to be of much use and the tracks through Glen Achal and Glen Einig which form a cross-country link between Ullapool and Oykel Bridge provide the best access from the north. The approach from the south by way of Strath Vaich and Strath Carron has been described in the previous chapter.

The area is practically all deer forest but up till now no attempt has been made by the various estate owners to restrict access by walkers or climbers ecxept during the stalking season. Habitations in

16. From A'Mhaighdean in March. Beneath is the Gorm
Loch, Ben Lair is in the centre, and to the left is the north side
of Slioch with the hills of Loch Maree on the horizon.

17. From Slioch, looking towards A'Mhaighdean (left) and Fionn Loch.

18. *Opposite:* The Dragon Climb on Carnmore Crag.

19. The view north from A'Mhaighdean; An Teallach distant, Ben Dearg Beag and Mor in the mid-distance.

the interior are few and far between, being limited largely to shooting lodges and estate workers' houses.

Ullapool is the main centre of population on the west side, and on the east, the villages of Ardgay and Bonar Bridge at either side of the head of the Dornoch Firth.

Ullapool is a busy fishing port and one of the most popular holiday resorts in the west. It offers several hotels and a variety of boarding-houses and overnight accommodation. There is a youth hostel on Shore Street and a large camping and caravan site. Its situation makes it an ideal centre for exploring the mountains within a radius of almost 25 miles.

The present-day port was established as an experiment in 1788 by the British Fisheries Association in the hope that it would become the chief centre for the west coast fishings. Previously, Inverlael at the head of Broom had been the main settlement in the immediate locality. Ullapool, however, as the name suggests must have been in existence still earlier. Pool is a form of the norse word 'bol' or town and Ullapool was the 'Olave's Town' of the early Viking Raiders who must have been attracted by the great, natural harbour stretching from Gruinard Bay to the head of Loch Broom and the easy pickings to be had from the rich grazing land along its sheltered sides.

There is access by sea to the Summer Isles off-shore from Coigach in outer Loch Broom, and beyond to Stornoway in the Island of Lewis. A ferry runs to Alltnaharrie on the west side of Loch Broom and a track connects across the headland to Dundonnell at the head of Little Loch Broom. This provides a possible approach to An Teallach and the great mountains of the Fisherfield Forest, but only operates when sea conditions are suitable and does not take cars.

Ardgay is the gateway from the east coast. This little village lies on the main rail-line to the north on the Ross-shire side of the Dornoch Firth. It connects by road bridge with Bonar Bridge, its counterpart on the Sutherland side of the Firth, 1 mile to the north. Here converge all roads leading through the whole of the far north-west. There is a wealth of accommodation in both villages but neither is a really good centre for exploration. They are important rather as a junction.

Farming, crofting, forestry and estate work form the main occupations and salmon are netted in season across the mouth of the Kyle at Bonar Bridge, where the great fishing rivers from Strath Carron and Strath Oykel merge.

H

It should be noted that there is no through road to the west coast from Ardgay itself. The road which leads up Strath Carron has already been described in conjunction with the path to Glen Beg. [Chapter 6]. A more north-westerly branch of this passes along Strath Cuileannach for 5 miles but again the connection with Strathmulzie is by track. A third road follows the south side of the Oykel valley past the Youth Hostel at Carbisdale Castle and continues for 13 miles to Inveroykel Lodge Hotel. A ford from below the hotel joins with the Lochinver road on the north side of the valley 2 miles past Rosehall, and a foot bridge crosses the Oykel a mile further up river. The Hotel caters for the climbing fraternity and both bunkhouse and camping facilities are available in the grounds. This is a good centre to explore the rock outcrops of Alladale and Glenbeag and gives reasonable access to Corriemulzie.

Strath Carron and Strath Oykel figure prominently in the chronicles of the Highland Clearances of the nineteenth century and from the introduction of the Cheviot sheep to the area in 1792 – known for long as 'Bliadhna nan Caorach' – 'The Year of the Sheep' – the surrounding glens were the scene of many of the more violent and pitiful episodes of the whole affair. In Glen Calvie, the names of those who sheltered in the churchyard after they had been evicted, can still be seen scratched on the window glass of Croick church.

The sheep walks were mostly turned over to the deer in the latter half of the century and the roads behind Ardgay serve a multitude of shooting lodges. Many of these are only used for a part of the year and are attended by estate workers for the remainder of the time.

Nearly all of the mountains in this group are most easily approached from the west side; the exceptions being those which lie at the head of Strathmulzie. This, however, only applies for parties who have only one day to spend and in the event of a longer stay in the area expeditions from either side are made feasible by the use of conveniently placed bothies and the wide choice of camp-sites.

The main group of 3000 ft. tops lie in a great crescent around the upper part of Gleann Squaib which open westwards to the head of Loch Broom 6½ miles south of Ullapool. Leave the main road just past the post office at Inverlael by a forestry road which is motorable for 2 miles as far as the gate in the deer fence on the north side of the River Lael. The road passes through dense conifers which stretch up the steep sides of the glen's entrance to a height of 750 ft.

Above the tree-line on the south end of the glen rises the conspicuous gneiss outcrop of Strone Nea. This can be reached by a branch of the forestry road and gives several rock routes of between 200 ft. and 300 ft. These were all first led by T. W. Patey in 1962–63 and are described in the *C.M.C. Rock and Ice Guide to Easter Ross*.

The most obvious climb *The Shaft* – 250 ft., Very Difficult, is on the steep pillar on the left of the main face.

Summit Slabs – 200 ft., Very Difficult – lie on the main crag right of the Shaft.

They are reached by the intervening gully and give a pleasant climb. Other routes are still possible here and the crag is worth visiting.

From the limit of the forest a well-marked track now leads steeply upwards along the glen but in its early stages gives little indication of the mountains. After $1\frac{1}{2}$ miles it forks above the water fall of Eas Fionn, and from here on the main feature of the great range around the head of the glen can be studied more clearly.

The left-hand fork continues to rise steadily for $2\frac{1}{4}$ miles on to the 2500 ft. pass between Eididh nan Clach Geala (3039 ft.) and Meall nan Capreachean (3192 ft.). From here, an ascent of either top can be made without difficulty.

Eididh nan Clach Geala has a certain amount of broken rock on its south face above the path at Lochan a'Chnapaich but there is no worthwhile cliff. It gets its name 'the hill of the white stone' from the quartzite boulders which sprinkle its summit slopes. The view to the north and west is quite fine, but to the east, the rolling slopes leading across to Seana Braigh are uninspiring from this direction.

Meall nan Ceapraichean has a subsidiary south top, *Ceann Garbh* (3063 ft.), which is named only on the 6″ Map. This sends a long shoulder eastwards into Cnap Coire Loch Tuath (2871 ft.), whose south slope drops steeply down into the head of Coire Lair. The east ridge of Cnap Coire Loch Tuath can be descended to the bothy at the head of Gleann Beag. From the summit of Meall nan Capreachean, easy slopes lead south-eastwards down into the bealach of Coire Ghranda which separates it from Beinn Dearg to meet the south fork of the path from Eas Fionn.

The climb from the bealach to the summit of Beinn Dearg is steep and rough but route finding is made easy by following the dry stone dyke which runs straight upwards on to the plateau to a height of 3400 ft., but not to the actual summit cairn. This lies 300 yds south of the angle made by the wall before it runs sharply right down the line of the south side of the glen towards Inverlael.

For 3 miles from the Eas Fionn junction to the Bealach Coire Ghranda, the south fork of the track passes below the main rock features of this side of Beinn Dearg.

The south side of Glen Squaib is formed by the long sloping shoulder of Beinn Dearg, Diollaid a'Mhill Bhric, which for most of its way is fringed by precipitous cliffs, terminating in 'an imposing corner tower' to the right of the wide scree gully known as Cadha Amadan or 'Fool's Pass'. This tower is the principal feature of the crags before they open out on to the great West Buttress of Beinn Dearg, and has given a fine rock climb – '*Tower of Babel*' – first climbed by T. W. Patey in 1962, giving 450 ft. of Difficult climbing on the best rock on Beinn Dearg, the climbing being airy and pleasantly varied.

It is possible to include a lower 100 ft. tier by starting below the entrance to the gully, but this has an awkward earth pull-up (Mild Severe) to the top where an easy terrace leads in from the foot of the gully, Cairn.

Climb the crest of the tower with no major divergences for 200 ft., on excellent holds. Then climb a cracked slab of peculiar rusty colour just left of the true crest for 60 ft. A mossy recess on the left leads round the steep wall ahead to a level promontory.

Beyond are two vertical steps, the first climbed direct, the second by a crack in the slab which forms the left wall of the ridge. Step up left into a square-cut recess and finish easily.

The West Buttress lies beyond the Cadha Amadan and has produced another long route on to Bein Dearg – *The West Buttress* – 1300 ft., Difficult, April 1962 (T. W. Patey.) Seen from the Glensquaib approach the aspect is uninviting, the true corner of the buttress being mainly steep vegetation. However, facing north-north-east and above the small loch is an extensive exposure of slabs bounded on the left by a shallow ill-defined gully coursing down the full height of the buttress. Immediately right of the gully and forming the left wall of the slabs is a poorly defined columnar rib offering the best line, the cleanest rock and a sporting line to the top of Beinn Dearg. Though vegetated in the lower reaches, it improves with height.

Climb the rib for 250 ft. to a cairn. Traverse 20 ft. right then continue up a secondary rib, turning two successive walls on the right, though they would go direct with increased difficulty. After some 300 ft. of this indeterminate climbing, the choice narrows and the rib becomes fluted. From a small cairn mount left to climb a hidden crack for 60 ft. behind a giant detached finger. The nose above on the right has good rock, so continue straight up on good holds. The angle then eases and the climbing becomes Moderate though pleasant. 200 ft. from the top is a small boulder, and easy scrambling follows. Numerous cairns left en route, but not at start.

An alternative route into the Beinn Dearg range from this side can be taken from Braemore Junction 5 miles further south of Inverlael. The junction lies close to the famous Corrieshalloch Gorge, which can be reached easily by a path from the roadside. The 400 ft. gorge is bridged by a suspension bridge near the roadside which gives a spectacular view of the Falls of Measach, which falls nearly 270 ft. in its main cascade. It is now the property of the National Trust for Scotland.

The subsidiary gorge from the south-west which carries the Adhainn Cuileig into the Abhainn Droma one mile below Measach is seldom visited and hardly known but in many ways equals the more famous Corrieshalloch and is worth visiting. The road to Dundonnell from Braemore Junction passes within 30 yds of the gorge which can be crossed with care by a semi-derelict footbridge. The view down into the 150 ft. chasm is both unexpected and spectacular. It is possible with care to descend to the river bed and traverse the foot of the gorge and at a higher level a path leads back to the Ullapool road about 1½ miles from Braemore Junction.

From Braemore Junction (the way towards Beinn Dearg follows initially) the road through the gates beside the keeper's house. Permission to use it can be obtained here and accommodation for climbers is available throughout the year at a reasonable charge. This is a useful base during the winter months. The road leads back along towards Loch Broom at a higher level along beautiful wooded slopes and in one mile reaches the flat site of what was once Braemore Lodge. Looking westwards from here the winter view over the trees across the Fannichs must be one of the finest in Scotland.

A stalker's track now leads north-east across open ground past the Home Loch and splits after ½ mile, sending a branch round either side of Beinn Enaiglair (2913 ft.), to join again on the saddle between the latter and Iorguill (2862 ft.) at a height of 2250 ft. Beinn Enaiglair tends to be overlooked by climbers on their way to the 'Munro' tops of the Beinn Dearg range, but it is well-worth ascending for the extensive view it gives to the Fannichs and it is easily reached from either of the two branch tracks.

The way on to Beinn Dearg now crosses the summit of Iorguill and on to meet the dry stone dyke already described. The dyke passes the top of the Cadha Amaden and stretches steeply upwards on to the summit plateau. Its line along the edge of the cliffs which drop along this south side of Glen Squaib makes it an invaluable aid in the event of bad visibility. The north western end, nearest Inverlael, terminates abruptly against a huge conspicuous boulder which is also a useful landmark for the hill-walker.

Conamheall (3200 ft.)

Conamheall is the fourth top over 3000 ft. in this great range of mountains and is easily reached from the Bealach Coire Ghranda after a dip of 2650 ft. The summit is at the northern end of the almost level ridge and is marked by a cairn. The western cliffs of the narrow, south-east ridge of Conamheall form with the eastern cliffs of Beinn Dearg, the walls of Coire Ghranda (The Gloomy Corrie), which contains the rock features of interest on this side of the range. The ridge itself ends in a steep, rocky bluff, overlooking Glen Lair and with care it is possible to find a way down southwards to the foot of Coire Ghranda.

Coire Ghranda can be approached equally we llby either of two paths which leave the roadside from the north-west and south-east end of Loch Droma, 3 miles from Braemore Junction towards Garve.

The north path leaves the road near Lochdrum – a useful bothy for both Beinn Dearg and the Fannichs – and climbs up on to the long sloping south-easterly tail of Beinn Enaiglair. One mile from the road the track forks; the main branch continues along the ridge for another 3 miles on to the saddle already mentioned between Enaiglair and Iorguil. The branch track leads down in the Long Corrie and crosses the Allt a'Charbhrain by stepping-stones. In wet weather this burn has been known to flood very suddenly and can provide an unexpected hazard to the walker. The way now leads up into the lower corrie on the north-east side – The Princess Coire – which contains a little lochan – Loch nan Eilean. The wild and rugged cliffs of the upper corrie – Coire Ghranda of Beinn Dearg and Conamheall can now be seen clearly. Those of Beinn Dearg rise almost directly from the west side of the loch on the corrie floor and are in two groups.

The Lower Crag rising from the loch-side is steep and slabby, with the slabs overlapping the wrong way like roof-tiles. The top section is steeper and is broken by a number of grooves and chimneys. At the south end is seen a deep, black gully which is blocked by a great chock-stone in its upper section.

The first route fully described on the crag is *Bell's Route*, which starts up the rocks close to their lowest point, above the largest of the two peninsulas on the south side of the Loch. The line continues directly above the peninsula throughout and has the best exposure of rock on the crag, but is spoilt rather at the top pitch by vegetation. It gives 500 ft. of Severe climbing, and was first climbed in 1946 by Dr and Mrs J. H. B. Bell.

The Upper Crag extends above the lower crag further up the corrie towards the Bealach Coire Ghranda, rising to a height of 400 ft. The steep dripping walls are frequently overhung and abound in vegetation and the outlook for rock-climbing on this forbidding crag is very slim.

The crags on the Conamheall side are drier and more feasible for climbing but offer little continuity. Most of the routes explored on the series of ribs and faces can be graded about Difficult.

The second of the two tracks from Loch Droma leaves the road 1 mile further south and crosses the Long Corrie past Loch a'Gharbhrain. It can easily be used to ascend into Coire Ghranda by way of Loch nan Eilean but also provides the best approach to Am Faochagach (3120 ft.) and Carn Gorm Loch (2980 ft.) on the east side of Glen Lair.

Continue up the glen to the south end of Loch Coire Lair. The ground is flat but boggy and the river from the Loch has to be forded. A steep shoulder rises from the Loch which can be climbed on to the rounded, domelike summit plateau. The climb is stiff and the final steep boulder slope below the summit is distinctly unpleasant and awkward when wet. The summit cairn lies to the west side of the plateau and offers a grand view across into Coire Ghranda. Carn Gorm-loch lies 1 mile north-east and can be reached by descending 600 ft. into the intervening saddle from which the Allt Glas Toll Beag flows down into Loch Vaich. A track from the loch-side follows the burn throughout and this provides an alternative route from Strath Vaich. To the south-east, Am Faochageach sends long grassy ridges down towards the head of Strath Vaich. On the west, the lower slopes are steeper, but it is possible to traverse around the head of Coire Lair by way of Loch Prille and include the main 3000 ft. tops of Beinn Dearg range in a long day expedition. This necessitates descending to Inverlael and requires organisation of transport.

The Beinn Dearg area offers fine winter mountaineering. The deep cut gully in the face of the West Buttress next to Cadha Amadan – *Inverlael Gully*, was climbed in January 1965 by J. M. Taylor, A. G. Nicol and T. W. Patey, giving an 800 ft. route, Grade II. The chockstone pitch at mid height was found to be covered with 20 ft. of 60 degree ice. Since then this side of the mountain has produced 9 firstclass routes – 5 to the right of the Cadha Amadan and 4 on the Buttress itself. All of the gullies have now been climbed in winter conditions. Their easy accessibility from Inverlael adds to the attraction – all were first climbed in the course of a series of afternoon outings from Ullapool.

In winter months the use of skis helps to cut out the tedium of the Glen Squaib track and it is possible to ski-traverse up both sides of the glen, on to the summits. Snow conditions can be remarkably good here and the ski-tourer would find the area of particular interest.

Seana Bhraigh (3040 ft.)

Seana Bhraigh is the most northerly of the mountains described in this chapter and is the highest point on the plateau which lies at the head of Strathmulzie. From the south this is seen as an unbroken heathery mass, but on the north side it drops in a series of steep rocky corries. Coire Luchd, the most westerly, falls 1300 ft, sheer from the summit of the mountain. Feich Coire, separated from the latter by the outstanding feature of Seana Bhraigh, the peak of An Sgurr (2950 ft. approx.) which juts out northwards immediately above Loch A'Choire Mhoir. Coire Mor, the most easterly from which the Allt Coire A'Choire Mhoir feeds down into the Loch.

The easiest approach is from the north-east, leaving the Lochinver road at Oykel Bridge. Follow the motor track for 4 miles to Duag Bridge along the south side of the River Einig. The road here passes an old corrugated iron building which was once a school but is now a hay shed with some open outbuildings which could be used as a bothy. The motor track stops at Corriemulzie Lodge 1¾ miles further on. The lodge is uninhabited during the winter but a shepherd lives nearby and permission can often be obtained to use one of the outbuildings. The path marked on the map leading up Strathmulzie runs out after about 2 miles but the going is easy for the remaining 3 miles to Loch a'Choire Mhor. There is a ruined bothy on the north-east side of the loch which is partially roofed and barely useable but there are plenty of camp-sites to choose from in the vicinity for a long stay.

The approach from the west is longer. Half a mile north of Ullapool a motor track leads along the River Ullapool to the west end of Loch Achall, which is crossed by a dubious wooden bridge. A right of way for pedestrians continues along the Loch into Glen Achall, but permission can usually be obtained from Major Scobie at Rhidorroch Lodge to take a car. The road continues for $5\frac{1}{2}$ miles to Rhidoroch Old Lodge which lies on the opposite side of the river and is reached by a wooden suspension bridge. A rough road rises steeply onwards for $1\frac{1}{2}$ miles past the lodge but is unsuitable for cars for any appreciable distance and the rest of the journey is on foot. At the second promi-nent track junction, take the right-hand fork leading down towards Loch an Damh. The way now leads up the side of the Allt nan Caorach, but is pathless for part of its way, between the south-east end of the cleft of the river and the head of Strathmulzie.

A combination of these two routes through Glen Einig and Glen Achall gives a magnificent east–west walk of almost 16 miles, which is to be recommended. From Duag bridge leave the Corriemulzie track by a footpath north-westwards along the River Poiblidh to Loch an Daimb. The path tends to be heavy in wet weather and at one point the River Poiblidh has to be forded. Four miles from Duag at the east end of the loch is Knockdamph bothy. This is in excellent condition and is frequently used by climbers and walkers. The key is on the wall by the door. The track continues along the north side of Loch Damph but it is advisable to take the north fork, the south one follows the edge of the Loch and is partially under water. This path links with the route from Rhidoroch already described. From the west path junction there is a fine view of An Sgurr on Seana Bhraigh, jutting out beyond the summit ridge. The walk along Loch Achall is especially fine, the way passing beneath the great crags of Creag Ruadh and Creag Grianach towards Rhidoroch Lodge. Once over the motor bridge at the end of the loch, the walk over into Ullapool along the river gorge is most impressive, and in the evening becomes almost eerie. For those who appreciate a long cross-country walk in peace and solitude the route is highly recommended.

A third possible route to Seana Bhraigh is from Glen Beag by path up to Loch Scruban Mora to cross the plateau and descend into the head of Coire Mhor. The distance from Glen Beag to Loch a'Choire Mhoir by this way is only 4 miles but is stiff going and the descent into the corrie is awkward, especially carrying a heavy load.

The summit of Seana Bhraigh is easily climbed by way of the grassy north shoulder and from there the plateau can be traversed with little difficulty, for 3½ miles take in the top of Carn Ban (2672 ft.), which rises as a rounded top to the east above the head of Coire Mhor. As has been observed previously it is possible to descend the head of the corrie and make back to Loch a'Choire Mhoir. At closer quarters the steep ridge on to An Sgurr becomes less forbidding and it is possible to ascend from the mouth of Loch Coire on the north-west aspect. The only unavoidable difficulties occur on the last 150 ft., from the summit tower to the plateau and here a rope may be required as a safeguard to the less-experienced scrambler.

Seanna Bhraigh has no outstanding potential as a rock-climbing area. The rock here is mainly schist, and the broken crags are highly vegetated in summer. Like Beinn Dearg however, its winter possi-bilities are great and only discovered in comparatively recent years. Despite its low-altitude, snow conditions are better than one might expect and the gullies of Luchd Coire have produced some fine routes. Most of the pioneer work here was done by members of the Corriemulzie Climbing Club who include the climbs here in their Snow and Ice Guide to Easter Ross and the area is included in the two new Scottish Mountaineering Club area guides for the Northern Highlands. Of the routes already climbed, and these by no means exhaust the possibilities, the following selection can be recommended:

The Traverse of An Sgurr from the corrie floor to the plateau. In summer conditions to the final stretch requires some scrambling but in winter conditions the difficulties increase considerably. The bad step, however, can be escaped by descending the south-east slope into the Feich Coire.

Sunday Post – 1000 ft., Grade II (W. D. Fraser and J. C. I. Wedderburn, 1963). This is the left-hand of the two obvious parallel gullies either side of a central rib on the Central Massif in Coire Luchd.

Pelican Gully – 800 ft., Grade II (C. S. M. Doake, P. N. L. Tranter and J. C. I. Wedderburn, 1964). This shares an easy first pitch of 200 ft. with Sham Gully, which slants up to the right between the summit buttress of Seana Bhraigh and the Far West

Buttress. 'Pelican Gully slants to the left and steep snow from the junction of the climbs leads to a short, awkward ice patch which may become snowed up. The only other obstacle is a 100 ft. broken ice and rock pitch near the top, and the cornice. It has been found that this route holds snow and ice better than any other route in Luchd Coire and is often the only climb in condition.'

Bodach Mor (2689 ft.). The large north-west quartzite cliff of Bodach Mor, 2 miles north-west of Carn Ban is still another climbing possibility, probably more so in winter. The summit is separated from Carn Ban by a 500 ft. dip leading up over Bodach Beag, but access to the foot of the crags is difficult from any direction, and is trackless for a greater part of the way.

8

Coigach

MAP: O.S. One Inch to the Mile (7th Series). Sheet 13 – Loch Inver and Loch Assynt.

The Parish of Coigach lies in the extreme north-westerly tip of the County of Ross and Cromarty. The name – Coigach – means the 'fifth-part'. The old Celtic custom was to divide land into five parts and Coigach is the Coigach of Ross – the fifth part of the Cromarties.

Its north-east boundary, formed by the River Kirkaig, the Fionn Loch and Loch Veyatie, is the county march with Sutherland and separates the area from the neighbouring parish of Assynt.

Access from the south is by way of the A835 from Ullapool, the nearest centre of population. This road has been reconstructed and widened within the past few years and now provides fast, easy passage from Ullapool to Ledmore Junction and beyond that northwards towards Lochinver and Kylesku Ferry.

From Drumrunie Junction, 10 miles north of Ullapool, a secondary road, single-tracked with infrequent passing places, cuts north-westwards to the isolated crofting community of Achiltibuie and the Summer Isles, following the line of well-stocked fishing waters formed by Loch Luragainn, Loch Bad a'Ghal and Loch Oscaig. This road conveniently divides the Coigach Hills into two distinct groups and is a useful means of access to both.

One other motorable road cuts off from the Achiltibuie road at Badagyle, on the west end of Loch Bad a'Ghal and winds its way through a maze of woodland and picturesque lochans to Inverkirkaig and the fishing port of Lochinver, the main township in the parish of Assynt. Scenically the road is to be recommended, but passing places often occur on awkward corners and drivers should take care.

The area as a whole is sparsely settled, the bulk of the population being concentrated along the seaboard north and south of Achiltibuie. Coigach suffered from the Clearances of the last century; its wealth of hill-grazing was a readily marketable commodity to the landowner, giving bigger and swifter monetary returns than the people who 'were altogether unable to occupy beneficially the large extent of hill pasture attached to their little allotments of land'. Despite resistance, the people went, leaving the hills to the sheep and the indigenous Red Deer. The pattern was similar to that which developed through-out most of the vast estates of the Northern Highlands, and now only a dwindling population remain along the perimeter of the area. The present population supplement crofting on a small scale with fishing and the passing tourist trade. Unfortunately it tends to be an ageing population, as the sadly reduced school rolls bear testimony and an infusion of new incentive is urgently needed if the young people who are still there are to be encouraged to remain. Security of tenure of croftland is now ensured but new legislation is needed to allow the linking of crofts into more viable working units if crofting as a way of life is to continue in even its present limited form.

The northern half of Coigach forms the Inverpolly Nature Reserve and includes the peaks of Cul Mor, Cul Beag, and Stack Polly – all over 2000 ft. The main parts of the 27,000 acre reserve, Drumrunie, Inverpolly and Eisg-Brachaidh, were declared in 1961 under agree-ment between the Nature Conservancy and the Polly Estates. A further 36 acres were purchased in 1962 to include Knockan Cliff on the Reserve's eastern boundary. The Reserve is second only in size to the Cairngorm Reserve and contains a wide range of natural habitats.

The wide range of mammals, representative of the mountains and woodlands of the north-west highlands, tend to be scattered and not immediately apparent. They include Red Deer, Wild Cat, Otter and Fox. Pine Martens have been observed in the area around Kirkaig.

Bird life includes the Black-throated Diver, Red-breasted Mer-ganser, Ptarmigan, Raven, Buzzard, Golden Plover, Ring-Ousel,

Cuckoo, Common Sand-piper, Stone-chat and Tree-creeper. The Red Grouse are not present in great numbers but woodcock are common in winter in the woods. Some Arctic Terns breed along the coast and geese and ducks visit the lochs in winter and on migration.

There is a wide range of plant habitats from the sea-coast to a summit of nearly 3000 ft., but the most interesting vegetation of the reserve is its woodlands. This consists mainly of Birch, Hazel, Rowan, Bird Cherry, Aspen, Alder and Holly and is a relic of a northern type of scrub once covering this region but now greatly reduced by heavy grazing and periodic burning.

Because of the high rainfall and the impervious underlying acid rock and glacial clay, large expanses of the reserve are covered with peat, bearing a species-poor moorland vegetation. The peat moorland of the lower reserve stops at the limestone outcrop of Knockan Cliff and here can be found some of the reserve's richest flora – Mountain Avens, Rock Sedge, Fairy Flax, Green Spleenwort and Moss Campion.

The sandstone cliffs and summits have a much poorer vegetation, but there are a number of arctic and alpine species including Alpine Lady's Mantle, Black Bearberry, Bearberry, Mountain Everlasting, Cloudberry, and Dwarf Juniper.

Access to the reserve is not normally restricted, but permission to visit Drumrunie between 15 July and 15 October should be obtained from the Assynt Estate Office (Lochinver 203), and for visits by parties of more than six at any time of the year. The Conservancy require that visitors to the reserve do not collect plants or animal specimens or disturb nesting birds.

Requests to carry out scientific work on the reserve should be addressed to the Regional Officer for North Scotland, The Nature Conservancy, 12 Hope Terrace, Edinburgh, 9. The Reserve Warden can be contacted at 'Strath-Polly' near Inverpolly Lodge – (Lochinver 204).

The structure of the southern part of Coigach is predominately Torridonian but as one moves northwards, one comes across some of the oldest rocks in Britain, occurring in an area which escaped the severity of the Caledonian mountain-building movements.

The oldest rocks, Lewisian Gneiss, underlie the north-west half of the Inverpolly Reserve, from Loch Sionascaig to Enard Bay. At some period a series of parallel north-west–south-east Dykes (ranging from granites to more basic dolerites and serpentines) intruded the gneiss and erosion of these produced a topography of ridges and troughs on which the latter deposits of Torridonian sandstone were laid down.

The more recent removal of the sandstone in this area has re-exposed part of the ancient surface – a fossil landscape modified by ice and river erosion at a later stage.

Torridonian Rocks form the south-east half of the reserve including most of Cul Mor, Cul Beag and Stac Pollaidh. Despite their great age these rocks have been little affected by Earth movements and are tilted only slightly eastwards.

After submergence and erosion of the sandstone, the marine deposits were laid down which now form the lowest layers of the Cambrian system. These rocks were tilted eastwards so that the layers now outcrop in strips along the east boundary of the reserve. The oldest layer, the Basal Quartzite, outcrops along the east slopes of Cul Beag, with an extension to the summit of Cul Mor. It is followed eastwards by successively younger strata, sandstone, shales and finally the Durness limestone, which all outcrop in the lower part of Knockan Cliff. Halfway up the cliff, however, the normal Cambrian succession is broken by the Moine Thrust Plane, one of the great structural lines of North-west Europe. Above this thrust occur the Moine Schists, highly altered rocks which were pushed westwards over the younger, relatively unaltered Cambrian strata by the force of the Caledonian mountain-building movements 400 million years ago. The line of the Thrust extends the full length of the north-western seaboard but its fine exposure at Knockan Cliff has played an important part in the development of Geological Science.

During the past few million years, erosion of these different rocks by ice, rivers, frost and wind has produced some of Scotland's most spectacular scenery. The lowland gneiss in north-west Coigach was heavily glaciated during the Ice Age. Ice scoured the rocky knolls and excavated deep rock basins which now contain lochs or pockets of drift with deep peat. This complex of lochs and bogs lies at a height of between 300 and 500 ft., and above it the isolated relic masses of Torridonian Sandstone which form the mountains of the area. Prolonged weathering of the nearly horizontal strata has produced impressive escarpments on these mountains. Erosion is most advanced on the ridge of Stack Polly where the vertical joints of the sandstone have been sculptured into weird rock pinnacles and chimneys.

The main catchment area for the reserve is Loch Sionascaig, 200 ft. deep and the largest of the multitude of lochs which abound in the region. Sionascaig has a short outlet to the sea via the River Polly.

Ben More Coigach (2438 ft.)

Seen from Ardmair Bay, 6 miles north of Ullapool, Ben More Coigach appears a continuous line of gully-seamed sandstone cliff stretching 2 miles in length from Speicein Coinich in the east to Garbh Choireachan at its western end.

Approaching from this direction, the easiest route on to Ben More starts 1½ miles north of Strathkanaird, leaving the A835 at the top of the rise just before it drops down towards Drumrunie. Cross the River Runie by a wooden bridge – NG.149036 – and an easy-angled shoulder leads upwards over firm ground to the foot of Speicein Coinich, by-passing Loch a'Chlaiginn en route. The summit ridge can be reached at a point west of the rocky outcrops or by contouring round on to the north side and climbing a steep, grassy slope to the top. This slope holds a good snow cover in winter.

The ridge is wide and fairly flat at this eastern end and the summit cairn is reached with little further ascent. From the road the distance is 4 miles.

From the cairn the ridge narrows westwards for ¾ mile towards Garbh Choireachan but presents no problems for the hill-walker. The succession of small rocky towers towards the west end can easily be by-passed on the north side and the outlook from the ridge is superb, both of the mainland hills curving in a great arc from north to south-west, and seawards across the lovely Summer Isles in Badentarbat-Bay to Lewis and the western Islands.

Looking down from Garbh Choireachan, one gets a bird's-eye view of the Holy Isle of St Martin standing guard at the mouth of Ardmair Bay. St Columba ministered here at one time but there is some doubt as to whether the island derives its name from the famous St Martin of Iona or from the Cleric who built his tiny chapel on the island having been banished as a student from Iona until such time as he could give proof to St Columba that he had changed to a more tasteful way of life. Whatever the case, he died on the island and the ruins of his chapel are to be found near the west corner, with the graves of his followers close by.

The way now drops down for 500 ft. in a southerly direction, following the line of the crags and passing the head of a prominent earthy gully – NG.094050 – before rising steeply for 700 ft. up the

20. Dubh Loch (foreground) and Fionn Loch from A'Mhaighdean.

21. Strath na Sheallag, with Ben Dearg Mor (left) and Beag (right).

22. *Opposite:* The An Teallach ridge in winter with the Corrag Bhuidhe pinnacles in profile.

23. Hay-fork Gully of An Teallach in March.

north-east slope leading to the summit cairn of Ben More. The ridge can then be followed westwards to Garbh Choireachan before descending to the road at Culnacraig.

Sgurr an Fhidhleir (2285 ft.)

Seen from Drumrunie, the steep, tooth-shaped peak of Sgurr an Fhidhleir is the most impressive feature of this western group of the Coigach hills.

The 3 mile approach route largely follows the winding course of the Allt Claonnaidh from the reedy Feur Loch at the south-east end of Loch Lurgainn. Leaving the road $2\frac{1}{2}$ miles from Drumrunie Junction, ford the burn leading into the loch and rise steadily westwards between the two long, rocky ended spurs flung out by Beinn an Eoin and Ben More Coigach. These are respectively, Cloch Beinn an Eoin and Beinn Tarsuinn. Sgurr an Fhidhleir rises up above Lochan Tuath, an excellent camp-site with sheltered sandy beaches. A good shelter stone for a small party can be found at the top of a boulder field on the north-east side of the lochan.

The prominent gully mentioned previously follows the south side of the rock face and provides a straightforward but dirty access to the saddle between Fhidhleir and Ben More Coigach. The rocks on the north side of the crag are broken and loose.

The first direct ascent of the 1000 ft. North Buttress of Sgurr an Fhidhleir in 1962 was the climax to a series of attempts spread over the last century and a milestone in the development of climbing in the North-west Highlands. A remarkable early attempt was that made by Messrs Ling and Sang, subsequent visits confirming the difficulties. overcome by these early pioneers.

The Pale Slabs, the key feature of the direct route up The Fiddler, cannot be seen during the approach or even from Lochan Tuath, as they lie just beyond the skyline edge at about mid-height on the buttress. They quickly come into view as one continues along the side of the small subsidiary lochan beyond Lochan Tuath. The Slabs, which appear to lie at an easy angle, are cut by three hair-line terraces composed of a lighter coloured rock than their surroundings. They mark the limit of the earlier attempts. Above the Slabs the buttress rears steeply for a further 300 ft. to the Upper Shoulder where serious climbing gives way to steep scrambling for the final 300 ft.

There is only one true direct line on The Fiddler, that which

I

continues unerringly up the central spur above the Pale Slabs. Earlier parties credited with the first ascent did ultimately succeed in reaching the top of the Buttress by following circuitous routes far to the right of the true line. These routes are now of historical interest only, and are highly dangerous on account of loose rock and friable vegetation.

The Fiddler, Direct Nose Route – 1000 ft., Very Severe (N. Drasdo and C. M. Dixon, April 1962).

Although the climbing, as far as the Pale Slabs at the start of the major difficulties is known to be unpleasantly vegetated, from this point upwards the rock is clean and superbly exposed. The difficulties are prolonged and serious. Dry conditions are recommended though a cross-wind on the exposed upper section could be intimidating. Pegs were twice used for belays, and the first party took between five and six hours to complete the climb.

The details of the route are as follows: 'Starting at the lowest rocks of the buttress follow cracks and corners (numerous lines) to gain the long grassy groove (an obvious feature) which twists up the centre of the buttress, passing two flat-topped overhangs en route (these are best passed on the right). The groove finally leads to a sweep of slabs (the Pale Slabs) which are not seen from below if approaching the buttress from the left (east) but are obvious when viewed from the screes to the right of and below the buttress. These slabs form the key to the steep upper portion of the buttress.

'From a grassy bay below the slabs climb the first slab centrally (Hard Severe) – or more easily climb a grassy groove in the right corner and then traverse easily leftwards along a level grass terrace – to reach the upper left corner of the slab. A large block belay, or a rusty peg (sign of earlier attempts) may be used. Turn the second slab above by climbing a steep right-angled grassy groove on the left. Hard Finish (Hard Severe or Very Severe) on to another good ledge below the third and largest slab. Limit of previous attempts. This could be climbed centrally, but the left-hand edge was used on this ascent. A hard step on to the undercut slab just right of the slab edge leads up and back leftwards for a few feet to a position where a nasty step can be made on to a large loose-looking block in a groove to the left (hard). Continue straight up, following the slab or the corner to another good ledge and various belays overlooking the steep left edge of the buttress. Continue up steeply on the right of the belays moving slightly left and then straight up a steep little wall with few holds to the top (Very Severe). From here easier climbing leads to the crest of the buttress and the top of the peak.'

The north-east Face of Sgurr an Fhidhleir which confronts Loch an Tuath is a formidable sweep of high angle slabs. There is a theoretical line of weakness, if such it may be called, a short distance to the left of the established line of the crest. Two equally fine routes have now been recorded on this side, *Magic Bow* (M. Boysen and T. W. Patey, 1966) and the *Phantom Fiddler* (T. W. Patey, 1967). Details of these appear in the *S.M.C. Journal*, 1970.

Needless to say, Ben More Coigach looks at its best in winter, but snow conditions are seldom good enough to offer any worthwhile climbing. There have been no rock routes recorded on the southern cliffs but varied scrambling is possible.

There is no great difficulty in finding a route down through the rocky outcrops of Garbh Choireachan to Culnacraig, a scattering of croft-houses lying 4 miles south of Achiltibuie at the end of the motorable road. A foot track leads from Culnacraig in a south-easterly direction, skirting the top of the sea-cliffs overlooking Isle Martin and Ardmair. The track crosses the River Runie near Blughasary where it joins a rough road back to Strathkanaird. From Culnacraig to Strathkanaird the distance is 6 miles and the track is in reasonable condition.

A fine walking circuit of the Ben More tops begins at the Allt a Choire Reidh where it crosses the road to Culnacraig – NG.137067, 18 miles by road from Drumrunie Junction. The route follows the right-hand side of the burn up a $2\frac{1}{2}$ mile firm, grassy slope to the summit of Sgurr an Fhidhleir. Looking northwards from the cairn which stands on the lip of the cliff, the hills of Coigach and West Assynt can be picked out in succession as far as Quinag by Kylesku.

Cona Mheall (1786 ft.)

Lying some 2 miles west of Sgurr an Fhidhleir, Cona Mheall forms part of the Coigach group and is distinguished by the prominent pinnacle, known as the Acheninver Pinnacle, which flanks the hill on its left. This formation has provided some rock-climbing.

The first recorded route starts 'From the lowest rocks up a large right-angled block and follows the right-hand edge of the pinnacle to the top. A wide crack about halfway up is turned by a left traverse. A short ascent from the pinnacle leads to the main top.' The route gives 300 ft. of climbing (Very Difficult) and was climbed in 1955 by D. Niven and G. F. Webster, who indicated the likelihood of other routes there.

In 1962, T. W. Patey climbed a 250-ft. Severe route on Middle Crag – 'The central slabby face enclosed by the two arms of a Y-gully and the second rocky buttress to the right of the Acheninver Pinnacle. Starting from the lowest rocks, a more or less direct line finishes up a wide shallow chimney which provides a severe straddling pitch.

'Other shorter routes of the 100 ft. variety have been made on the right-most buttress. The Buttress is south facing and accessible; the rock though sound and rough, is surprisingly scant of holds.'

Beinn an Eoin (1973 ft.)

This twin-topped hill is the smallest of the Coigach group in height. Sgorr Deas, the south top, is broken and rocky on its south west side but on close inspection, the rock is dirty and vegetated and offers little in the way of satisfactory climbing. Sgorr Tuath, the north top, is rocky on its northerly side overlooking Loch Lurgainn and looks promising from the road but again, closer contact proves otherwise. A tiny lochan lies in the saddle between the two tops which are best approached by following at first the route along the Allt Claonnaidh then traversing easily upwards on to Cloch Beinn an Eoin. The complete circuit covers $3\frac{1}{2}$ miles.

Cul Beag (2523 ft.)

Cul Beag rises as a long dip slope of moorland in a north-westerly direction from Drumrunie Junction. The easiest approach to the summit is from this direction, starting at a point past the bridge over the River Runie about 1 mile from the road junction on the way to Achiltibuie. The final slope leading to the summit cairn is steep and boulder-strewn but presents no difficulty to the walker. The distance from the start is about $2\frac{1}{2}$ miles and the view from the summit is extensive.

Cul Beag presents a line of steep gullied cliffs on its North side overlooking Gleann Laoigh but no climbs have been recorded. To the west overlooking Loch Lurgainn, the crags stretch gradually higher from Creag Dubh, providing varied scrambling broken by the usual heathery ledges. As one moves westwards, the rock becomes more continuous and holds better possibilities for more serious climbing.

The main west face of Cul Beag is split in its upper reaches by a prominent Y-shaped gully which sends a long scree tail down to the lower slopes. The gully encloses a wedge-shaped buttress with its apex below and is easily identified from the road by Linneraineach. Early descriptions of climbs on or near this face are too vague to be used as a sure means of identification. In 1914, Messrs Inglis Clark and Ling started from Loch Lurgainn, making for a 'vivid green patch at 1400 ft. where a chimney began'. They reached the summit in $2\frac{1}{4}$ hours. In 1920, L. W. and T. H. Somervell climbed on the Buttress up a series of 50 ft. pitches divided by broad heather ledges, finishing up a long gully which gave interesting climbing and led on to a short arête near the summit of the mountain.

Dr Bell's lucid account in the *S.M.C. Journal of 1959* describes a climb named Lurgain Edge. 'The route had a lower section on the lower rocks to the left of Y-gully, and the upper section was on the right of the shallow upper gully and above the Y, where there is a long steep cliff face. Lurgainn Edge, almost a true ridge, separates the easier rocks facing the upper gully from the wall extending south-eastwards. The Lower introductory part gave little over 150 ft. of climbing and would be improved greatly by going up a sharp rather holdless arête on the left of Y-gully. Start up behind a detached flake more to the left, with one or two difficult pitches on steep, good rock followed by scrambling. Above this, cross Y-gully above the wedge and then to the base of Lurgainn Edge which gave 200–250 ft. of delightful climbing on good steep rock with fine, airy situations. After 100 ft., a difficult chimney to a platform. A cairn was left at the big platform about 100 ft. higher. Then there was a really difficult 30-ft. chimney and some roof-tile slabs to the finish at the top of the rocks. From here a little grassy ridge runs up to the subsidiary southern summit of the mountain with a little dip before the top.'

Other routes have been recorded on the tier of rock below Wedge Buttress, and there is undoubtedly room for further exploration here.

Stac Pollaidh (Polly) (2009 ft.)

Although the smallest of the Coigach group, Stack Polly (correctly but rarely spelt, Pollaidh) undoubtedly holds greater attraction for the mountaineer than any of its neighbours. It is truly a 'mountain in miniature'. The summit ridge rises from an encircling apron of steep talus slopes, lying at an angle of 45 degrees and is an outstanding example of sandstone in the final stages of erosion. The weird variety of weathered shapes and pinnacles sprouting out throughout its half mile length gain in appeal by virtue of the comparative isolation of the mountain from the mainder of the Coigach group. The enthusiasm which it arouses is both remarkable and understandable and has resulted in a wealth of enjoyable literature. James Fisher, the naturalist, is among its most ardent admirers, and his article in *Portraits of Mountains* by E. Molony is strongly recommended.

The proximity of the mountain to the road along the north shore of Loch Lurgainn greatly facilitates access, the choice of routes on to the summit ridge is wide. In an earlier edition of this Guide, W. N. Ling gives a good general introduction to Stack Polly – 'The summit ridge may be easily attained on the north or south by the numerous scree gullies which lead up between the shattered pinnacle ridges. On the east and west the ridge terminates in very steep cliffs, that to the east being somewhat broken up by vegetable ledges. The western cliff has afforded a very difficult and sporting climb, the ascent was made up the true terminal arête of the ridge. An ascent has also been made on the south-east face of the arête and another still on the north-western face. The angle is very steep, but for the most part the rock is sound, though from its nature not many hitches are available and the climbs are only those to be tried by a strong party. To traverse the summit ridge from end to end is an interesting and by no means easy bit of rock-climbing, and from the spectacular photographic point of view is unique in the British Isles.'

The easiest approach is from Linneraineach, 4 miles from Drumrunie Junction on the north side of Loch Lurgainn at its western end. The start of the route is marked by a prominent lay-by beside a solitary cottage – locked and uninhabited for the greater part of the year. From this point a direct line can be taken towards the East Buttress, a distance of 1 mile over open moorland, giving easy walking even in wet weather. A prominent stone cairn stands on exposed slabs near the foot of the buttress. Their succession is complex and route finding needs continuous attention if the climber does not want to find himself in a 'blind alley'. Care should be taken after rain when the ledges can be tricky for a spell.

A path leads round the foot of the crag into a steep dirty shoot which leads on to the saddle already mentioned. This is a better exit than a means of ascent. Easier going is found by traversing round the cairn to the north side of the east buttress to pick up a track leading steeply up on to the saddle at the same point as the other routes. From the cairn, the distance is $\frac{1}{2}$ mile.

Once on the ridge, the tracks along to the west summit, the highest point on Stack Polly, are well-defined and offer countless combinations of walking, scrambling and climbing. Most of the rock problems encountered in the course of the traverse from east to west can be by-passed easily at a lower level if need be, but care should be taken at the west end of the ridge on the step across to the small rock tower that blocks the way to the summit. The holds here are beginning to disintegrate and even the larger blocks need to be tested for security.

On a clear day, the view from the summit is superb. Looking backwards along the ridge itself, one is amazed how the pinnacles just passed have changed in character seen from a different angle. Every hollow in the surrounding floor of gneiss seems to hold its own lochan, many ringed with little sandy beaches. To the north-east, across Loch Sionascaig with its little wooded islands, the whole length of Suilven dominates the view, while closer at hand the muralled western cliffs of Cul Mor rise steeply above Glen Laogh.

The whole of Coigach is unfolded, and beyond that the more distant peaks of Sutherland and Wester Ross.

Stack Polly seldom holds much snow, but when it does, the path on the north side should be treated with care. In normal weather conditions routes back down to the road can be found down most of the many gullies on either side of the ridge. A descent down the large gully to the east of the second buttress from the west and leads past some of the mountain's most spectacular pinnacles. Described by Frank Cunningham in an article in the *S.M.C.J.* (1951) as Pinnacle Basin, three of the pinnacles were seen to resemble the Sphinx, Tam O'Shanter and Madonna and Child. The latter was climbed in 1957 by I. S. Clough and D. Pipes of Kinross Mountain Rescue Team and was called 'The Virgin Pinnacle'. It gave 60 ft. of Severe climbing and was described as follows – 'This slender pinnacle, rising almost 100 ft. above the screes in Pinnacle Basin, was climbed in continuous drizzle by an obvious crack on its shortest side – nearest the mountain – the ledge below the crack was reached (artificial) and the crack was climbed by artificially inserted chock-stones to the gap between the two summit blocks. In good conditions the crack might go by lay-back and jammings giving a very severe pitch.'

The traverse from west to east necessitates rock-climbing, and most of the rock routes on Stack Polly have been concentrated around

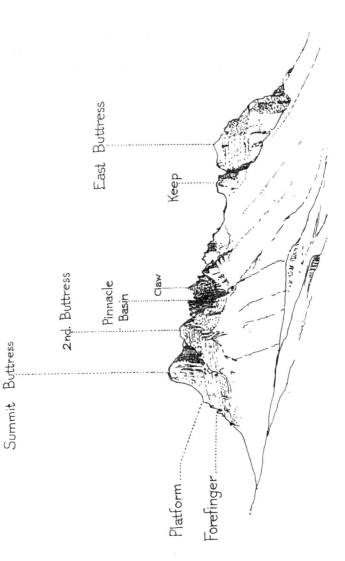

Summit Buttress

2nd. Buttress

Pinnacle
Basin

Claw

East Buttress

Keep

Platform

Forefinger

Fig. 11   Stack Polly from Loch Lurgainn.

24. *Above:* The rock face of Sgurr an Fhidhleir.

25. *Below:* The mountains of Coigach and Assynt, seen stretching from Sgurr an Fhidhleir.

26. Stack Polly from across Loch Lurgainn.

27. The Virgin Pinnacle, Stack Polly.

28. Sandstone pinnacles of Stack Polly.

the West Buttress. The usual route follows the south-west corner of the buttress above the conspicuous rock pinnacle known either as 'The Forefinger' or 'Baird's Pinnacle'. The first ascent here was done in 1906 by C. W. Walker and Dr Inglis Clark. Dr T. W. Patey records that the corresponding northerly corner of the west face of the Buttress may also be climbed more or less directly by a narrow rib of no great difficulty, but of less merit than the south-west corner. This was climbed by him in 1962 and gave 300 ft. of Difficult climbing.

Most of the mountain's main features have now been explored, and a variety of new routes have been recorded. Details of these will be found in the appropriate volume of the *S.M.C. North Rock Guide*.

Cul Mor (2789 ft.)

Cul Mor is the most northerly of the Coigach group, rising steeply from the shore of Loch Veyatie on the Ross-shire–Sutherland border, 2 miles west of the dwindling crofting communities of Knockan and Elphin. Seen from the east, its twin peaks, joined by a smoothly curving saddle and capped with quartzite, form a distinctive land-mark. To the west, Cul Mor drops in a line of steep muralled preci-pices split by deep gullies into Gleann Laoigh. This lovely glen separates the mountain from Cul Beag and is by far the most inter-esting line of approach. Below the main top, from Sròn Garbh (2786 ft.) on the north side of the mountain lies Coire Gorm – the blue corrie – circled by cliffs and hidden from the road. A deep gully formed by a weathered-out dyke drops steeply from the north-west shoulder of Cul Mor and near the point where it meets the ridge is to be seen a distinctive rock pinnacle known as Bod a'Mhiotailt or 'the Old Man' from its likeness to a human figure when seen in profile. The ascent of this Pinnacled Ridge affords pleasant scrambling of a moderate nature but care should be taken on the pinnacle itself – the top blocks are far from secure. The best line of approach to this north side of the mountain is from Elphin School-house, fording the burn which runs into Loch Veyatie just west of the school and rising upwards along the side of the Loch towards Lochan Dearg – NG. 162132 – a distance of 4 miles over good ground. From here a steep ascent leads round into the foot of the gully bounded by Pinnacle Ridge.

The usual approach to Cul Mor starts at the well-marked stalker's track which leaves the A835 ½ mile north-east of the Nature Con-servancy viewpoint at Knockan Rock. This gives good walking for a mile and then the broad south-east ridge can be followed to the base of the summit cone of Sròn Garbh. A series of steep traverses takes one steadily upwards to the final quartzite boulder field and the summit cairn. This involves 3 miles of walking from the road.

Descend into the saddle between the two tops and an easy climb leads in ½ mile on to the south top, Creag nan Calmon (2578 ft.). The actual summit plateau is broad and flat and affords rough hill grazing for sheep. From Craig nan Calmon it is worth detouring on to the west side of the mountain. A small jutting platform gives a spectacular view down into the deep gullies on that side and across to Cul Beag. This can be descended on its west side into Gleann Laoigh with no great difficulty.

Gleann Laoigh provides the most rewarding approach to the western crags of Cul Mor and is in itself one of the loveliest walking routes in the whole area. It can be approached either from the A835 at Knockan Rock or from Linneraineach on Loch Lurgainn. From Knockan Rock the route passes between Loch an Als and Lochan Eada to skirt the south end of Loch nan Ealachan and then crosses the Alt an Loin Duibh at the head of the glen. Traverse the lower slopes of An Laoigh, the rocky southerly satellite of Cul Mor to rise gradually past Lochan Dearg. The boulder field at the north end is a good bivouac site.

If the intention is to reach the west crags of Cul Mor, make for the prominent waterfall which drops over the lowest crags and ascend it to Loch Dearg a'Chuill Mhoir which lies at the foot of the main crags. The choice of route to the top is governed by personal ability and there is undoubtedly scope for climbing routes.

If one continues along the glen, the way leads through woodland and flat meadows to Loch Gainmeich with its sandy beaches. There is a keeper's hut at the north-west end of the loch which is kept locked, but the ground around has many fine camp-sites. The path crosses the narrow neck of water between Loch Gainmeich and Loch Sionascaig by a dubious single-plank bridge and then joins to the well-marked stalker's track which passes over between Cul Beag and Stack Polly to Linneraineach. The distance either way to the foot of the crags is 3 miles and the route is to be recommended.

9

Assynt

(1)   **Suilven** (2399 ft.).
 (2)   **Canisp** (2779 ft.).
 (3)   **Quinag** (2653 ft.).
 (4)   **Glas Bhein** (2541 ft.).
 (5)   **Beinn Uidhe** (2410 ft.).
 (6)   **Beinn a Fhurain** (2824 ft.).
 (7)   ***Conival** (3234 ft.).
 (8)   ***Ben More Assynt** (3273 ft.).
 (9)   **Brae Bag** (2670 ft.).
(10)   **Ben Leoid** (2597 ft.).

MAP: O.S. One Inch to the Mile (7th Series). Sheet No. 13 – Loch Inver and Loch Assynt and Sheet No. 14 – Lairg.

Assynt forms the south-west portion of the county of Sutherland and is separated from Coigach by the boundary line along Loch Veyatie and the River Kirkaig.

Sutherland is the 'Suderland' or 'Southland' of the Norsemen who were the scourge of the northern mainland of Scotland for over 400 years from A.D. 800 to A.D. 1263. Their influence in Assynt, as in other parts of the Sutherland and Caithness areas which came under their power is still to be seen in many of the place-names – often a corrupted combination of Norse and Ancient Gaelic.

The name 'Assynt' itself has been suggested as deriving from the Norse 'A-ssynt' – seen from afar, in reference to its mountains. The Norse word 'Ass' means 'rocky'.

An alternative meaning of 'Assynt' comes from a vague legend that at one time there were two brothers – Unt and Ass-Unt – meaning Man of Peace and Man of Discord. In olden days they fought for the mastery of Assynt and Unt was slain, his brother then giving his name to the parish. Equally likely is the contraction of the Gaelic compound – Agus Unt – to As-int – In and Out –

which is descriptive of the broken nature of the surface of the area.

On its northern border, Assynt is separated from the neighbouring parish of Eddrachillis by the great sea loch of A'Chairn Bhain (Anglicised into Cairbawn) which opens westwards into the broad bay of Eddrachillis with its host of sandy inlets and low-lying islands.

In the past these islands were used as grazing grounds for the mainland, and here sheep and cattle were fattened – the old statistical accounts of the eighteenth century detail the number of animals which each of the many islands could carry.

Oldany Island lying just off the Assynt shore near the mouth of the bay is the largest of these, and in the days when Assynt swarmed with wolves it was used as a burial ground for the mainland settlements. At its inland end Loch Cairnbawn narrows to less than $\frac{1}{4}$ mile and a free ferry now operates seven days a week across from Kylesku to Kylestrome on the north side of the channel. In the past, drovers from the north swum their cattle across the narrows and nineteenth-century prints of the area show a sizeable fleet of herring-boats anchored in Unapool Bay, once the centre of a thriving fishing industry.

East of the narrows, Loch Cairnbawn divides, sending two fingers probing inland for almost 4 miles. The northerly inlet is Loch Glendhu; the southerly inlet Loch Glencoul. This is an area of especial attraction to the geologist. Aird da Loch, the headland, dividing the two lochs, shows a classic exposure of the Glencoul Thrust plane, and of the great earth movements which took place in the development of the mountain ranges of the Northern Highlands. Here the displacement of the native gneiss over the sedimentary layer of Cambrian strata can be clearly seen.

The parish boundary on the east side follows the watershed along the ridges of Beinn Uidhe, Conival and Braebeg paradoxically excluding Ben More Assynt, the highest mountain top in Sutherland. To further exclude it from this chapter on the Assynt mountains would be illogical and for similar geographical reasons we include here mention of Ben Leoid. This mountain officially lies in the parish of Edrachillis (in the Glen Coul–Glen Dhu hinterland).

At the south-eastern corner of Assynt, the Ross-shire border makes a strange, wedge-like invasion north into Sutherland as far as Conival and the slopes of Ben More Assynt. The road from the south crosses the border by the well-known fishing hotel at Altnacealgach. A dispute took place here in the past over the demarcation of the county boundaries. When two witnesses were called they maintained that while walking the boundaries their feet had never left Ross-shire soil. This was true. They had first filled their shoes with Balnagowan earth. Altnacealgach means 'the burn of the cheat'.

From Enard Bay in the south around the peninsula of Rubh a'Stoer to Eddrachillis, the Assynt coastline is indented by numerous sandy-bayed sea lochs of which the most important is Loch Inver. The village of Lochinver which lies at its head is the main centre of population in the area and has become an important port for the landing of white-fish. Its central location at the junction of motor roads from north, south and east make it a popular centre for summer visitors and superb sea-angling ranks high among its many attractions.

The Rubh a'Stoer peninsula culminates in the Point of Stoer, which juts out into the Minch, eight miles north-west of Lochinver. The 'Old Man of Stoer' – not to be confused with the 'Old Man of Storr' in Skye – stands half a mile south of the Point. This 220-ft. sandstone sea stack was considered 'unclimbable' until it was ascended for the first time in 1966 by T. W. Patey, B. Robertson, B. Henderson and P. Nunn. It was found to give a 'fine free climb of Severe Standard on the best Torridonian Sandstone in Scotland'.

From its slender base, the pinnacle bulges at mid-height, before it begins to taper and, from its appearance, might suggest a more exacting climb than its better-known namesake in Skye (which it overtops by about 60 ft.). Huge, rough-grained holds flatter the climber, so that almost anything may be attempted.

Puking Fulmars elevate the standard during the nesting season.

Scramble down steeply for 300 ft., to the broad shelf opposite the Old Man. To gain the supporting plinth, a deep channel 25 ft. wide at its narrowest point, must be crossed. A 30 ft. ladder, a Tyrolean traverse rope, and swimming offered different solutions on different visits, but tidal currents and underwater seaweed could often hamper swimmers. Twelve feet up the landward face, twin horizontal cracks are followed left round the first corner, then go straight up excellent rock to a large platform on the corner (60 ft.).

Above the platform climb a steep slab (crux) to a fringe of overhangs. Pass the overhangs by a crack and step delicately left to reach easy ledges. Continue for 30 ft. to a cave below, above a large chockstone (70 ft.). Traverse round the airy corner to the right on the landward face and veer up rightwards avoiding the first upward break, to reach a small ledge and block belay (40 ft.). Climb the prominent

V-chimney above, facing left, to easy ground. Finish up obvious corner-crack (50 ft.). Descent by Rappel: go straight down the line of the south-east corner to the first belay platform (150 ft.). Move along a thin ledge on the landward face to an abseil piton. Go down to the starting point (60 ft.) – 220 ft., Hard Severe.

Two good motor roads lead into Assynt from the south. The road from Ullapool with its branch road to Lochinver has been described in a previous chapter. This links with the Bonar Bridge–Lochinver road – (A837) – at Ledmore Junction, 2 miles north-west of Altna-cealgach Hotel. The road from Bonar Bridge leaves the A9 at the head of the Kyle of Sutherland and follows the Oykel valley for most of its way north-westwards. This wide river valley, running roughly north-west–south-east, separates Sutherland and Caithness from the rest of the southern mainland and inspired early geographers to name the area 'Innismor' – 'The Great Island'.

The road rises steeply out of the river valley on to the watershed at Craggie then continues past Ledmore northwards through Inchna-damph and on along Loch Assynt side to Lochinver. Its route con-veniently passes through the main mountain mass of Assynt providing easy access to both east and west.

Two miles north of Inchnadamph, at Skiag Bridge, a branch road leads northwards to Kylesku Ferry and the Reay country, crossing between Quinag and Glas Bheinn at its highest point.

A secondary road branches westwards some 2 miles from the Ferry passing along the coastline and across the neck of the Stoer Peninsula to link the crofting communities of Need, Drumbeg, Clashnessie, Culkein and Stoer with Lochinver. This circuit is one of the most picturesque in the area and should not be by-passed. The road passes beneath the great northern buttresses of Quinag then winds and switchbacks its way westwards to Stoer, the largest of the villages through which it passes. Stoer lies 7 miles north of Lochinver and has a good camping site by its broad sandy beach. One mile north of the village a side road branches on to the Point of Stoer. A car can be taken as far as Culkein, which is a scattered community of croft houses but the final 2 miles to the sea is by peat road and moorland.

From the road south of Stoer one gets a fine panoramic view of the Coigach and Assynt hills rising in all their varied shapes from the surrounding moorland. One can well believe the legend that this is where the old Norse gods came when the world was still young and malleable to practice mountain building. They are said to have returned and modelled Norway with more experienced hands.

The country stretches inland for 10 miles to Loch Assynt and is a maze of fresh water lochs of every shape and size – a paradise for fishermen but difficult to navigate.

The roads throughout Assynt pass few inhabited communities. The population is scattered mainly around the coastal region from Lochinver north to Drumbeg. Here crofting and fishing are the main occupations and most houses will provide overnight accommodation for the tourists.

Once away from the coastal strip, Assynt is virtually uninhabited apart from the scattering of houses around Inchnadamph Hotel at the east end of Loch Assynt, the tiny village of Unapool by Kylesku Ferry and along the stretch of road from Ledmore to the village of Elphin.

Assynt is the legendary hunting grounds of the Thanes of Sutherland and is still almost entirely divided among great sporting estates which are let throughout the season for their fishing and stalking rights.

The exception is the limestone area lying east of Inchnadamph Hotel to the slopes of Ben More where 3200 acres of the Assynt Estate are managed by the Nature Conservancy. Here vegetation changes are being studied and the existing herb-rich pastures maintained by strict control of burning and grazing.

In the past, much of Assynt was covered by dense forest which provided hunting for its early overlords – the Thanes of Sutherland. Evidence of still earlier inhabitants is to be seen close to the roadside from Ledmore to Loch Assynt in the relics of early burial chambers and in the isolated standing stones in the neighbourhood of Clachtoll, while later ruins of brochs are to be found at Clashness and Stoer Bay on the coastline.

During the twelfth century the area was pillaged by the Norsemen and was defended by the neighbouring MacNicholl family who held the land around Ullapool during the Thanes' absence. In gratitude for their help, Assynt was given to the MacNicholls to be held in vassalage, and remained under their control for centuries until passing into the hands of a son of Macleod of Lewis as dowry on his marriage to the only daughter of the MacNicholl chief.

Macleod received a charter for the land from King David II with the approval of the Thane of Sutherland in 1346 and fourteen successive Macleod lairds ruled Assynt until the end of the seventeenth century.

Ardvreck Castle, the stronghold of the family, was built in 1597 and the ruins still stand out into the waters of Loch Assynt on a narrow, easily defended peninsula 1½ miles north-west of Inchnadamph. The devil is reputed to have had a hand in both its building and its ultimate fate.

The downfall of Macleod power began with the part played by Neil Macleod, in the betrayal of the Marquis of Montrose in 1650. After his little army of 1200 men had been cut to pieces at Carbisdale by Strachan's cavalry, the wounded Marquis fled westwards with three companions and wandered the hills for two days and nights. Separated from his companions, Montrose was forced to beg food at a herd's shieling on the third day and was captured by Macleod's men. He was imprisoned in a dungeon in Ardvreck Castle and then taken to Edinburgh where he was executed on 21 April, 1650. Though Macleod tried to vindicate himself it is a recorded fact that he accepted payment for his service and his fortunes and those of his family declined from that time on. A dispute with the Mackenzie lairds of Seaforth came to litigation and was upheld in Mackenzie's favour by the law court. Mackenzie was given permission to exact the pledge by force of arms, and after a prolonged siege, Ardvreck Castle fell and the Macleod laird fled, allegedly to Holland.

After the Jacobite risings the Mackenzie estates were forfeit to the crown and in 1760 passed back into the hands of the Sutherland family by purchase. The ruined house on the roadside near Ardvreck is Calda House – known locally as the white house – a stronghold built and burned by the Mackenzies allegedly rather than see it pass into the hands of the Sutherlands.

In 1760, Assynt passed back into the hands of the original Sutherland family by purchase and on the marriage of Elizabeth, Countess of Sutherland to Lord Stafford, who was to become the first Duke of Sutherland and the owner of almost the entire county. Like the remainder of his estates, Assynt suffered in his schemes for Agricultural Improvement, and between 1812 and 1820, large numbers of the inhabitants were 'cleared' to make way for sheepwalks.

The major part of the area now forms the Assynt Estate whose present owner is Mr E. H. Vestey. The estate offices are in Lochinver.

The mountains of Assynt fall into two distinct groups – west and east – divided by the road from Ledmore Junction to Kylesku. This is no artificial division. From Ullapool to Kylesku the road follows the boundary of the Great Thrust Planes and one cannot fail to observe the change in rock formation and scenery on either side of it. To the west is the undisturbed Lewisian Gneiss and to the east the crystalline schists of the Moine Series.

The gneiss forms a platform for the western mountains – which are predominantly sandstone monoliths capped in varying degrees with Cambrian Quartzite.

To the east, the gneiss is found rising to a much greater height as a result of the great thrust movements, and on Ben More Assynt (3237 ft.) rises close to the summit, the highest occurrence of this formation in Britain.

In the north-west there are four main formations which go to build the mountain slopes.

The oldest (oldest in the world) is the Lewisian Gneiss. On top of it rests the younger Torridonian Sandstone. Next is the Cambrian (certain fossils) which here take the form of white quartzite and a series of limestones.

After the Cambrian had been laid down came a series of vast movements which thrust forward great slabs of rock and piled them up, older rocks overriding on younger rocks, upsetting the natural sequence and sometimes causing complete inversion to the confusion of early geologists.

Last and greatest of these thrusts was the Moine Thrust which brought forward the great series of schists – the Moine Schists – over the Lewisian, Torridonian and Cambrian strata. This thrust runs on a sinuous line from Whitten Head on the north coast of Sutherland (Outer Loch Eriboll) to Sleat in Skye – a distance of 120 miles. The width of the thrust varies from 12 miles in Skye to 1 mile in Sutherland. In Assynt it is 7 miles wide.

It is not known for sure whether the pressure built up from the south-south-east to pile up the schists on the fringe of a stable area of older rocks or whether the older strata moved from the west-north-west and pushed the schists up over them.

The minimum distance through which the Moine Schists have been displaced westwards relative to the formation beneath the Moine Thrust Plane is estimated at 10 miles.

Full information of the movements and the manner in which they affected the Northern Highlands is to be found in *Basic Regional*

Geology: Scotland: The Northern Highlands (2nd Edition), by J. Phemister; H.M.S.O. Publication.

WEST ASSYNT

Suilven
(1) *Caisteal Liath* (2399 ft.). 5 miles S.E. of Lochinver.
(2) *Meall Mheadhonach* (2300 ft.). ½ mile E. of (1).
(3) *Meall Bheag* (2000 ft.). ½ mile E. of (2).

Suilven is the most westerly of the Assynt mountains and dominates the surrounding landscape. It is one of the most remarkable and best known peaks in the British Isles.

Viewed from east or west it appears as a solitary peak. This is how the Vikings saw it coming into the Assynt coast from the sea and causing them to name it Sul-Fjal – the Pillar Mountain. To the native Gael the great rounded western dome became Caisteal Liath – the Grey Castle – a fitter name for this splendid sculptured sandstone tower than the 'Sugar Loaf'. Seen across the Cam Loch from Elphin in the south-east it appears as a sharp cone with only a glimpse of the precipices on Caisteal Liath with the ridge greatly foreshortened. Seen from north or south, the whole splendour of its triple-peaked ridge is unfolded, rising in splendid isolation from the surrounding lochan-strewn moorland like a ship riding at anchor.

The ridge extends for 1½ miles. The rounded red flanked tower of Caisteal Liath lies at the western end, the sharp peak of Meall Mheadhonach in the middle and the much smaller peak of Meall Beag with its sharp drop facing Meall Mheadhonach at the eastern end. Between Caisteal Liath and Meall Mheadhonach lies the Bealach Mor – a prominent col from which steep stone-shoots drop down to north and south. The easy route on to the summit ridge lies up either of those; that on the north side is possibly a little easier but there is nothing to choose between them. The descent should be treated carefully. Loose stone.

Approaching Suilven from the north-west, there is a choice of three starting points.

From Little Assynt at the west end of Loch Assynt on the Inchnadamph–Lochinver road – A837 – River Inver is crossed by a footbridge and a stalker's track is followed for 2½ miles to Suileag in Glen Canisp.

The same point can be reached from Lochinver. A private road leads for almost 2 miles to Glencanisp Lodge, owned by Mr Vestey, the Estate proprietor, and a stalker's track leads to the junction with the Little Assynt track near Suileag. Continue along the north side of Amhainn na Clach Airigh for 1¾ miles to the bridge at the head of Loch na Gainimh. The main track continues for a good 2 miles along the north shore of the Loch towards Lochan Fada below Canisp. From the bridge a steep climb over rough ground leads to the foot of the stone-shoot leading to the north side of Bealach Mor.

The stone-shoot on the south side of the Bealach is reached from Inver Kirkaig at the bridge over the River Kirkaig 3 miles south of Lochinver. A good track follows the river of the Fionn Loch – 3 miles. The track passes the Falls of Kirkaig – a 60 ft. perpendicular fall – continue along the north side of the loch for another mile before making a way upwards to the foot of the stone-shoot on the south side of the Bealach Mor.

Once on the Bealach an easy climb westwards leads to the summit cairn on Caisteal Liath, passing en route through a gap in the dry-stone dyke which amazingly enough has been built for some indefinite reason across the line of the ridge at this point.

Retrace the route to the bealach and a splendid ridge walk with some scrambling leads on to the summit of Meall Mheadhonach giving spectacular views down either flank. The route drops steeply between Mheall Mheadhonach and Mheall Bheag and the ascent of the latter from the col requires some care. An exposed corner is turned on the north side along a rocky shelf and a way can then be made up to the top of Mheall Bheag on the same side by way of a series of terraces. The situation is slightly exposed but affords no great difficulty. A little way down the east ridge a narrow transverse gap is easily crossed and the difficulties are over.

A way may be made with care, down the south side of the col between Mheall Mheadhonach and Mheall Bheag but this is loose and dirty and care should be taken in the lower stretches where a steep drop is by-passed by keeping eastwards. The east ridge can be followed down to the head of Cam Loch and from there along the south side of the loch for a little over a mile. The loch is indented by a wide bay on this side and a line overland from the southern corner brings on to the waterfall between Cam Loch and Loch Veyatie. The water can be forded at the head of Loch Veyatie from where a track leads up to Elphin School house and the road to Ledmore Junction.

The approach to Suilven from this eastern direction is long and arduous. An alternative is to go by canoe along Loch Veyatie for about 2½ miles to an obvious natural harbour on its north shore – NG. 178141. A direct line north is then taken overland to the end of Loch nan Rac – a distance of 1½ miles. A steep but straightforward ascent then leads on to the east ridge of the mountain and Mheall Bheag. This makes a delightful day's expedition. The traverse of Suilven from west to east involving the ascent of Caisteal Liath with its near vertical cliffs is undoubtedly a classic of its kind. The problem posed by the 800 ft. terraced sandstone which encircles the north-western end of Suilven already has produced a variety of solutions but the possibilities are by no means exhausted. It can be tackled by way of several of the numerous gullies which reach the walls but these eventually run out and the climber must be prepared for steep regulation, exposure and little protection.

The original climbing route on Caisteal Liath lies up the steep open gully on the southern side of the North-west Buttress. It has no technical difficulty but is exposed and vegetated, as are many of the subsequently recorded routes. The first people to climb this way were C. Pilkington and H. Walker in 1892.

A 'fine route up the middle of the North West Buttress itself' was recorded by R. Gray in the *Rucksack Club Journal*, 1935. This began at an open groove in the middle of the face. At few points was there much technical difficulty, but there was considerable exposure, and it was necessary to accept and to use with care whatever holds there were, whether vegetation or quartz pebbles projecting from the sandstone.

A more recent climb on the North-west Buttress is *Rose Route* – 400 ft., Mild Severe (A. Smart and A. Mitchell, 1957).

Start at foot of North-west Buttress, right of the prominent central rib:

(1) 40 ft. – Climb steep 8 ft. wall and turn steeper one to the right, to reach the foot of a fine red slab. Climb obliquely upwards for 20 ft., and to the ledge above – dubious flake belay.

(2) 40 ft. – up 8 ft. from ledge and traverse left round a nose to the foot of two narrow slabs, the right set back from the left. Climb 20 ft. up between them to a larger ledge at the edge of the nearest water-slide. Jammed Stone Belay.

(3) 30 ft. – A spectacular and exposed (but not technically hard) traverse left round a corner and along ledges more secure than they

look, leads to the broken ledges of the traverse directly below the south edge of the main buttress. The remainder of the climb more or less follows this edge.

(4) 65 ft. – Start at the obvious corner of the buttress. This corner is taken throughout as being the edge of the buttress, as against a lesser corner further right (cairn). Climb 12 ft. and then over or round a large block. At 25 ft., a small slab leads to a mantelshelf movement on to a large block on the right. Traverse right to the buttress edge, and go up 20 ft. further to a notable stalactite belay at the foot of a small chimney.

(5) 85 ft. – Climb the chimney and by-pass a small wall on the right leading back to a dark corner on the left at 35 ft. Traverse right, round a projecting block (hands above, feet beneath) to a good ledge, again near the buttress edge.

30 ft. – of easier climbing leads to a broad ledge above which the angle obviously lessens.

Three long run-outs over more broken rocks leads in 200 ft. to the top of the climb. Some distance from the top of the buttress the climbing is easier and variation possible.

The rock is sound and the climb, which is a good one, is always steep and generally exposed.

Canisp (2779 ft.). 5 miles N.E. of Ledmore Junction.

In itself, Canisp holds little of interest to the climber, but its position some 3 miles east of Suilven across Glen Canisp makes it an ideal viewpoint for the latter mountain. Its long south-eastern slope is best approached from the road some 2 miles north of Ledmore Junction. The River Loanan which flows out of Loch Awe can be crossed at the end of the loch by a footbridge and the summit of Canisp is easily reached in just over one hour. The distance from the road is $3\frac{1}{2}$ miles. The view across to the ridge of Suilven, especially in winter, is in itself ample reward, but the northern side of Canisp drops unexpectedly in broken quartzite cliffs in its upper reaches, and here the golden eagle can be seen. The derivation of Canisp is doubtful but in view of its quartzite capping the old Gaelic word 'Can' meaning 'white' may well form part of the name. The rock is too shattered to offer any climbing. The return to the road can be made down the side of the attractive Allt Mhic Mhurchaidh Gheir which drops in series of falls and pools, natural bathing pools into Loch Awe.

Quinag

(1) *Spidean Coinich* (2508 ft.). 4½ miles N.N.W. of Skiag Bridge.
(2) *Centre Top* (2448 ft.). ¾ mile N.N.W. of (1).
(3) *Main Top on East Ridge* (2653 ft.). ½ mile N.E. of (2).
(4) *Sail Gharbh* (2414 ft.). ½ mile N.N.W. of (3).
(5) *Sail Ghorm* (2551 ft.). 1 mile N.W. of (2).

Quinag stands as a mighty sentinel guarding the northern border of Assynt and is the last distinctive 'Mountain' in that chain of Torridonian Sandstone which stretches from Applecross along the western seaboard of the Northern Highlands. Only around the Cape Wrath Peninsula in the extreme northern tip does the sandstone again reach a height of any impressive proportions.

Quinag is shaped like a gigantic 'Y'. The main leg is formed by the mile and a half long dip slope running north-westwards from Loch Assynt on to Spidean Coinich (2508 ft.), the southern peak which stands out boldly like a giant water spout. This peak gives the mountain its name Cuinneag in Gaelic as a narrow-mouthed bucket. The slope has an overlying cover of white quartzite widely exposed in many places and giving pleasant walking. The quartzite also appears as an impressive cliff falling from the north-east side of Spideac Coinich. The ridge continues slightly north-westwards for 1 mile to the centre unnamed top (2448 ft.) dropping on the way into the Bealach a'Chornaidh, the deep saddle which bisects the ridge and provides an easy route across the ridge from east to west.

The ridge divides and sends out two broad areas containing in their fork the deep corrie out of which flows the Alt a'Bhathaich – the burn of the Byre. Then the spur continues north-westwards in the main line of the ridge and terminates in a rocky buttress of Sail Ghorm (2551 ft.). Here on the north face the underlying gneiss rises to a height of 2000 ft. The north-east spur rises to the highest top of Quinag (2653 ft.), and terminates in the great sandstone buttress of Sail Garbh (2414 ft.). The main top has a capping of white quartzite; the deeply gullied face of Sail Garbh is of sandstone, which drops down in a series of bold steps, broken here and there by heathery terraces.

The entire western side of Quinag extends for some 2 miles as a line of well-seamed crags, rising to a height of 700 ft. in places, abounding in broken ribs and gullies as yet barely touched by rock climbers.

The mountain is easy of access from all sides. The south-east dip slope rises from the Junction of the Lochinver and Kylesku roads at Skiag Bridge some 2 miles north of Inchnadamph Hotel on the north shore of Loch Assynt. The Kylesku road is followed northwards for 2 miles and from any convenient point the line of the slope can be followed to the summit of Spidean Coinich.

Alternatively, a stalker's track leaves the road near by NG.232274 – and leads into the north side of Lochan Bealach Ghornaidh on to the Saddle below the centre top Bealach Chornaidh. The distance is 2¾ miles and the track goes in further than is marked on the map. This is a good escape route from the ridge if need be, and gives a fine view of the great north cliff of Spidean Coinich.

The nearest point of access to the rock faces of Sail Garbh is from the Kylesku road where it crosses the Unapool burn – 1½ miles across the Alt na Saodbeidh Mor – the way is largely across moorland but eventually a track is joined which leads to the foot of the rocks.

Other routes are possible from a variety of points along the Drumbeg road which branches off from the Kylesku road 2 miles before the ferry. The most obvious starting point is from the bridge over the Alt a Ghamhna – 2 miles from the junction.

From Tumore on the Lochinver road, 3½ miles west of Skiag Bridge, a stalker's track leads through Gleann Leireag to join the Drumbeg road 5 miles from the junction near Kylesku. This passes along the foot of the western cliffs of Quinag giving a fine view of the length of the ridge with its succession of rounded subsidiary tops.

From Criag na H'Iolaire on the 750 ft. contour the Bealach lies ½ mile east of the track and to reach it from this point involves only 1200 ft. of ascent.

Further north, the track passes Loch an Leathaid, and from here one can make a way up the long slope leading on to Sail Ghorm.

The western cliffs of Quinag abound in ribs and gullies which should produce a variety of new rock routes. The prominent rib seen rising from right to left immediately below the small truncated top north-west of the central top of Quinag has been climbed by C. R. Ambler and J. R. Sutcliffe and is named *Tenement Ridge* – 500 ft. (Very Difficult).

This rib is separated from the main face of the mountain by a deep gully branching left from the Geodha Rudha; it rises in a series of steep rock steps divided by spacious ledges and can worthily be considered a 'ridge'.

The scree gully – Geodha Rudha – is crossed to gain a heather ledge at the base of the rock ridge. The climb starts up a sloping corner with a slab on its left. Minor variations are possible on most pitches. Thread, or block belays were found on all but the third platform, when a piton was used. In the prevailing weather condition of heavy rain, the final steep rock step before the ridge levels out was passed by a short rightward traverse above the gully and the crest regained by a chimney. Easy scrambling along the final section of the ridge before it joins the mountain is interrupted by steep 15 ft. wall which provides an unavoidable problem to the finish of the climb.

More recent exploration by T. W. Patey and H. MacInnes has produced several other routes on this side of Quinag, details of which appear in the *Scottish Mountaineering Club Journal*, 1970.

The most impressive view of Quinag is that of the great northern buttresses of Sail Ghorm and Sail Gharbh which rise in huge vertical steps split by deep gullies and broken occasionally by narrow terraces. The great Barrel Buttress of Sail Gharbh starts at a height of about 1700 ft., and is best approached by leaving the Kylesku road near Loch an Geinmhich and across the moor past Loch nan Dueun where a sheep track leads to the foot of the buttress. The original climb by Messrs Raeburn, Mackay and Ling in 1907 is now of historical interest only, broken by ledges and highly vegetated. The same holds true of the Buttress east of the Barrel Buttress first climbed by Messrs Goggs, Arthur and Young in 1914. Although there are some interesting pitches these can be avoided and the frequent ledges allow for variation of the original lines taken. The nature of the climbing makes accurate description of these early routes difficult. Two more recent routes on the Barrel Buttress itself to the right of the original route give some of the best climbing on this side of Quinag to date. Both of these are of about 300 ft. in length. *Mild* – Mild Very Severe (T. W. Patey) lies to the right of original route. *Bitter* – Very Severe (T. W. Patey and G. Nicol) lies to the right of Mild.

EASTERN ASSYNT

(1) *Glasbheinn* (2541 ft.). E. of road from Inchnadamph to Kylesku.
(2) *Beinn Uidhe* (2410 ft.). 2¾ miles N.E. of Inchnadamph.
(3) *Beinn an Fhurain* (2824 ft.). 3¼ miles E. of Inchnadamph.

Overleaf
29. The Old Man of Stoer.

30. *Above left:* Suilven ridge from the River Kirkaig.

31. *Above right:* Quinag: Sail Garbh and Sail Gorm and the great line of the western cliffs.

32. *Opposite:* Quinag and Sail Garbh, showing the main routes on the Barrel Buttress. 1 and 2 are original lines, 3 Mild, 4 Bitter.

33. The unclimbed 600 ft. cliffs of Clo Mhor on the north coast of Sutherland near Cape Wrath.

(4) *Conival* (3234 ft.). 3½ miles E. by S. of Inchnadamph.
(5) *Ben More Assynt* (3273 ft.). 4¼ miles E. by S. of Inchnadamph.
(6) *South Top of Ben More* (3200 ft.). ⅜ mile S.E. of (5).
(7) *Carn nan Conbhairean* (2850 ft.). 1 mile S. of (6).
(8) *Meall an Aonaich* (2345 ft.). 1 mile E. of S. of (7).
(9) *Creag Liath Braebag* (2670 ft.). 3 miles S.S.W. of (4).
(10) *Ben Leoid* (2597 ft.). 6½ miles N.E. of Inchnadamph.

The mountains of the eastern part of Assynt form a continuous range stretching more than 11 miles in a north-west–south-east direction. Throughout its length, the range never drops below 2000 ft., rising upwards from either end to over 3000 ft., on the summits of Conival and Ben More Assynt, the highest points in Sutherland. Despite its greater height, Ben More does not stand out as conspicuously in the Assynt landscape as the isolated sandstone peaks of the western area. Even from Inchnadamph its summit is hidden by Conival and from most points along the roadside it is almost completely concealed by its own foothills. Only when viewed from a distance, is the greater part of the ridge unfolded at one time – from the top of the Oykel watershed just east of Altnacealgach; from Rosehall at the south end of Glen Cassley: from the road along the north side of Loch Shin.

Gneiss and quartzite are the main rock formations in this eastern area and on Ben More Assynt the former extends almost to the summit of the mountain, the highest point it reaches in Scotland.

The lower western slopes at the head of Gleann Dubh are of Cambrian Limestone which outcrops in both dark blue and lighter varieties all along the Moine Thrust, and along the Traligill Burn is burrowed by underground rivers and caves as mentioned previously.

The 3000 ft. tops are usually climbed from Inchnadamph. The main road is left 200 yds past the hotel and a rough motor road leads for a mile along the River Traligill to the shepherd's cottage at Glenbain. Cars are best left at the concrete ford ½ mile from the start. There is a good camp-site here in a sheltered hollow beside the water.

From Glenbain, a faint track continues along Gleann Dubh for ½ mile to cross the Traligill at the Nature Conservancy sign. If the track is followed for ½ mile south-east, one of the main entrances to the Traligill caves and underground river is easily found at the head of a short limestone gulch (NG.276206).

Traligill has a Norse derivation – Troll's Gill meaning Giant's

Ravine – the name can be aptly applied to many of the water-sculptured limestone formations in the immediate area. In particular the fine hollowed out cavern entered by a gigantic arch which lies some distance south of the main cave entrance along the obvious dried-out river bed.

For the ascent of Conival and Ben More, leave the track at the signpost already mentioned and keep to the east bank of the Traligill River traversing upwards for just under 2 miles on to the saddle between Conival and Beinn an Fhurain. Even in wet conditions the going is firm and the 2000 ft. of ascent to the cairn on the saddle requires no great effort. A direct line up the side of the burn which drops down from the saddle further to the west is not recommended.

Three-quarters of a mile and a further 800 ft. of climbing up a steep quartzite ridge leads to the summit cairn of Conival. A narrow ridge now turns eastwards and continues for 1 mile on to the main top of Ben More. The way is rough and requires some mild boulder scrambling in places but presents no difficulty to the climber in dry weather. Extreme care should be taken, however, in winter conditions or in poor visibility. The connecting ridge between Conival and Ben More drops steeply on the south into the head of Glen Oykel and is precipitous in stretches in its initial stage.

From the main top, the view to the east across the deserted central part of Sutherland is broken by Ben Klibreck and further north by the mountains of Reay.

The view westwards brings in the mountains of the Inverlael forest and beyond that the Fannichs and the peaks of Wester Ross. On a clear winter's day the panorama is particularly fine.

The south top is reached in $\frac{1}{2}$ mile and involves two or three bad steps across exposed slab. Here the Ben More ridge drops steeply down into Dubh Loch Mor – a good example of a corrie loch – from which originates the River Oykel – one of the finest fishing rivers in the country. The slopes are of deeply gullied gneiss but with care a way can be made down into the Glen, the slopes becoming progressively easier as one moves southwards.

From the loch, a stalker's path follows the course of the water down into the glen leading to Benmore shooting lodge on the shores of Loch Ailsh, and from there to the road – an overall distance of over 8 miles.

If, however, one wishes to return to Inchnadamph, traverse round from the loch-side into the Bealach between Conival and Tarsuinn

Braebag, an ascent of just over 200 ft. There is no well-defined track but this narrow picturesque defile can easily be followed back to rejoin the outward route. However, in bad weather the going is decidedly boggy.

The Braebag ridge can also be climbed from the Bealach. The route passes from Beinn Tarsuinn (2044 ft.) for just under three miles to Creag Liath (2670 ft.), the highest point on the ridge, giving pleasant hill-walking alternatively over rough hill pasture and broken rocky pavements of gneiss. The ridge is broad and flat for most of its length, but drops unexpectedly in great vertical cliffs into the head of Glen Oykel. These could well afford some rock-climbing.

The traverse of the entire range from north to south is undoubtedly the most worthwhile expedition in this easter part of Assynt. Start from the stalker's track 4½ miles north of Inchnadamph at the highest point on the road to Kylesku beside Loch na Ghainmhich. The track is followed eastwards for a short distance before climbing directly up the steep slopes on to the flat grassy richly vegetated summit plateau of Glas Bheinn. One and a half miles and 1800 ft. of ascent. Descend on to the saddle between Glas Bheinn and Beinn Uidhe by way of the steep and narrow east ridge and continue up the long boulder-strewn slope to the summit of Beinn Uidhe. The going here is rather unpleasant for 2 miles past Mullach an Leathaid Riaghaich then dip into the saddle above Loch an Caorach. From here a long heavy trudge leads up on to the highest point of Beinn an Fhurain – almost 3 miles involving 600 ft. of ascent. On the north, an impressive rock buttress falls steeply down into Coire a'Mhadaidh which is worthwhile exploring. The ridge drops past some rocky outcrops and an attractive little lochan to the saddle leading up on to Conival. From the south top of Ben More the ridge continues in a southerly direction for a mile to Carn an Conbhairean, becoming progressively broader and less rocky in character. A further mile leads over Meall an Aonach – Eagle Rock – the south end of the range, then down on to the track to Benmore Lodge. The descent to the track and thence to the road – 2½ miles south of Altnacealgeach – is a distance of 6 miles.

The main Benmore Assynt ridge is often described as resembling the Aonach Eagach ridge in Glencoe. While not presenting the same rock problems it should not be treated lightly and in winter conditions a pleasant ridge route becomes a serious mountaineering exercise. The isolated nature of the area, which is virtually devoid of habitation throughout its one hundred odd square miles is a factor which should be kept well in mind in adverse weather conditions.

Creag Liath Braebag (2670 ft.) is the highest point of the hills on the west side of Glen Oykel which form a subsidiary branch of the main Ben Assynt range. Tarsuinn Braebag (2044 ft.) at the north end of the ridge can easily be climbed from the Bealach Traligill. The approach to the south end of the ridge involves a rather uninteresting moorland walk from Altnacealgeach Hotel.

The Braebag mass slopes upwards from the western moorland forming a broad flat ridge, alternating between rough hill pasture, rich in herbage, to broken rocky pavements and drops unexpectedly into the Oykel valley in a line of steep, cleanly cut cliffs which could well provide some worthwhile climbing routes.

Three miles past Ledmore Junction at the Nature Conservancy signpost on the east side of the road, a track strikes inwards towards Braebag along the Allt nan Uamh. A prominent limestone cliff a mile up the glen on the right-hand side contains the well-known Allt nan Uamh bone caves. Continuing up the side of the water provides a straightforward and interesting approach into the Braebag ridge.

The most spectacular feature on the Ben More Range is the great waterfall of Eas Coulin or Eas a 'Chual Aluinn which leaps over the cliff line of Leiter Dubh $1\frac{1}{2}$ miles north-west of Glas Bheinn, into the basin of Loch Glencoul. The Eas Coulin can rival the more familiar Falls of Glomach in Kintail as the highest fall in Britain. The claim can only be disputed by difference in interpretation of the continuity of the 500 ft. vertical drop which cascades still further for yet another 150 ft. at the foot of the cliffs.

From the Inchnadamph–Kylesku road there are two ways to the fall. The south side of Loch Glencoul can be reached from the bridge over the Unapool burn. The route along the lochside is virtually trackless and at one point the walker is forced to traverse on steep grass some 200 ft. above the loch. This can be awkward in bad weather.

It is also possible to hire a boat from the proprietor of Kylesku Hotel. This drops you at the head of Loch Glencoul at a ruined jetty beside the empty keeper's house. The $3\frac{1}{2}$-mile trip gives magnificent views of the Quinag range and allows close inspection of the geological structure of the area along the Aird da Loch cliffs where the action of the thrust plane is clearly seen.

Seals are often seen playing in the secluded expanse of water and the journey culminates in the spectacle of the full drop of Eas Coulin into the head of the glen.

It is possible to climb up the side of the fall on to the top of the Leiter Dubh from the floor of the glen with little difficulty.

The head of the falls can be most easily reached by a track leaving the road 3 miles past Skiag Bridge along Loch na Gainmich (sandy loch) which rises steeply from the east end of the loch over the 1600 ft. Bealach a'Bhuirich (the pass of the roaring), which derives its name from the roaring of stags during the rutting season. The path gives a fine walk through the gneiss scenery of the lower foothills of Glas-bheinn and is left ½ mile past the head of the Pass. A cairn marks the point where the path crosses a stream beside a fair-sized lochan but this can easily be missed. The stream which feeds the fall is followed past a huge split boulder and the fall can be crossed with care at the lip of the cliff. It is worth continuing along the cliff top for about 100 yds and descending the series of grassy terraces to get a full side view of the drop. The basin formed by the head of the glen is a gathering place of stags during the rutting season and their roaring echoing up from the basin at the foot of the waterfall underlines the aptness of the name of the Bealach.

Beinn Leoid (2597 ft.)

Beinn Leoid is usually climbed from the landing place at the head of Loch Glencoul. A well-marked track passes prominent Stack of Glencoul and continues upwards along the glen to Loch an Eirciol. A distance of 3 miles involving 1000 ft. of ascent. The Stack has a steep western face but has more to offer the geologist than the climber. Like the Aird na Loch it is a show-piece of the thrust move-ment and the natural rock sequence here has been completely re-versed, the gneiss lying on top of the Cambrian strata. From Loch an Eircoll one and a half miles leads on to the summit of Ben Leoid and opens up the view across to the Reay Forest.

The return journey can be made north-westwards to the head of Loch Glendubh where a good track is joined to lead for 5 miles along the north side of the Loch to Kylestrome and the Ferry.

This makes a fine day's walking expedition through the north-east corner of Assynt.

10

The Reay Forest

FOINAVEN is the name of the range embracing the following five peaks:
(1)   **Ceann Garbh** (2952 ft.). 4 miles E. of Rhiconich Hotel.
(2)   **Ganu Mor** (2980 ft.). $\frac{1}{2}$ mile S. of 1.
(3)   **A'Cheir Ghorm** (2839 ft.). $\frac{3}{4}$ mile S. of 2.
(4)   **Unnamed Top** (2646 ft.). 1$\frac{1}{4}$ miles S. of 2.
(5)   **Creag Dionard** (2554 ft.). 2 miles S.E. of 2.

Arkle (2580 ft.). 5 miles S.E. of Rhiconich Hotel.
Meall Horn (2548 ft.). 3 miles E. of Arkle.
Saval More (2288 ft.). 1 mile S.E. of Meall Horn.
Saval Beg (2393 ft.). 1$\frac{1}{2}$ miles S.E. of Saval More.
Meallan Liath Coire Mhic Dhugaill (2625 ft.). 2 miles N.E. of Loch More.
Carn Dearg (2613 ft.). 1 mile E. of Meallan Liath.
Ben Hee (2864 ft.). 3 miles N.E. of Loch Merkland.
Ben Stack (2364 ft.). $\frac{1}{2}$ mile W. of Loch Stack.
Cranstackie (2630 ft.). 6$\frac{3}{4}$ miles N.E. of Rhiconich Hotel.
Beinn Spionnaidh (2537 ft.). 1 mile N.E. of Cranstackie.

MAP: O.S. One Inch to the Mile (7th Series). Sheet No. 9 – Cape Wrath, No. 10 – Tongue, No. 14 – Lairg, No. 13 – Lochinver and Loch Assynt.

The mountains of the Reay Forest are situated in the north-west corner of Sutherland, one of the wildest and most remote parts of the Scottish mainland. The area falls into the parishes of Eddrachilles and Durness.

On the north and on the west, the sea forms a natural boundary, the deeply indented coastline stretching from Eddrachillis Bay around Cape Wrath to the eastern shore of Loch Eriboll – measured straight a distance of 40 or so miles, but double that if all the numerous bays and sea lochs are taken into account.

The southern boundary with Assynt can be taken as a line drawn eastwards from the head of Loch Glencoul to the north end of Loch Shin. The main road north from Lairg to Tongue passes through Altnaharra, one of the rare communities of any size left in central Sutherland. A branch road travels north-westwards by way of Glen

Mudale and Strathmore along the side of Loch Hope to meet the north coast road at the mouth of Loch Eriboll and this forms the eastern boundary.

The natural centre of Sutherland and of the whole of the North of Scotland is the market village of Lairg at the south end of Loch Shin and here the majority of roads from north and west converge to meet with those coming from the south. Roads in the north-west follow natural rather than direct lines from point to point and are forced by the nature of the country to by-pass obstacles by devious routes. They are mostly single-tracked, twisting and not built for speed.

Lairg has a railway station on the main line north from Inverness to Caithness and is the depot for the daily mail-bus service which covers the outlying districts of Sutherland.

The A836 by way of Altnaharra has already been mentioned. This leads to the eastern side of the Reay Country. Two miles north of Lairg the road forks and the A838 leads north-westwards to Laxford Bridge following the continuous line of waterway which stretches diagonally across Sutherland from the Dornoch Firth on the North Sea to Loch Laxford on the Atlantic coast. For 16 miles the road follows the north shore of Loch Shin, the largest freshwater loch in Sutherland, then winds between Loch Ghriama, Loch Merkland, Loch More and Loch Stack to the road junction at Laxford Bridge.

From Laxford Bridge the A836 continues north-eastwards by way of the scattered community of Rhiconich to Durness then follows the coastline around Loch Eriboll to link up with the road through Strathmore. The majority of the mountains of the Reay Forest lie within this circuit.

From Kylesku Ferry, the A894, a narrow twisting road, follows the western coastline by way of the crofting village of Scourie to join the Lairg road at Laxford Bridge. This road is currently undergoing major reconstruction.

The Cape Wrath Peninsula is virtually roadless. The only direct route leaves the A836 at Rhiconich and follows the north shore of Loch Inchard to Kinlochbervie. Situated on an isthmus between Loch Inchard and Loch Clash, its natural harbour and up-to-date ice plant make it one of the busiest fishing bases on the west coast. The road continues for another 5 miles to serve the crofting communities of Oldshore and terminates abruptly at Sheigra. There is one other road on the north coast of the peninsula but this has no motor link with the mainland. A ferry for pedestrians operates over the Kyle of

Durness from Keodale, near the Cape Wrath Hotel, and links with the Cape Wrath Minibus Service, to the Cape Wrath Lighthouse. The Ferry runs daily, Sundays included, weather permitting.

The principal mountain ranges of the Reay Forest lie almost wholly to the east of the Lairg–Laxford road. Ben Stack, rising from the west shore of Loch Stack is the only notable exception. These formed the traditional hunting forests of the Lords of Reay, chiefs of the clan Mackay, one of the great families who ruled in Sutherland in the past.

A seventeenth century account of the area by a Sir Robert Gordon gives a full and picturesque account of the variety of wild life to be found here in the days of these early Lords of Reay:

'All these forrests and schases are verie profitable for feiding of bestiall and delectable for hunting. They are full of reid-deir and roes, woulffs, foxes, wyld catts, brocks, skuyrells, whittrets, weasels, otters, martrixes, hares, and fumarts. In these forests, and in all this province, there is great store of patridges, pluivers, caper-calegs, blackwaks, murefowls, heth-hens, swanes, bewters, turtle-doves, herons, dowes, steares or starlings, lairigigh or knag (which is a fould like unto a paroket or parret, which maks place for her nest with her beck in the oak trie), duke, draig, widgeon, teale, wild grouse, ring-house, routs, whaips, shot-whaips, woodcock, larkes, sparrows, snyps, blackburds, or osills, neireis, thrushes, and all other kinds of wild-foule and birds, which are to be had in any pairt of this kingdom.'

In 1829, the area passed into the hands of Lord Stafford, later created first Duke of Sutherland, who, in the course of his great schemes of 'Improvement', swallowed up vast tracks of land in the north and west of Sutherland and was one of the instigators of the Clearances of the first half of the nineteenth century. The area is now divided among several smaller estates but the main mountain mass falls largely into the great estates belonging to the Duchess of Westminster, one of the country's biggest landowners. The estate office is in the village of Achfarry, at the head of Loch More.

The area is still preserved for its sporting facilities and is virtually uninhabited. Apart from a few forestry and estate workers' houses the only habitations are some seasonal shooting lodges and stalkers' bothies. The few centres of population of any size are to be found along the coastline and to the west of the Lairg–Laxford road. Crofting and fishing and tourism are the main means of livelihood.

The western coastline is rich in history and is well worth visiting. For the 400 years, from the A.D. ninth–thirteenth centuries, the

34. Cape Wrath, the north-west tip of the Scottish mainland.

35. Am Buachaille, Sandwood Bay

Vikings raided here, penetrating every inlet, and eventually ruling the whole of the North of Scotland from their Jarldom of Orkney. They have left behind them a legacy of place-names throughout the whole of Sutherland and Caithness: Vik, Ness, Stac, Cleit, Bol, Geo, Sgeir, Tunga, Dal, Fjord, Gil, Setr, Ob, Smoo, all indicate the Viking influence in a locality.

The five great fjords or sea-lochs which indent the north-west coast bear purely Norse names. Laxford was Lax-fjord – the Salmon Loch and the name is still apt after all those years. The river Laxford is one of the finest salmon rivers in the country. Inchard was Engi-ford or Meadow-loch. Durness was the Deer's point. Eriboll was Eyrr-bol or Beach Town. Tongue was Tunga or Tongue of Land.

The great sea-cliffs around Cape Wrath, the ultimate point on the mainland, were the 'Hvarf' or Turning Point of the Norsemen. Once around the point the raiding longships were clear of the treacherous tides and storms of the 'Pettland' or Pentland Firth.

Gneiss is the predominant formation of southern part of the coastal region, from Kylesku to Rhiconich and the country here is a maze of hillocks, hollows and lochans.

From Kylestrome on the north side of the ferry, a stalker's track leads north-eastwards across the moorland to come out at Loch More on the Lairg–Laxford road. A lower branch of the track initially follows the north shore of Loch Glen Dhu then rejoins the main track by way of the fine waterfall which drops spectacularly into the Loch from the Maldie Burn.

Another useful cross-country track leaves the road some 2 miles further north past the forestry plantation at Duartmore Bridge. This passes across for a little more than 6 miles to reach the Laxford road on the north side of Ben Stack. A locked shooting bothy is maintained by the estate halfway along it.

The road follows the coast to Scourie, which is the main village in this part. Two miles south of Scourie it passes Badcall Bay which at one time was a safe anchorage for cargo vessels but is now unused. Scourie lies 9 miles north of Kylestrome at the head of a wide sandy bay. Scourie was the birthplace of General Hugh Mackay – a famous soldier of the seventeenth century who saw service in the European campaigns of the times and was the author of a manual on infantry tactics. He commanded the forces which were defeated by Graham of Claverhouse at the Battle of Killiecrankie in 1689. The name is a corruption of Norse and Gaelic: Skoga – copse and Airge – shieling

L

or summer grazing. Crofting is carried on here in the traditional manner and the sheltered sandy hollow is a favourite with summer visitors. Hotel and other accommodation is available and Scourie is the best centre from which to visit the famous island bird sanctuary of Handa lying 2 miles off-shore to the north-west.

The island is approached by sea from the tiny clachan of Tarbet, 2 miles due north of Scourie by track but 5 miles by road. The honorary warden lives here and operates a boat-hire service to the island, weather permitting. There are excellent camping facilities at the head of the Bay. Handa is composed of stratified sandstone, which has been tilted up from east and south-east to the heathery moors rising gradually upwards to Sithean Mor (406 ft.) – the great hill of the fairies, on the north-west corner of the island. The sea-cliffs rise to their highest point here under Sithean Mor and stretch towards the furthest north-west point of the island. On the east side of the point a geo (Norse – inlet) with walls of almost 350 ft., encloses the famous great Stack of Handa which rises from the sea to almost the same height – a distance of 80 ft. from the shore at its closest west side.

In 1876 a party of Lewismen secured a rope over the top of the Stack and one of the number, Donald Macdonald, made an epic crossing, hand-over-fist, legs locked around the rope, solely dependent on strength and nerve and unbolstered by any type of safety device. Once across, his companions threw him a line by which wooden stakes and a block and tackle were passed to him. The stakes were driven into the top of the Stack, the block and tackle fixed, and the remainder of the party joined him by the breeches buoy. They then went about the main business of the expedition, the culling of sea birds from their hitherto impregnable sanctuary. These were later to be salted and used both for home consumption and export to immigrants abroad. They taste not unlike kippers. When the load was complete the party returned to the island leaving behind only the two stakes on the top of the Stack as an undeniable proof of this remarkable feat of early cragmanship. The feat was repeated in July 1967 by T. W. Patey. A 600-ft. length of climbing rope was carried outwards on either side of the geo until the middle lay across the top of the stack. The ends were anchored, one to rock the other to spikes driven into rock. The shortest rope length across the gap was 150 ft., and this he crossed using sliding clamps.

In the light of the second crossing using modern equipment, the incredible original feat is undoubtedly without parallel in mountaineering as practised at that time, nor is there anything comparable in the present era in Scotland.

The Stack was climbed from the seaward side for the first time in August, 1969 by Hamish McInnes and party, who timed their attempt opportunely with essential calm sea conditions. The climb starts from the boat to the right of the obvious ledge some 60 ft. up the north-east face and ascent leftwards leads to the ledge in one or two pitches (Very Difficult). The route continues up a steeper wall to gain the traverse line to the left on a ledge. An ascent is made to the left of the Nose to gain a small ledge and belay (Very Severe). The route now goes directly up steep rock (Difficult) to gain a traverse line right. Then the easy route is taken to the summit of the Stack. On the descent abseil down from a point directly above small stance above (Very Severe) pitch to gain this ledge. From here abseil directly into the boat.

The near-by 'Mini Stack' which appears to have been scooped out of the lower cliffs of Sithean Mhor and deposited slightly off-shore remains unclimbed.

Six miles north-west of Scourie is the road junction at Laxford Bridge. Laxford Bridge is not a village, only a junction with an A.A. Telephone point.

From here the road continues north-westwards for 5 miles to Rhiconich, a scattered crofting community with a small hotel and shop. The lonely peninsula of Ardmore lies between Loch Laxford and Loch Inchard on the north-west side of the road. Its broken coastline has some fine harbours and is surrounded by islands. There is no through motorable road on to the peninsula which in the Gaelic is Ceuthramh Garbh or Rough Quarter.

From Rhiconich, the road leads north to Durness past Gualin Lodge, a distance of 14 miles. Gualin means 'shoulder' and this point is the summit of the road. When you descend into Strath Diouard towards the Kyle of Durness, the Archaean gneiss gives way to limestone and the scenery changes – this is a region of flat sheep lands, green fields, wide waters and homely hills and the ruins of Brochs line this strath – relics of earlier inhabitants.

Durness is still basically a collection of crofting townships but it has developed in recent years into one of the most popular tourist centres on the north coast. Hotel and guest-house accommodation is readily available and there is a Youth Hostel.

West of the village the sandy Kyle of Durness broadens into the bay of Balnakiel. At the head of the bay stands the old church of Balnakeil, built in 1619 on the site of a still older cell associated with the monastery in Dornoch – Balnakeil means a place of the kirk. Near by is the house of Balnakeil, once the hunting residence of the Bishops of Caithness and later passing into the hands of the Lords of Reay. In the churchyard is buried Rob Donn (1714–78), the celebrated, unlettered Celtic Bard. His works were handed down by word of mouth through the years until 1829 when the first collection of his poems was published in book form.

The former Air Ministry Station at Balnakiel some ½ mile from Durness has now been developed as a craft village.

The Durness peninsula is bounded on the east by the great sea loch of Eriboll, one of the finest natural harbours in Britain. Its potential has so far been neglected. There are rich unworked deposits of dolomite in the area but the uneconomic process of producing magnesium and the limited market for the product in the light of new technological development in the field of carbon-fibre makes their development unlikely.

The Viking fleet anchored off Loch Eriboll after its defeat at Largs in A.D. 1263. Legend has it that a party landed to raid the mainland and were driven off, their leader Urradal being slain in the skirmish. Strath Urradale bears his name still. This was the end of the Viking rule on the north-west mainland of Scotland. Pestilence was already aboard the fleet and the Norse King Hakon died of the disease in Kirkwall some months later.

One mile west of Durness at the head of a small bay is to be found the Smoo Cave. The name is derived from the Norse word – Smjuga – a narrow cleft to creep through.

From the sea-shore the cave is entered under an arch, 50 ft. high and 40 yds wide. An inner cave extends from the right of the waterfall which drops into the main limestone cavern some 80 ft. from the entrance. This was explored as early as 1833.

As one would expect the cave has numerous legends. The first Lord Reay, like many Scots of his time, served under Gustavus Adolphus in his continental wars, in the middle of the seventeenth century. While abroad he is reputed to have met the Devil and bested him in several battles of wit. The Devil pursued him to Scotland and planned to waylay him while he was visiting the Smoo Cave which lay within the Reay domain. Lord Reay got into the second cavern, when his dog which had raced ahead of him returned howling and hairless. Lord Reay realised what lay ahead but then the cock crowed, and the Devil and his three attendant witches were powerless. They blew holes in the roof of the cavern and so escaped facing Lord Reay in the outer cave. This is the reputed origin of the holes through which the Alt Smoo falls into caverns.

The road from Rhiconich to Durness passes across the neck of the great north-west peninsula which culminates in Cape Wrath. Wrath is purely a map-maker's name – a corruption of the Norse 'Hvarf' (turning point). In Gaelic this becomes Parbh or Parph and in many texts this derivation is the one used. The northernmost of the two roads on to the peninsula passes near the great sandstone sea cliffs of Cleit Dubh which runs to a height of 850 ft. – the highest sea cliffs in Britain. For 2 miles they stretch westwards, falling down towards the sandy bay at Kearaig where there is a solitary croft house. Along their length at Clo Mor, they attain a height of 600 ft. The surrounding area is the Parph Moor proper, an awe-inspiring wilderness – where fact and legend draw close together. One can well believe that hereabouts can be met the terrible monster Cu-Saeng whom no one has lived to describe – unlike the 'Grey Man of Ben MacDhui – the Cu-Saeng wanders throughout all the wilder parts of the Scottish Highlands. One man hereabouts is reputed to have seen his shadow on the hillside – it had two heads.'

The Cape Wrath Lighthouse, built in 1828, stands on a 400-ft. cliff of Archaean gneiss veined with pink pegmatite known as An Dunan – the small fort. This is the end of mainland Scotland – there is no land between here and the North Pole.

In clear weather the Nature Reserve of North Rona can often be seen 45 miles to the north-west, a breeding ground for the Atlantic Grey Seal and the Stormy Petrel.

Six miles south along the coastline is Sandwood Bay, one of the loveliest and certainly most private in the country. There is no track to Sandwood from Cape Wrath, but the possibility of constructing one is currently being explored.

One mile south, two rock stacks rise up from the sea. They are A'Chailleach and An Bodach – the Old Woman and the Old Man.

Another stack rises out from the south side of Sandwood Bay. This is Am Buchaille – The Shepherd, which has recently been climbed in the current spate of sea-cliff exploration along this coastline.

Sandwood (from the Norse – Sand Vat or Sandy water) lies 4 miles north of Sheigra, the last inhabited community on the road from Rhiconich along the side of Loch Inchard. The Norse fleet anchored near here on 10 August, 1263, on its way to the battle of Largs. Its defeat there ended the Norse domination of the North of Scotland and the Hebrides. Three years later at Perth, they were ceded to Scotland for a payment of 4000 marks down, and a further yearly sum of 100 marks. Orkney and Shetland, however, remained part of Norway until 1468.

A peat road leaves the motor road between Blairmore and Sheigra leading to Loch a'Mhuillin and then on by track to Sandwood Bay and the freshwater loch behind it. At its widest point the beach stretches about 2 miles and the shore rocks here are rich in semi-precious stones.

Strath Shinary which stretches south-eastwards from Sandwood Loch produces a feasible cross-country route to reach the Durness road at Gualin House. The way is trackless as indeed is the whole of the inland part of the peninsula. Cross-country explorers here should be sound in navigational skills.

Ben Stack (2364 ft.)
Ben Stack is the only summit within the Reay Forest on the west side of the Lairg–Laxford road, to reach a height of over 2000 ft. It rises above the road along the side of Loch Stack just north of the village of Achfarry, its relative isolation bestowing on its conical peak a grandeur disproportionate to its size.

It can be climbed from all sides with little difficulty. Two tracks already mentioned leading cross-country to the road from Kylestrome to Scourie pass along its north and west ends and from either of these a steep direct route can be made on to the summit in just over an hour from the road.

The north-eastern side of the hill above Ben Stack is flanked by two bands of cliff which provide scope for scrambling and rock-climbing within easy access from the roadside.

The higher band starts at about 800 ft. above sea-level and four short routes were climbed on its left end in 1958 by members of Kinloss Mountain Rescue Team – I. Clough, J. M. Alexander, A. Flegg and B. Halpin. The main feature is 'a big right-angled corner about 100 ft. high, well seen from the road near the south end of Loch Stack. This gives enjoyable short climbs on good rock.

Cracked Slab – 80 ft., Very Difficult. Climb the big right-angled corner for 20 ft. and then go up slab – 60 ft. This forms the left wall of the corner, finishing up well above on good holds.

Eastern Buttress – 100 ft., Very Difficult. Goes up buttress to right of corner. Start 15 ft., right of lowest part of buttress. Up to flake, mantelshelf on to it, and trend right over small overhang to groove. Up short chimney then diagonally left to top of buttress.

Halpin's Route – 100 ft., Very Difficult. Reach the same stance as on previous route by a difficult crack to the left of that route. Up short chimney, then straight up or slightly right.

The Groove – 80 ft. An obvious groove with overhangs on left of big corner. Mostly artificial – A2. Finish up wall as for Cracked Slab.

The main mountain mass of the Reay Forest is contained in an area roughly rectangular in shape measuring approximately 14 miles by 7 miles, the whole being tilted so that the longer sides run in a north-west–south-east direction.

Motor roads already described form the north and west sides of the area. The south and east side of the rectangle run through the great cross-country glens which converge on Gobernuisgeach Lodge in the south-eastern corner.

The eastern side passes through the Strath Dionard and Glen Golly but there is no continuous through track.

Half a mile beyond Gualin House on the Laxford–Durness road a well-maintained track leads into Strath Dionard from a stone road-bridge. This continues up the Strath along the river side for 4 miles but stops at the Allt Coire Duaill. From here the going is bad for 2 miles to Loch Dionard. The path gives good access to the relatively new climbing area in the eastern corries of Foinaven.

At the south-eastern end of Glen Golly – a deep rocky glen skirted by birchwood through which the River Golly drops in a series of small waterfalls–lies Gobernuisgeach Lodge. This is used throughout the stalking season and is inhabited by the estate keeper for the rest of the year. It is reached by private road from a junction with the Altna-harra – Hope road near the ruined bothy at Altnabad – 8½ miles from Altnaharra. The road to the lodge has a gate which is sometimes locked but enquiries should be made at the Lodge for access.

The track which passes along Glen Golly north-westwards is one of three which spread out from Gobernuisgeach Lodge through the southern part of the Reay mountains. It rises upwards for 7½ miles on to the saddle between Creagon Meall Horn and Plat Reidh on the lower slopes of Foinaven to a height of 1700 ft., but has no direct link with the Dionard track. The Ordnance Survey Map shows the track as stopping before the saddle. In fact it continues across south-westwards to connect with another track from Achfary which will be described later.

The south side of the Reay area passes over the Bealach nan Meirleach – the Robber's Pass – which connects the valley of Strath-more with that of Loch More and Loch Shin. It stretches for over 7 miles from Gobernuisgeach to the north-east of Loch Merkland, reaching 800 ft. at its highest point.

This was an old drove road and is still the only right of way through the Reay Forest. The track is only suitable for Land-Rovers. The gate at the Loch Merkland end is usually unlocked but enquiries can be made at the nearby shepherd's house.

This track separates Ben Hee (2864 ft.) – The Fairies' Hill – from the main mountain mass. The ascent from the track is straightforward. Follow the track for 1 mile to the first bridge and an obvious hill path leads upwards along the Allt Coir a'Chruiteir for just over 1½ miles to the 2000 ft. contour. Another ½ mile and 850 ft. of steep but easy climbing brings out on to the summit cairn. The view from here eastwards is across the central Sutherland moors to Klibreck. The ridge can be followed for a mile to the subsidiary top (2796 ft.), and the descent to the track by way of the broad shoulder of Sail Gharbh. The hill has no special features and is more interesting in winter when the Coire Allt a Ghorm provides some snow climbing on to the summit, from the east.

From this direction it can be approached by private road from Loch Shin to Fiag Lodge at the south side of Loch Fiag but this involves a 4-mile cross-country pathless walk to Loch Ghormcoire.

From the west, the mountains are best approached from Achfarry at the head of Loch More on the Lairg–Laxford road. Half a mile north of the village, a motorable branch road turns off across the river to the right, reaching the keeper's house at Airgachuillin in 1 mile. The road continues for another mile to the disused steading at Lone, the junction of two cross-country tracks. This road is private and although the gate is seldom locked, permission should be obtained before using it.

From Lone, the north fork of the track rises along the Allt Horn for nearly 3 miles to connect on the saddle with the track to Glen Golly previously described.

This is the easiest approach to the main tops of both Arkle and Foinaven. Continue past Lone for 1 mile then take to the slabby ridge leading on to the saddle overlooking An Garbh Coire, the steep rocky corrie between Arkle and Foinaven. The line now runs up between two burns for about 900 ft., a distance of 1 mile. The ground to the left may look tempting but the going here is bad. The first cairn on the Arkle ridge (2468 ft.) is reached in another half mile.

The ridge of Arkle is sickle-shaped bending to the north-east and narrows considerably with steep drops to the east and gentler slopes to the west. The main top is almost a mile further on and any difficulty which may be encountered by the three small 'towers' guarding its approach can be easily turned by descending slightly westward in the event of high wind or wintry conditions.

The terminal ridge of Arkle can be descended on to the corrie over Sail Mhor of Arkle from Loch Stack Lodge for 5 miles.

Arkle's western flank is split by several gullies which are prominent from the road past Achfary. The largest of these, *Arkle South Rib*, was climbed by T. Weir and A. D. S. Macpherson in 1951. This rib encloses a prominent gully and is the largest piece of rock on this face. It can be reached after a short walk from Lone. The rib is the right edge of the first gully on the right and makes a pleasant scramble for 600 ft. By its easiest route it is no more than moderate and is a pleasant way of gaining height on the peak, but difficulty can be found if required.

The approach route to Foinaven is dictated by the nature of the expedition.

To traverse the complete ridge, the best start is from Achfary by way of the north track from Lone. From the saddle the ridge is followed to Creag Dionard (2554 ft.) and thence taking in all the tops to Ceann Garbh na Beuchaich but the rocky tower can be turned on the west side.

A detour should be made at the named top (2839 ft.), to the head of the cliffs of A'Cheir Ghorm, the mile-long quartzite spur which juts out in a north-easterly direction from the main ridge. This gives a fine view of the rock faces of the eastern flank.

The north end of the ridge can be descended from Ceann Garbh and thence to Gualin on the Durness road in 3 miles. The going here is wet and boggy and is not recommended.

In adverse weather conditions the narrow summit ridge of Foinaven with its almost continuously precipitous eastern flanks requires good navigation and should not be attempted by an inexperienced party.

The approach from Gualin has already been described. An alternative route is the north track from Lone which gives access to Creag Ubhard and the cliffs to the south of it.

A third route into the area starts at the head of Loch Eriboll. A track leaves the north coast road to Durness below the crags of Creag na Faoilinn which is motorable for about half a mile, inland along Strath Beag. Rough going, it leads for a mile from the end of the motor track to Strabeg Cottage. This is locked but the outhouse is open and has been used as a bothy. Its availability however, cannot be guaranteed.

The track continues past Strabeg on the east side of the river beneath the cliffs of Shomhairle for more than a mile then an ill-defined track leads over the lower Cranstackie foothills by the Bealach na H'Imrich to Strath Dionard.

Both Creag na Faoilinn and Creag Shormaile are of quartzite and have produced several rock routes.

Descriptions of these can be found in the Foinaven Supplement produced by the Corriemulzie Mountaineering Club.

Foinaven's potential as a rock-climbing area is only apparent from the Strath Dionard track.

From the west the ridge rises steeply from the surrounding moorland but gives no hint of the great rock faces which stretch along the eastern flanks.

From north to south, the cliffs of the eastern side of Foinaven are:

1. *Creag Dubh* – A gneiss cliff on the east face of Ceann Garbh at the head of Coire Duail.

2. *A'Cheir Ghorm* – the long easterly ridge which stretches from the unnamed point on the Foinaven Ridge (2839 ft.) next to Ganu Mor. Seen from Strath Dionard, three ridges converge on the apparent summit and each of these has been climbed. The *South* and *North Ridge* in 1954 by Messrs T. Weir, L. S. Lovatt, and A. D. S. Macpherson, and the Centre Ridge by I. G. Cumming and Miss H. Rose in 1959. This latter was named Cave Ridge. A small cave is visible from below.

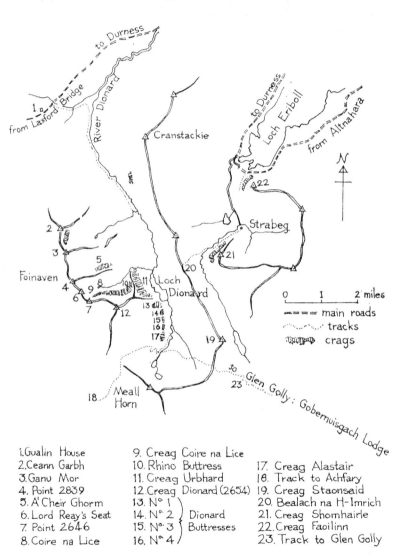

Fig. 12 Sketch Map of Foinaven and its approaches.

1. Gualin House
2. Ceann Garbh
3. Ganu Mor
4. Point 2839
5. A'Cheir Ghorm
6. Lord Reay's Seat
7. Point 2646
8. Coire na Lice

9. Creag Coire na Lice
10. Rhino Buttress
11. Creag Urbhard
12. Creag Dionard (2654)
13. Nº 1
14. Nº 2 } Dionard
15. Nº 3 } Buttresses
16. Nº 4

17. Creag Alastair
18. Track to Achfary
19. Creag Staonsaid
20. Bealach na H-Imrich
21. Creag Shomhairle
22. Creag Faoilinn
23. Track to Glen Golly

The *North Ridge* route started at the cairn, right of the lowest rocks and gave 550 ft. of Difficult climbing.

Start at the cairn a bit right of the lowest rocks. Two pitches of insecure rock lead to a belay in 150 ft., below a prominent grey overhang. Traverse right, round the steep nose, and climb a steep wall. Continue on exposed rock to the foot of a formidable overhanging tower. Start left of its nose and traverse left along a ledge on to the nose. Climb the steep exposed edge of the tower on good holds to an easier arête. Keep on the crest and finish shortly under the summit cairn.

3. *Lord Reay's Seat* – This is unmarked on the O.S. Map and stands north of Cadha na Beuchaich at the head of Coire na Lice (also unnamed). The 700 ft. east face has so far produced only one route. This was climbed by W. D. Fraser and the late P. N. L. Tranter (who was responsible for much of the exploration of this area) in 1964. The route is named 'Fishmonger' and gives 750 ft. of Severe climbing, described in the Corriemulzie Guide as follows:

The obvious chimney to the right of the central nose is the general line. The route goes straight up the cliff and is very steep in its lower half. Odd places are loose but all the harder climbing is sound. Start at the foot of the chimney.

(1) 80 ft. up chimney to small wet overhang. To left is good platform and peg belay.

(2) From belay traverse 10 ft. left, then delicately 20 ft. back right, into the chimney again above the overhang. Then climb up right 50 ft. to a large platform clearly visible from the belay.

(3) The line of the chimney now continues straight up a little to the left as a very steep broken wall, but this defeated the original party. Instead traverse a big ledge 60 ft., right to the foot of the next chimney. Peg Belay. Climb this chimney to a scree shelf. Belay to left at 80 ft.

(4) 120 ft. Climb the obvious long Difficult chimney (loose) to belay on grassy ledge.

(5) The final tower lies ahead, with an obvious chimney up its centre. Climb holdless, awkward rocks for 30 ft. to foot of chimney. Peg belay.

(6) Traverse 10 ft. right and climb the 25 ft. crack (crux) between a detached pillar and the main cliff. Then traverse 20 ft. horizontally left to regain the line of the chimney to the left of the nose, where belay.

(7) Above is a right-angled corner with a crack. Climb it.
(8) Moderate climbing leads from here up the narrow summit arête to an amusing gap in 100 ft., crossed by bridging to belay beyond. Thence scrambling to the top of Lord Reay's Seat. This still awaits a direct ascent – the party left the chimney in pitch 3 to the right.

4. *The North Face of Creag Dionard* – the south wall of Coire Lice, unnamed on the O.S. Map.
5. *Creag Urbhard* – The east face of Creag Dionard, has been described as having the greatest potential of any cliff north of Carnmore and most of the routes done on Foinaven are to be found here. There is still room for further exploration.

Fingal – 900 ft., Mild Severe (T. W. Patey, 1962).
Start up the rocks left of the bottom of the Second Waterfall and follow a virtually direct line up the crags diverging left from the Second Waterfall, crossing two diagonal fault lines and finishing up the right hand edge of a large V-depression in the top tier, easily seen from the lochside.
(1) Start from a small amphitheatre at the foot of the Second Waterfall. Climb rocks on the left to a terrace at 120 ft. Return along this to the Second Waterfall above its main pitch.
(2) Just before re-entering the waterfall twin cracks forming a shallow fault line split the wall on the left. Climb these and follow the direct line of cracks for 250 ft. of exposed Very Difficult climbing to the first true terrace, more an indeterminate rock shelf (the continuation of the Upper Pavement). Shaky cairn.
(3) Follow the line of least resistance rising leftwards for 50 ft. towards a shallow inconspicuous gully with a little vegetation, which after an awkward start is easier than it looks. This breaches the next tier for 250 ft., with Very Difficult to Mild Severe climbing to the upper terrace (cairn directly below the huge wet V-shaped amphitheatre).
(4) No easier routes exist to the right, contrary to appearances. Climb on to a flake 40 ft. up on the right-hand enclosing wall of the amphitheatre and continue climbing within its confines a huge rock fang 120 ft. above the cairn. (Invisible from below.) Now escape right from the amphitheatre by a traverse round the exposed edge to an inset slab in a corner (crux), leading to easier broken rocks halfway up the great slabby wall to the right of the amphitheatre. The final section of the wall may go direct, but an obvious chimney in the right corner was followed for 50 ft. This narrows above to an overhanging cleft,

but one can traverse horizontally leftwards for 30 ft. over the slabs to emerge with surprising suddenness at the top of the main cliff. Cairn. Scrambling.

Route-finding is difficult throughout. The detailed description is intended to avoid ambiguity with harder alternatives.

North Ridge – 1000 ft., Very Difficult (L. S. Lovat and T. Weir, 1954). Start at the lowest rock beyond a large highly coloured outcrop. Slabby Moderate rock gradually steepens. Climb fairly direct by short walls to the foot of a recess with a tree above. Climb left wall to tree and a mossy overhang. Continue up steep rock, with much variation possible.

About 300 ft. below the top the rock becomes broken and easier. Other lines would be possible, of a similar standard.

6. *The Dionard Buttresses* – These four buttresses face upper Strath Dionard between Creag Urbhard and Creag Alistair.
7. *Creag Alistair* – forms the east face of Plat Reidh one mile south of Loch Dionard.

The south fork of the track from Lone cuts almost due east for 8 miles through the centre of the southern part of the Reay Forest to Gobernuisgeach Lodge, crossing the Bealach na Feithe between Saval Beg and Mheall Garbh at a height of 1471 ft.

From Lone to the highest point of the pass is just over 4 miles. The hills to the south form a pleasant hill walk stretching for 8½ miles towards Loch Merkland.

A similar circuit from the same point takes in the remainder of the tops to the north of the Bealach and from Creagan Meall Horn descends to join the north fork back to Lone. A distance of 7 miles.

Cranstackie (2630 ft.) and **Beinn Spionnaidh** (2537 ft.)
Cranstackie and Beinn Spionnaidh lie on the north-east side of Strath Dionard and are the highest points on the long grassy ridge of hills which drop gradually downwards to the coastline between Loch Eriboll and the Kyle of Durness.

They offer pleasant hill walks and wide views across the Parph peninsula. On a clear day North Rona can be seen 40 miles beyond Cape Wrath.

The western slopes are steep and grassy and can be easily climbed from Carbreck, 2½ miles past Gualin on the road to Durness. A car track goes into the croft at Rhigolter for 1 mile and from there less than 2 miles of ascent leads on to either top.

A rough band of gneiss and quartzite is exposed along Cranstackie's long south-western flank above Strath Dionard but there are no prominent crags.

Legend has it that Robb Donn, the Celtic Bard, filled his beloved gun with tallow and buried it in the rocks of Carn an Righe on Beinn Spionnaidh when his poaching days were over, rather than have it handled by anyone else. If he did, it could still well be there.

11

Ben Hope and Ben Loyal

(1) *Ben Hope (3040 ft.). 10½ miles N.W. of Altnaharra.
(2) Ben Loyal (2504 ft.).
    (1) An Caisteal (2504 ft.). 5 miles S.S.W. of Tongue.
    (2) Sgor Chaonasaid (2320 ft.). ½ mile N. of 1.
    (3) Top (2465 ft.). Heddle's top, ½ mile S. of 1.
    (4) Carn an Tionail. ½ mile S. of 3.
    (5) Sgor a'Chleirich (1750 ft. contour). ½ mile N.W. of 3.

MAP: O.S. One Inch to the Mile (7th Series). Sheet No. 9 – Cape Wrath, Sheet No. 10 – Tongue.

These two fine mountains lie in the area immediately to the east of the Reay Forest between Strath More and Strath Naver. The coast-line stretches from Whiten Head on outer Loch Eriboll eastwards to Torrisdale Bay at the mouth of the River Naver and is broken at its mid-point by the Kyle of Tongue stretching inland for almost 7 miles. The landward boundaries converge in the south on the village of Altnaharra, which is the road centre for the area.

From the crossroads on the north of the village, three roads stretch out to meet with the north coastal road. The west road passes through Glen Mudale and Strathmore along the side of Loch Hope to Loch Eriboll. The east road follows Loch Naver through Strath Naver to reach the coast at the township of Bettyhill. A central route passes directly northwards to the village of Tongue on the east side of the Kyle following the shore of Loch Loyal for part of its way.

From Loch Eriboll, the coastal road cuts eastwards across the great peat-moss peninsula of a'Mhoine to the Kyle of Tongue. At Whiten Head on the north-west corner, Loch Eriboll opens into the Pentland Firth and the 500 ft. cliffs mark the end of the 120-mile long line of the Moine Thrust Plane, which along with the great series of Schists has derived its name from the peninsula. Whiten Head to the native Gael was known as 'Kennagall' – the headland of

36. *Above:* Ben Stack from the road to Laxford Bridge.
37. *Below:* Arkle from Achfarry.

38. Ben Klibreck from Altnahara.

the strangers. The strangers were undoubtedly the Norsemen who name the point 'Hvitr' or White headland. From here to Loch Eriboll is to be found the only mainland breeding ground of the Atlantic Grey Seal.

The road winds round the head of the Kyle of Tongue which differs from the other communities in the north and west. It is rich and green and is well-wooded.

The Gaelic name for Tongue was Geann-T-Saile A'Mhicaoidh – The head of Mackay's Salt Water – and the ruined Castle Varrich west of the village was once a Mackay stronghold. Tongue House, north of the village, was built in 1678 by Lord Reay, chief of Mackay, but later passed into the hands of the Sutherland family.

At the mouth of the Kyle of Tongue stand several islands. Eilean nan Roan, the largest of these, was inhabited until fairly recently, and on the sands of Rabbit Island, which can be reached by walking at low tide, the French sloop 'Hazard' carrying gold for the Jacobite Cause ran aground and held fast.

Tongue itself is fairly well populated and provides a variety of tourist accommodation including two Hotels and a Youth Hostel but the rest of the population is scattered along either sides of the Kyle and the coastal strip east to Bettyhill. The crofting township of Melness which stands on the west side of the Kyle, can be reached by road from Tongue. This owes its origin to the evictions from Strathmore. The bleak peat-moss of A'Mhoine has few houses other than those connected to the estates.

The two mountains which lie within this area are similar only in the manner in which they gain in appearance from their isolation. Geologically they are entirely different. Ben Hope is composed of rocks of the Moine Series – granulite and horneblende schist. Ben Loyal is the only mountain of the igneous group of rocks to fall within the area of the Northern Highlands. It is largely composed of synenite which has many of the characteristics of the granite of the Cairngorms. The mountain has magnetic tendencies which can distract compasses and this was blamed for the aircrash which killed the Duke of Kent here in 1942.

Ben Hope (3050 ft.)

Ben Hope is the most northerly mountain in Scotland included in Munro's 3000 ft. Tables and rises from only 12 ft. above sea-level, east of the roadside at the south end of Loch Hope. The name Hope is derived from 'hop' the Norse word for a 'bay'. This name has obviously worked its way inland from the bay on Loch Eriboll formed by the mouth of the River Hope, to both the loch and the mountain beyond.

Ben Hope rises in two great terraces from the loch side. The lower terrace has a fine natural birch wood covering and reaches the 1000 ft. contour. The upper terrace starts at 2000 ft., and rises in a series of steep rocky ridges and buttresses. The west and north-west faces of Ben Hope are both steep and craggy but to the east and south-east the mountain slopes away more gradually.

For the hill-walker, the long gently sloping south ridge gives the easiest approach to the summit, the northern ridge is both steep and narrow and requires greater care. The two eastern ridges present no difficulty but are too remote to provide a useful means of ascent to the top.

It should be noted that the road marked on the map from Loch Eriboll to the keeper's house at Cashel Dhu does not give access to Ben Hope. The ferry previously operating has long been out of use.

Ben Hope can be approached equally well from the north or from the south by way of the road from Altnaharra to Loch Eriboll already mentioned.

From the south this road passes by way of Glen Mudale into the broad valley of Strathmore. Two miles down the strath stands the Broch of Dun Dornaigil which is one of the few structures of its kind of which part of the wall stands more than 20 ft. high. The interior measures 27 ft. in diameter and the wall is some 14 ft. thick. An interesting feature is the large triangular lintel covering the outer opening of the entrance passage on the north-east side. The interior of the Broch is now largely blocked by fallen masonry.

From the Broch a track leaves the road by the scattering of houses at Altnacaillich, and follows the burn upwards into the Leiter Mhuiseil – the lower part of the south ridge of Ben Hope.

The stream of the Allt na Caillich – the burn of the old woman – drops in a great waterfall above the houses – near here is the reputed birthplace of the Celtic Bard Rob Donn.

The broad ridge can be followed directly up to the summit along the head of the western crags. The cliff edge is marked by several cairns but the summit cairn lies 150 yds north-east of the largest of these – from the Broch the distance is 3½ miles.

An alternative route begins at a track rising from the south end of

Loch Hope. This can be followed for a sharp distance and then is left to climb steeply towards Dubh Loch na Beinne – the black loch of the Ben – which nestles on the first of the two terraces.

The route now passes north-eastwards below the line of the rock cliffs on to the narrow north ridge which is followed to the summit. There is one 'bad' corner on the line of this ridge which requires care – especially on the descent.

A possible, though longer, escape route to the east necessitates dropping into the corrie and then following the next ridge running due east-west on to the summit.

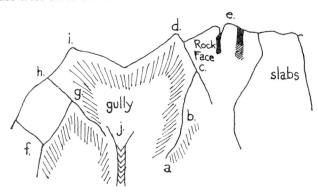

Fig. 13   North-west Face of Ben Hope (the letters relate to text).

Rock climbing on Ben Hope is mainly on the north-west face of the mountain and seen from the loch-side the main feature is a wide gully flanked by two rocky ridges. The accompanying diagram out-lines the possibilities around this feature which was first explored by J. H. B. Bell in 1933.

The south ridge was the most interesting and gave 800 ft. of climbing from A to just below the summit. Some difficulty was found in the lower section AB and a traverse was made across the face of the buttress to the right. From B to C excellent climbing rock was encountered, with occasionally difficult situations. C to D was pleasant and airy. Between D and E the ridge is narrow and has one exposed corner. The summit of Ben Hope lies just beyond E. The line FGHL provides an easier route.

Another straightforward route on this face is described as 'Petticoat Ridge' and was climbed by S. and M. Johnstone. The route is of no great difficulty and provides an excellent way to the summit. The ridge of Bell's climb is bounded on the left by a funnel-shaped gully and on the right by a steep grassy rake (a gully near its bottom) from which the right-hand wall of the ridge apparently rises in a series of steep slabby towers. One of these towers, on which lies a prominent square-cut pinnacle, rises in a ridge from the grassy saddle at the top of the rake, while a lower tower rises in a ridge from the rake about 200 ft. below the saddle. This latter ridge was climbed. It proved to be Moderate Difficult if the lower steep section is climbed and disappointingly artificial as easy ground was always accessible on the right. The grassy rake was difficult of access. Further exploration here could prove rewarding.

Ben Loyal

The isolated position and impressive profile of Ben Loyal which rises from the moorland to the south of the Kyle of Tongue has earned it the title of 'Queen of the Scottish Peaks' despite its comparatively modest height.

To the north and east, only Beinn Stumanadh rises to any great height, while to the west and to the south, its nearest rivals, Ben Hope and Ben Klibreck, both over 3000 ft., lie 6 and 12 miles distant.

The finest view is undoubtedly the one from the north. From this direction the full splendour of the ridge with its four granite peaks can be seen dipping and rising south-westwards from Sgor Chaonasaid. Seen from the east, Ben Loyal loses its clearly defined outline, and while there is no difficulty in climbing on to the summit ridge from any point from the roadside along Loch Loyal it is not recommended. From this direction the way passes across boggy moorland for over 2 miles and is unpleasant at any time of the year.

The best approach is from Tongue. The road to Durness is left after 1½ miles and a farm road followed to Ribigill. From here a good track leads for just over a mile to the shepherd's house at Cunside. Steep grassy slopes lead upwards on to Sgor Chaonasaid (2320 ft.), the northern top of the ridge. Alternatively, one can follow either of the two gullies which run up to its highest point.

Rock routes have been attempted in the past on the rocky north buttress of Sgor Chaonsaid but the rock was not found to be very suitable and parties had to traverse off into the gullies. The traverse of the ridge from Sgor Chaonasaid need present no difficulty and a circuit of the main tops and the return to Cunside covers a distance of 6 miles with little intermediate re-ascent. A'Chaisteal (2504 ft.), the highest point on Ben Loyal, lies half a mile south of Sgor Chaonasaid and drops in steep, smooth faces of up to 40 ft. on its south side. The way to it passes the twin tors of Sgurr a'Bhatain (The Boats), which lie slightly more to the west and these have produced one rock-route, *Row Boat* – 190 ft., Mild Severe (K. Richardson and D. Dewell, 1959).

The climb lies on the upper tor and the rock was found to be 'steep, impressive and sound'. This is probably the easiest line on the main rampart of the crag, and follows the left-hand bounding ridge. Starts 3 ft. left of extreme bottom left-hand corner of the crag.

(1) 110 ft. on to ledge immediately above corner, continuing up corners until line of ridge merges with that of gully on left; belays.

(2) 50 ft. – A prominent ledge now crosses the main face (it gives a sensational walk); climb on to it into a corner and climb the 15 ft. left wall. Continue up grassy groove to belay.

(3) 40 ft. – Move right from belay, step on to ledge on arête and continue up easy rocks.

From Sgurr a'Bhatain the ridge continues south for $\frac{1}{2}$ mile over a top of 2465 ft., which has been named Heddle's top, and then in another $\frac{1}{2}$ mile to Carn an Tionail (2250 ft.) the featureless southerly point on the main ridge.

From Heddle's top, a branch ridge dips west-north-westwards on to the sharply defined peak of Sgor a'Chleirich (2100 ft.) and this is the best crag on the mountain. The south-west face overlooking Loch Fhionnach has produced one climb – *Priest's Rake* – 850 ft., Very Severe (D. D. Stewart and R. Tombs, 1958).

A rake, ill-defined at first, rises from left to right across the crag, and another fault divides it in a vertical plane. Below the rake this second fault forms a groove, above it a steep, broken, dirty-looking dièdre.

Start at a small cairn below the lowest rib, a few feet left of the dirty groove (peg, 100 ft.). Traverse right here and climb into groove. Follow the groove until escape on the left leads to overhung grass patch. Exit on left leads out over exposed slabs to a larger grass patch which is the start of the defined section of the rake. Follow it up to the right to its highest point, whence a rib leads directly to the top of the crag.

As far as the rake, the climbing is serious and difficult; the rake itself is narrow but easy and the final section is straightforward. A direct continuation from the rake up the steep dièdre would give a difficult but elegant finish.

To the west, Sgor a'Chleirich drops steeply for almost 700 ft. to a saddle which connects it with the 1750 ft. terminal cone of this branch ridge of Ben Loyal. The dip is only seen when the mountain is viewed from the north or from the road south of Altnaharra and is unapparent from the main ridge.

East Sutherland and Caithness

(1) ***Ben Klibreck** (3154 ft.). 3½ miles S.S.E. of Altanharra.
(2)   **Ben Armine** (2338 ft.). 11 miles S.E. of Altnaharra.
(3)   **Morven** (2313 ft.). 8 miles N.W. of Berriedale.
(4)   **Scaraben** (2054 ft.). 4 miles N.W. of Berriedale.
(5)   **Maiden Pap** (1587 ft.). 2 miles E. of Morven.
(6)   **Beinn Dhorain** (2060 ft.). 6 miles W. of Helmsdale.
(7)   **Ben Griam Beg** (1903 ft.). 3½ miles W. of Forsinard.

MAP: O.S. One Inch to the Mile. (7th Series). Sheet No. 10 – Tongue, Sheet No. 11 – Thurso, Sheet No. 14 – Lairg, Sheet No. 15 – Helmsdale, Sheet No. 16 – Wick, Sheet No. 7 – Orkney.

This chapter deals with the easter part of Sutherland which together with the county of Caithness forms the north-east corner of the area of the Northern Highlands.

The area is bounded on the west by the main road from the head of the Kyle of Sutherland which passes north and north-eastwards through Lairg and Altnaharra to reach the coast at Bettyhill on the mouth of Strath Naver. The coastline, stretching more than 100 miles around the great headland of Duncansby, provides some of the finest sea-cliff scenery in the country.

Although the most northerly county on the Scottish mainland, Caithness is easy of access. 100 miles of good road travels the length of the east coast from Inverness. This is supplemented by a network of cross-country roads which mostly connect with the north coastal road leading towards the west of Sutherland.

A passenger service runs daily to the north from Inverness and the track meanders through the centre of Sutherland before turning north-eastwards to Wick and Thurso. Use of the numerous request stops en route will open up the more interesting inland parts.

Daily flights from the south to Wick Airport have opened up a new mode of travel into the area and there is an authorised landing-strip available for private planes at Dornoch on the Kyle of Sutherland. Doubtless further air links will be available in the future.

One important road bisects the area in a northwards direction from Helmsdale through Strath Kildonan and Strath Halladale to meet the north coast road by Melvich. This road is still in Sutherland, but follows the county border with Caithness which lies some 4 miles to the east along the watershed. From Kinbrace Junction at the head of Strath Kildonan one other useful road passes north-westwards of Syre on Strathnaver, the only direct east-west road link in the area.

In the past, Caithness with Sutherland formed the Pictish province of Cat or Cataobh, one of the seven great provinces of Pictland, but as the name implies, Caithness was once more Scandinavian than Highland. The Norse settled along the coastline and the fertile area which ran inland along the straths and here the place-names keep their Norse flavour. The terminal 'byster' common in many of the place-names is the Norse word for 'farm'. On the inland heights the names are mainly the Gaelic of the native Celts who were pushed there by the invaders.

Caithness has few characteristics in common with the rest of the area of the Northern Highlands, which it resembles only along its inland border with Sutherland. This can be accounted for when one looks at the geology of the area. Two main rock formations make up the surface of the county. The hilly inland region consists mainly of stratified schists and Cambrian Quartzites – the lowland country stretching to the coastline is composed mainly of Old Red Sandstone.

The Lowland area of Caithness is similar in many ways to the Orkney Islands to the north and to East Ross and the country around the Morayshire coast. The underlying Old Red Sandstone breaks down to produce rich farming land and agriculture plays an important part in the economy of the country. Like the Orkneys, there are few trees, and the inland areas tend to be featureless and uninspiring.

Inland, the gradually rising moorlands attain their greatest height along the south-west border and here where the Archaean metamorphic rocks prevail, the country consists of heath-clad hills, peat moss, lochs and bogs in direct contrast to the cultivated flats of the north-east angle.

The coast line more than compensates for the uninspiring outlook across the flat farming lands and inland moors. Throughout its length it is indented with deep gorges or bays, lined with heather-topped cliffs and ending in great headlands of near-vertical weathered

39. Ben Loyal from near Tongue (winter).

41. *Above:* Dunnet Head on the north coast of Caithness, east of Thurso.

Overleaf
40. Ben Hope.

sandstone cliffs, the nesting grounds of countless varieties of sea-birds. The action of the sea has in many cases isolated completely from the mainland strange–shaped stacks and where the process is incomplete, great natural arches have been formed to add to the variety of the scene.

The coast holds countless possibilities for the enthusiastic sea cliff climber and there are still many 'first ascents' to be recorded.

On the north coast the great headlands of Holborn and Dunnet enclose Thurso Bay, and to the east around Clardon Head, lies Dunnet Bay with its 4 miles of golden sand. Dunnet Head is the most northerly point in Scotland and stands over 400 ft. above the sea giving splendid views along the north-east coast.

The great head of Duncansby forms the north-eastern corner of Scotland 2 miles east of John o' Groat's house and from here the view over the Pentland Firth to the Orkneys includes the only island on the Caithness coast – The Isle of Stroma.

The south-east boundary of Caithness is impressively marked by the great Headland of Ord, whose 747 ft. cliffs are famous for their breeding sea-birds. The way to the Ord leads over the famous Berriedale Hill, which in winter becomes a motorist's nightmare. On a Monday in the year 1513 the Sinclair Earl of Caithness with 300 men crossed the Ord by this route on his way to the ill-fated battle of Flodden. No one made the return journey.

The inland border of Caithness runs in a southerly direction from Drumholliston on the north coast to the Ord Point, 1 mile north of Helmsdale on the A9. Pont's map of 1608 has the boundary along Strath Halladale and Kildonan, but the watershed is the officially recognised line.

The three highest mountains in Caithness lie within the extreme south corner between the county boundary and the Berriedale water. This comes under the Braemore and Langwell estate which is a strictly preserved deer forest. The estate proprietors insist on permission being asked to enter the forest, which can be obtained from the Factor's office at Berriedale – 3 miles north of Helmsdale on the A9.

Morven (2313 ft.)

Morven is one of the few mountains of Old Red Sandstone to obtain a height of over 2000 ft., and is the highest point in Caithness. Its regular cone-shape makes it a prominent landmark standing up from the surrounding moorland.

It is best approached from Berriedale by a motorable road up the Langwell Water to Wag – a distance of 8 miles. The summit lies in a north-westerly direction from here and is easily climbed although the last 1000 ft. are very steep. The way lies over wet moorland and it is best to make for the depression between the main top and the conspicuous knob of rock which is Morven's only irregular feature.

Permission to use the road to Wag must be obtained as mentioned previously.

Scaraben (2034 ft.)

Scaraben lies 4 miles north-west of Berriedale and is a different type of hill from Morven. It consists of three smoothly rounded tops of quartzite of the Moine Series.

It is most easily reached from a track along the west side of the Berriedale River which also gives access to Maiden Pap (1587 ft.) almost two miles further north-west. Two miles to the east of Maiden Pap lies Morven.

The western part of the area of this chapter lies entirely within the county of Sutherland. The mountains here lie along the western boundary, the road from the south to Bettyhill, and from these the land falls down gradually to the north and east coast along the sides of five great open Straths. To the north – Strathnaver and Strath Halladale; to the south – Strath Kildonan, Strath Brora and Strath Fleet.

The floors of the Straths are rich in archaeological remains dating back to the time of the earliest inhabitants but of greater interest is the underlying reason for the considerable number of more recently ruined settlements to be found along the now deserted upper valleys.

This is the classic area of the famous Sutherland Clearance which, by the middle of the nineteenth century, created an uninhabited wilderness where once there had been thriving communities. The story of the Clearances and the events leading up to them have produced a wealth of reading material and it is not the intention of the Guide Book to examine the matter in detail.

It is of interest to note, however, that the Clearances and the subsequent developments in the Highlands were included in the prophecy of the famous seventeenth-century Brahan Seer, the Ross-shire soothsayer whose prophecies cover most of the highland areas

'The day will come when the jaw-bone of the big sheep (Caorich Mhore) will plough on the rafters. The bleating of sheep will cover the highlands, great prices will be got, then they will go back until a man finding the jaw-bone of a sheep in a cairn will not be able to tell what animal it belonged to.

'The ancient proprietors of the land shall give place to strange merchant proprietors. Then the country is to be given over to deer and not a man left.

'The crow of a cock shall not be heard north of Druim-Uachdair; the people will emigrate to islands now unknown but which shall yet be discovered in the boundless oceans, after which the deer and other wild animals in the huge wilderness shall be exterminated and drowned by a horrid black rain.

'The people will then return to take possession of the land of their ancestors.'

A great part of his prophecy is now historical fact. The sheep did come and the men were forced to leave to make way for them. The people did emigrate to lands overseas – New Kildonan was founded on the Red River in Canada by evicted tenants from Strath Kildonan and is now the city of Winnipeg. Some of the earliest settlers to New Zealand left from Brora. Whole communities left together for the growing lands of the new continents.

Those who remained were resettled on the poorest lands of the coastal strip where they had to learn new skills to make a livelihood from the sea. This is the origin of many of the north and east coast communities still in being. Bettyhill was one example of this, the land having been set aside by a repentant Duchess of Sutherland who gave her name to the new township for her evicted tenants from Strath-naver.

The previous homes can still be found in the pre-Clearance villages along the Strath at Grummore, Grubeg and Rossal.

The deer did oust the sheep in the latter nineteenth century and saw the creation of the great sporting estates which still exist to the present day having been sold and re-sold through a succession of mainly seasonal landlords.

Whether the last part of the prophecy will come about remains to be seen.

Ben Klibreck (3154 ft.)

(1) *Meall nan Con* (3154 ft.). 3½ miles S.S.E. of Altnaharra.
(2) *Creag an Lochan* (2650 contour). 1½ miles S.W. of (1).
(3) *Cnoc Sgriodain* (1780 ft.). 1½ miles W.S.W. of (2), above Crask Inn.

(4) *Meall Ailein* (2367 ft.). 2 miles N.E. of (1).
(5) *Meall nan Eoin* (2502 ft.). 1 mile S.W. of (1).

Ben Klibreck rises from the east side of the road between Lairg and Altnaharra, between Loch Naver and Loch Coire. Together with the hilly tract which comprises Ben Armine, it forms the main mountainous mass of the area covered by this chapter of the Guide. The main ridge of Ben Klibreck extends in a south-west to north-east direction with Meall nan Con, the highest point, at its midpoint. Three broad shoulders are flung out in a south-easterly direction to form a huge E shape. These enclose two large corries which drain into Loch Coire and its subsidiary Loch a'Bhealaich (the loch of the pass).

Ben Klibreck is a conspicuous landmark in this central Sutherland landscape, which is predominantly one of low-lying moorland, but it has few pronounced rock features.

The western slopes are steep but mainly heathery. The head walls of the south-east corries hold little continuous rock. The climb on to the ridge is usually made from the west side, either from Altnaharra or Crask Inn.

From Altnaharra the road from Lairg is left about half a mile before reaching the Hotel and a rough motor track leads in along the south side of Loch Naver for 1 mile to Klibreck Farm. A good track leaves the back of the farm and this can be followed easily for just over 2 miles on to the north end of the ridge. The traverse of the ridge from here presents no difficulty and the main 'Munro' top is reached in 2 miles.

The approach from the Inn at Crask, 13 miles north of Lairg, is equally straightforward. The little Inn lies at a height of 700 ft. above sea-level and the road here tends to be blocked easily by snow during the winter months. Its height is of advantage to the hill-walker; the $2\frac{1}{4}$ mile climb on to Cnoc Sgriodain, the western spur of Klibreck, involves only 1000 ft. of gentle ascent over moorland and heathery slopes.

The main top is reached in $1\frac{1}{2}$ miles with only another 900 ft. of climbing. The view westwards is of the whole range of Ben More Assynt and the surrounding mountains. If one follows the central shoulder south-westwards to Meall and Eoin, there is a fine view down into the Loch Coire Forest and across over the rolling range of Ben Armine to the mountains of Caithness.

It is now possible to descend to the shores of Loch Coire by way of either of the south-east corries of Klibreck and a path through leads along the loch-side over the Bealach Easach along Strath a'Chraisg to the Inn over $3\frac{1}{2}$ miles of flat moorland.

Klibreck looks at its best in winter and the mountain can often be approached and ascended on skis thus cutting out the otherwise long and rather uninteresting approach walks over the surrounding moorlands.

One interesting rock feature on the west side of Ben Klibreck is the buttress visible from the road to Altnaharra which rises on to the main ridge at a point below the main summit. A prominent gulley at the foot of the buttress is conspicuous from the road and rocks here afford the possibility of some climbing. This was tackled in 1933 by J. H. B. Bell and in 1965 H. M. Brown and M. Barnes recorded a route named *Eyrie* which gave them 400 ft. of fine climbing, difficult and airy at the start on the lowest rocks to the right of the gully. An eagle's eyrie is to be found on the upper rocks to which a descent can be made equally well from the ridge above.

Ben Armine

(1) *Creag Mhor* (2338 ft.). $10\frac{3}{4}$ miles S. of E. from Crask Inn.
(2) *Creag a'Choire Ghlas* (2311 ft.). 2 miles N. from (1).
(3) *Meall nan Aighan* (2287 ft.). $1\frac{1}{4}$ miles N.W. from (2).
(4) *Creag na H'Iolaire* (2278 ft.). $\frac{1}{2}$ mile W. from (3).
(5) *Meall Ard* (2061 ft.). $\frac{1}{2}$ mile W.N.W. from (4).

Ben Armine is the collective name given to the ridge of hills which runs in a line roughly south-south-east from the north end of Loch Choire towards the great straths which open on to the east coast of Sutherland. The hills lie entirely within the Armine Forest which is part of the great Sutherland Estates. The area is solely maintained for its sporting potential and enquiries about permission for access should be made at the Estate Office in Golspie.

There is no outstanding feature to catch the eye, but the wide expanse of rolling moorland rising gently upwards from the south holds a peculiar attraction for those unaccustomed to such solitude. To the west the outlying hills of the ridge drop steep heathery slopes into the Loch Choire basin and to the east and north the main ridge drops unexpectedly in a series of almost precipitous walls enclosing five large corries. The ridge drains southwards to feed the Rivers Blackwater and Brora which join at the head of Strath Brora and open into the North Sea. The fishing in the area is excellent.

A well-kept system of tracks encircles the Ben Armine ridge, connecting Ben Armine Lodge at the south-east end with Loch Choire Lodge on the north shore of the Loch. These in turn connect with tracks leading westwards and south-westwards towards the Lairg road and provide a variety of possibilities for long but pleasant cross-country walking expeditions. This area is indeed one for the foot-traveller by virtue of the distance of the hills from main motor roads and the limitations of estate vehicle tracks serving the shooting lodges.

Three possible approach routes into the area can be suggested.

(1) From Sciberscross, 10 miles inland along Strath Brora from the east coast. An estate track leaves the keeper's house on the west side of the road and travels 8 miles inland over the open moorland to Ben Armine Lodge, in Strath na Seilige. The gate at the road is seldom locked but drivers should note that only vehicles with high clearance should attempt this route.

There is a fine unobstructed view to the north of Morven.

(2) By way of Strath Kildonan or Strath Naver, leave the Syre–Kinbrace road at Loch Badanloch – 4 miles from the remote Garbhalt fishing hotel. An estate road similar in condition to the road from Sciberscross reaches Loch Choire Lodge at the north end of the loch in 10 miles.

(3) From the Lairg–Crask road, an estate road branches off at the river bridge 5 miles north of Lairg. Four miles inland lies Dalnessie Lodge and the road continues over to the River Brora for another mile. A shooting path follows the east bank of the river for $1\frac{1}{2}$ miles and then cuts across country to meet with the Ben Armine track at Greenface.

Two other hills occur in places of special interest –

Ben Griam Beg (1903 ft.)

Ben Griam Beg, lying $3\frac{1}{2}$ miles west by south of Forsinard Hotel between Strath Halladale and Strath Naver, has on its summit the highest hill fort in Scotland. The remains consist of a stone wall about 6 ft. thick which encloses an area of 500 by 200 ft. at the top of the hill with an entrance on the north side. The remains of other walls are found on a lower level on the south flank of the hill. From Forsinard, it is possible most years to enjoy some ski-ing on the surrounding slopes.

Beinn Dhorain (2060 ft.) and **Ben Uarie** (2046 ft.)

Beinn Dhorain and Ben Uarie lie 6 miles west of Helmsdale. A rough track up Glen Loth is barely motorable. It leaves the A9, 5 miles north of Brora and rises up along the eastern slopes of these two rounded hills of Old Red Sandstone to almost 1100 ft. at its highest point before descending into Strath Kildonan to cross the railway line north, and the River Helmsdale by a bridge near Kildonan Lodge. Glen Loth provides some ski-ing in most winters.

Kildonan in 1869 was the scene of a gold rush. The Kildonan and Suisgill burns yielded limited quantities but the rush eventually petered out. Recent mineral surveys in Sutherland have included the area in their work and this has resulted in a renewed interest into the possible development of the natural resources of the area, including the gold deposits. It would seem unlikely, however, that there is another Klondyke hidden beneath the Sutherland glens.

Mountain Names and Meanings

The following list attempts to give the meanings of the mountain names mentioned in the Guide. Gaelic spellings as in the guide itself, are those commonly used by the Ordnance Survey. In many cases these are found to be a corrupted form of the original Gaelic name, which adds to the difficulty of accurate interpretation. It must be remembered that the original Gaelic names for the mountains are local names and often lose their aptness if taken out of context.

As has been mentioned in the text of the Guide, there is a strong Norse influence in several of the place-names in the Northern Highlands, and an attempt has been made to indicate this where it is applicable.

Many of the meanings are already well accepted but in the case of those where there is some doubt, either the most appropriate alternative has been given or a blank has been left.

A'Chailleach: *The Old Woman.*
A'Choinneach Mhor: *The Big Moss.*
A'Mhaighdean: *The Maiden.*
Arkle: *The Mountain of the level top.*
Am Bodach: *The Old Man (Spectre).*
Am Buachaille: *The Shepherd (Herdsman).*
Am Faochagach: *Centre of Forehead (Brow). The Wilk-shaped Mountain.*
Am Fasarinen: *The Teeth, or Fasgadh an eun – The shelter of the birds.*
An Cabar: *The Stake (or Antler).*
An Coileachan: *The Cockerel.*
An Grianan: *The Sunny Place.*
An Laoigh: *The Calf.*
An Liathanach: *The Grey Headed Man.*
An Ruadh Stac: *The Red Steep Hill.*

An Sgurr: *The Rocky Peak.*
An Socach: *The Projective Place (The Snoot).*
An Teallach: *The Forge.*

Baosbheinn: *The Wizard's Mountain or The Mad Mountain.*
BEALACH or B(H)EALAICH: *pass.*
Bealach nan 'Arr (Faradh): *The Ladder Pass.*
Bealach na Ba: *Pass of the Cattle.*
Bealach Ban: *The White Pass.*
Bealach na Bhiurich: *The Pass of the Bellowing.*
Bealach a'Chonnaidh: *The Pass of the Firewood.*
Bealach a'Chornaidh: *The Pass of the Folds (Corn is a folding like in a skirt).*
Bealach a'Chuirn: *The Pass of the Cairn.*
Bealach na Croise: *The Pass of the Cross.*
Bealach Easach: *The Pass of the Waterfall (Marsh).*
Bealach na Feithe: *The Pass of the Bog Channel.*
Bealach a'Ghlas-Chnoic: *The Pass of the Green Hillock.*
Bealach Gorm: *The Blue Pass.*
Bealach na H'Imrich: *The Pass of the Removing.*
Bealach na Lice: *The Pass of the Flat Stone.*
Bealach nan Meirleach: *The Thieves' Pass.*
Bealach Mhor: *The Big Pass.*
Bealach A'Chomla: *The Pass of Meeting.*
BEINN, BEINNE, BEANN: MOUNTAIN.
Beinn a'Chaisgean Mor: *The Mountain of the Great Stillness.*
Beinn a'Chaisteal: *Castle Mountain.*
Beinn a'Chlaidheimh: *Mountain of the Sword.*
Beinn a'Chearcaill: *Circular Hill or the Mountain of the Girdle.*
Beinn a'Ghrianain: *Sunny Mountain.*
Beinn a'Mhuinidh: *The Mountain of the Heath.*
Beinn Airigh Charr: *The Mountain of the Rocky Sheiling.*
Beinn Alligin: *The Jewel Mountain.*
Beinn an Eoin: *Mountain of the Bird.*
Beinn an Fhurain: *Mountain of the Well or Spring.*
Beinn Bhan: *The White (Fair) Mountain.*
Beinn Damph: *The Mountain of the Stag.*
Beinn Dearg: *The Red Mountain.*
Beinn Direach: *The Steep Mountain.*
Beinn Dhorain (Dhobhrain): *The Hill of the Otter or The Hill of Pain.*

N

Beinn Eighe: *The Mountain of the File.*
Beinn Enaiglair: *The Hill of the Timid Birds.*
Beinn Ghoblach: *The Forked Mountain.*
Beinn Lair: *The Mountain of the Mare.*
Beinn Leoid: *The Sloping Mountain.*
Beinn Liath Mhor Fannaich: *Big Grey Mountain of Fannich.*
Beinn nan Caorach: *The Mountain of the Sheep.*
Beinn na h'Eaglaise: *The Mountain of the Church.*
Beinn Spionnaidh: *The Mountain of Strength.*
Beinn Stumanadh: *The Modest Mountain?*
Beinn Tarsuinn: *The transverse mountain (lying across, oblique).*
Beinn Uidhe: *Mountain of the Slowly Moving Water (Place where the Burn leaves the Loch).*
Ben Armine: *The Mountain of the Warrior.*
Ben Griam Beg: *The Small Dark Mountain.*
Ben Griam More: *The Big Dark Mountain.*
Ben Hee: *The Fairies' Mountain.*
Ben Hope: *The Mountain of the Bay.*
Ben Klibreck (Clibreck): *The Mountain of the Fish.*
Ben Loyal: *The Mountain of the Elm Tree.*
Ben More Assynt: *The Great Mountain of Assynt.*
Ben Stack: *The Steep Mountain.*
Ben Strome: *The Steep (abrupt) Mountain.*
Ben Wyvis: *The Noble Mountain.*
BIDEIN: PINNACLE.
Bidein a'Ghlas Thuill: *The Sharp Peak of the Grey Hollow.*
Bidein Toll a'Mhuic: *The Sharp Peak of the Pig's Hollow.*
Bodach Mhor: *The Great Old Man (Spectre).*
Braebeg: *The Little Upland.*

CADHA: PASS *or* STEEP PLACE.
Cadha am Adan: *The Fool's Pass.*
Cadha na Beucaich: *The Pass (Steep Place) of the Roaring.*
Cadha Ghoblach: *The Forked Pass.*
Canisp: *White Mountain.*
CARN, C(H)UIRN, C(H)AIRN: KEEP OF STONES APPLIED TO A ROUND ROCKY HILL.
Carn an Fheidh: *The Deer's Hill.*
Carn an Righe: *The King's Hill.*
Carn an Tionail: *The Gathering Hill.*

Carn Ban: *The White Hill.*
Carn Chuinneag: *The Hill of the Churn.*
Carn Dearg: *The Red Hill.*
Carn Gorm Loch: *The Hill of the Blue Loch.*
Carn na Criche: *The Boundary Hill.*
Carn na Feola: *The Hill of Flesh.*
Carn nan Conbhairean
Ceann Garbh: *The Rough Head.*
Cearcall Dubh: *The Black Circle.*
Cioch Beinn an Eoin: *The Breast of the Mountain of the Bird.*
Cnoc Sgriodain: *Scree Slope.*
Cona' Mheall (Meall Conaidh): *The Enchanted Hill.*
Corrag Bhuidhe: *The Yellow Pinnacle (Finger).*
Cramstackie: *The Rugged Hill.*
CREAG: ROCK, CRAG *or* CLIFF.
Creag a Choire Ghlais: *The Rock of the Green Hollow.*
Creag a Duine: *The Rock of the Fort.*
Creag an Fhithich: *The Raven's Crag.*
Creag Gorm: *The Green Crag.*
Creag Ghrianach: *The Sunny Crag.*
Creag, Liath, Braebag: *The Grey Crag.*
Creag an Lochan: *The Crag of the Loch.*
Creag nan Calmon: *Crag of the Dove.*
Creag na Faoilinn: *Seagull Crag.*
Creag na H'Iolaire: *Eagle Crag.*
Creag na H'Uidhe: *The Crag of the Ford.*
Creag Rainich: *Bracken Crag.*
Creag Riabhach: *The Dun Crag.*
Creag Ruadh: *The Red Crag.*
Creag Shomhairle: *Samuel's Peak.*
Creag Urbhard: *From Urabhallach – the herb 'Devil's Bit' found on
    many hills.*
Cul Beag: *The Little Hill-Back.*
Cul Mhor: *The Big Hill-Back.*

Dun Caan: *The Fortress.*

Eididh nan Clach Geala: *The covering of the white stones.*

Fashven: *The Rise.*

Fiachlach: *The Tooth.*
Fionn Bheinn: *The White Mountain.*
Fuar Tholl: *The Cold Hollow.*

Ganu Mor: *The Great Wedge.*
Garbh Choireachan: *The Rough Circular Hollow (Cauldron).*
Glas Bheinn: *The Grey Mountain.*
Glas Leathad Beag: *The Little Grey Slope.*
Glas Leathad Mor: *The Big Grey Slope.*
Glas Mheall Liath: *The Pale Grey Hill.*
Graban: *The Obstruction.*

Iorguill: *The Battle Hill.*

Liathach: *The Grey One.*

Maol Chean Dearg: *The Bald Red Head.*
MEALL, M(HILL): LUMP (AS APPLIED TO A ROUNDED HILL).
Meall a'Aonaich: *The Hill of (The Heath-Reconciliation).*
Meall a' Bhraghaid: *The Sloping Hill.*
Meall a'Chrasgaidh
Meall a'Cleireach: *Hill of the Priest.*
Meall an Eoin: *Hill of the Bird.*
Meall an Fheadain: *Hill of the Whistle.*
Meall a'Ghuibhais: *Hill of the Fir Tree.*
Meall Ailein: *The Beautiful Hill.*
Meall Ard: *The Prominent Hill.*
Meall Bad a'Mhuidhe: *The Hill of the Churn-shaped Thicket.*
Meall Beag: *The Little Hill.*
Meall Dearg: *The Red Mountain.*
Meallon Don: *The Brown Hill.*
Meall Each: *The Hill of the Horse.*
Meall Gorm: *Green Hill.*
Meall Horn: *The Eagle's Hill.*
Meallon Liath Coire Mhic Dhugaill: *The Grey Hill of Dugald's son's Coire.*
Meall Mheadhonach: *The Middle Hill.*
Meall Mheinnidh: *The Grassy Hill; The Solitary Hill.*
Meall nan Aighean: *The Hill of the Hind.*
Meall nan Bradhan: *The Hill of the Swelling (Salmon).*

Meall nan Ceapraichean: *The Hill of the Stumps or little hill tops.*
Meall nan Con: *The Hill of the Dog.*
Meall nan Cra (Crath): *The Hill of the Earthquakes or tremblings.*
Meall nam Peithirean: *The Forester's Hill.*
Meall na Saobhaidhe: *The Hill of the Fox's Den.*
Morven: *The Big Hill.*
MULLACH, M(H)ULLAICH: TOP OR SUMMIT.
Mullach an Rathain: *The Top above the Horns.*
Mullach Coire Mhic Fhearchair: *The Top above son of Farquhar's Coire.*
Mullach an Leathaid Riabhaich: *The Top above the speckled slope.*

Quinag (Cuinnaeg): *The Water Spout (Bucket).*

Ruadh Stac Beag: *Little Red Peak.*
Ruadh Stac Mhor: *Big Red Peak.*

SAIL: HEEL.
Sail Garbh: *The Rough Heel.*
Sail Ghorm: *The Green Heel.*
Sail Liath: *The Grey Heel.*
Sail Mhor: *The Big Heel.*
Saval More: *The Big Barn.*
Saval Beag: *The Little Barn.*
Scaraben
Seana Bhraigh: *The Old Mountain.*
Seana Mheallon: *The Old Round Mill.*
Sgribhis Beinn: *Rocky-sided mountain.*
SGORR, SGURR: A ROCKY PEAK.
Sgurr a'Chadail: *The Peak of Sleep.*
Sgurr Creag an Eich: *Peak of the Horses.*
Sgurr a'Chaorachain: *The Sheep's Peak.*
Sgurr a Gharaidh: *The Peak of the Beast's Lair.*
Sgurr an Fhidhleir: *The Fiddler's Peak.*
Sgurr an Fhir Duibhe: *The Peak of the Black Men.*
Sgurr an Tuill Bhain: *The Peak of the White Waters.*
Sgurr Ban: *The White (Fair) Peak.*
Sgurr Breac: *The Speckled Peak.*
Sgurr Creag an Eich: *The Peak of the Horses.*
Sgurr Dubh: *Black Peak.*

Sgurr Fiona: *Peak of the Wine.*
Sgurr Mhor: *The Great Peak.*
Sgurr na Bana Mhoraire: *The Peak of the wife of Morar.*
Sgurr nan Clach Geala: *The Peak of the White Stone.*
Sgurr nan Each: *The Horse's Peak.*
Sgurr na Laocainn: *Peak of the Little Hero.*
Sgurr Deas: *South Peak.*
Sgurr nan Lochan Uaine: *Peak of the Green Loch.*
Sgurr Ruadh: *Red Peak.*
Sgurr Tuath: *North Peak.*
Sithean Mhor: *The Great Fairy Knoll.*
Slioch: *The Spear.*
Spidean a'Choire Leith: *The Peak of the Grey Coire.*
Spidean Coire an Laoigh: *The Peak of the Calf's Coire.*
Spidean Coire nan Clach: *The Peak of the Stony Coire.*
Spidean nam Fasarinen: *The Peak of the Teeth.*
Sron Garbh: *The Rough Nose.*
Stac Pollaidh: *The Peak of the Peat Moss.*
Stob Cadha Goblach: *The Point of the Forked Pass.*
Strone Nea: *The Nose of the Nest.*
Stuc a'Choire Dhuibh Bhig: *The Peak of the Little Black Coire.*
Stuc Loch na Cabhaig: *The Peak of the Loch of Haste.*
Suilven (Norse): *The Pillar.*

Toll Beag: *The Little Hollow.*
Toll Mhor: *The Big Hollow.*
Tom na Caillich: *The Old Woman's Hillock.*
Tom a'Choinnich: *The Mossy Hillock.*
Tom na Gruagaich: *The Maiden's Hillock.*

Advice to Hill-Walkers

The Association of Scottish Climbing Clubs consider it desirable to give advice to hill-walkers – especially to those with limited knowledge of conditions in Scotland – as an increasing number of people make use of the Scottish mountains in summer and in winter.

The Clubs are constrained to give this advice owing to the accidents in recent years which led to serious injury or death, caused trouble and anxiety to local residents called from their ordinary vocations, and to experienced climbers summoned from long distances to render assistance. Such assistance must not be regarded as always available, and it is only fair and reasonable that local helpers be paid adequately for their assistance.

The Guide books issued by the Scottish Mountaineering Club describe routes which range from difficult climbs to what are in fine weather mere walks. It cannot be stressed too strongly that an expedition, which in fine weather is simple, may cease to be so if the weather becomes bad or mist descends. In winter, conditions on the hills change – what in summer is a walk may become a mountaineering expedition.

In many cases accidents are caused by a combination of events, no one of which singly would have been serious. Ample time should be allowed for expeditions, especially when the route is unknown. Further, before setting out on an expedition, parties should leave information as to their objectives and route and, without exception, have the courage to turn back when prudence so dictates.

In expeditions of any magnitude a party should consist of not less than three members, and they should never separate. If the party is large, two of the experienced members should bring up the rear.

If one member of the party is injured, another member should stay with him with all available food and spare clothing, while the remainder go to secure help. Great care should be taken in marking the spot where the injured man is left. Unless a conspicuous landmark is chosen, for example the junction of two streams, it is difficult to locate the spot, especially if the return is from a different direction or by night.

Some common causes of difficulty are:
Underestimation of time required for expedition.
Slow or untried companions or members who are in poor training.
Illness caused through unwise eating or drinking.
Extreme cold or exhaustion through severe conditions.
Poor, soft snow; steep hard snow; snowstorms; mist.
Change in temperature rapidly converting soft snow into ice – involving step cutting.
Rain making rock slippery or snow filling the holds when rock-climbing.
Frost after snow or rain glazing rocks with ice.
Sudden spates rendering the crossing of burns dangerous or impossible and necessitating long detours.

Hints – Equipment:
All parties should carry:
Simple First Aid equipment, torch, whistle, watch, One-inch Ordnance Survey Map, compass, and be able to use them.

Except in a few spots in Skye where the rocks are magnetic, the compass direction is certain to be correct even if it differs from one's sense of direction.

Ice-axes should be carried if there is any chance of snow or ice, and a rope unless it is certain not to be required.

Clothing: At all times reserve clothing should be carried. Temperatures change rapidly, especially at high levels. Clothing should be warm; in winter a Balaclava helmet and thick woollen gloves should be carried. Well-shod boots should always be worn.

Food: Each member of a party should carry his own food. Climbers will find from experience what kind of food suits their individual need. Normally, jams and sugar are better than meat as more rapidly converted into energy. Most people will find it advisable to avoid alcohol on the hills, but a flask may be carried for emergencies. Light meals at frequent intervals are better than heavy meals at long intervals. In winter it may be advisable to make an early stop for food if shelter is found.

It is essential at all times to respect proprietary and sporting rights, especially during the shooting season, and to avoid disturbing game in deer forests and on grouse moors.

Issued with the authority of:

Scottish Mountaineering Club;
Dundee Rambling Club;
Ladies' Scottish Climbing Club;
Moray Mountaineering Club;
Creagh Dhu Mountaineering Club;
Edinburgh University Mountaineering Club;
Cairngorm Club;
Grampian Club;
Lomond Mountaineering Club;
Junior Mountaineering Club of Scotland;
Etchachan Club.

APPENDIX III

Bibliography

The following selection of books provides a useful source of further information and interesting general reading:

Autumn in Skye, Ross and Sutherland, Ratcliffe Barnett – John Grant, Booksellers Ltd, Edinburgh, 1946.

A Progress in Mountaineering, J. H. B. Bell – Oliver & Boyd, 1950.

Scotland's Western Seaboard, G. Douglas Bolten – Oliver & Boyd, 1953.

Caithness and Sutherland, M. F. Campbell – Cambridge University Press, 1920.

The Crofting Problem, Adam Collier – Cambridge University Press, 1953.

Corriemulzie Mountaineering Club – *Rock and Ice Guide to Easter Ross and Foinaven Supplement,* 1966.

Inverewe – A Garden in the North West Highlands, May Cowan – Bles, 1964.

The Highlands and Islands, F. Fraser Darling and J. Morton Boyd – Fontana New Naturalist Series, 1969.

Pre-historic Scotland, Richard Feacham – B. T. Batsford, London, 1963.

Scotland, Ian Finlay – Chatto & Windus, 1957.

Western Highlands, Arthur Gardner – Batsford, 1947.

Highways and Byeways in the West Highlands, Seton Gordon – Macmillan, 1955.

The Trial of Patrick Sellar – The Tragedy of the Highland Evictions, Ian Grimble – Routledge & Kegan Paul, 1962.

Sutherland and the Reay Country, Rev. A. Gunn, M.A., and John Mackay – Glasgow, 1897 (Out of Print).

Highland River, Neil Gunn – Faber & Faber.

The Drove Roads of Scotland, A. R. S. Haldane – Nelson, 1952.

Prophecies of the Brahan Seer – Eneas Mackay (Stirling), 1957.

Mackay's Regiment, John Mackay – W. Blackwood.

A History of Scotland, Prof. J. D. Mackie – Penguin Books Ltd, 1969.

A Short History of Scotland, Robert L. Mackie – Oxford University Press, 1930.

Torridon Highlands, Brenda G. Macrow – Robert Hale, 1969 (Reprinted).

A History of the Highland Clearances, A. Mackenzie – Maclaren & Sons, Glasgow, 1st edn., 1883, 2nd edn., 1946.

A Hundred Years in the Highlands, Osgood Mackenzie – Bles, 1965 (Reprinted).

The Roads from the Isles, D. D. C. Pochin Mould – Oliver & Boyd, 1950.

In Scotland Again, H. V. Morton – Methuen, 1933, 1952 (Reprinted).

Undiscovered Scotland, W. H. Murray, 1951 – Dent.

Highland Landscape, W. H. Murray – National Trust for Scotland, 1962.

Companion Guide to the West Highlands of Scotland, W. H. Murray – Collins, 1968.

The Highlands and Islands of Scotland, A. C. O'Dell, and K. Walton – Thos. Nelson & Sons Ltd, 1963.

The Highland Clearances, John Prebble – Penguin Books, 1969.

Where to Climb in the British Isles, E. C. Pyatt – Faber, 1960.

The Highlands and Their Legends, Otto F. Swire – Oliver & Boyd, 1963.

The Northern Highlands, 1967 Edition – The S.Y.H.A., 7 Glebe Crescent, Stirling.

The S.Y.H.A. Annual Hand-Book, The S.Y.H.A., 7 Glebe Crescent, Stirling.

The Future of the Highlands, D. C. Thomson and I. Grimble, 1968 – Routledge & Kegan Paul.

On Hills of the North, Walker, 1940 – Oliver & Boyd.

Highland Days, Tom Weir – Cassell, 1948.

Rocks and Minerals, Zim and Shaffer – Paul Hamlyn, London.

H.M.S.O. Publications

Place Names on Map of Scotland and Wales by Director General, Ordnance Survey, Southampton.

Mountain Rescue – 1968.

Training Handbook for R.A.F. Mountain Rescue Team.

British Regional Geology – Scotland: The Northern Highlands (3rd Edition), J. Phimister, M.A., D.SC.

The Geological Structure of the North-West Highlands of Scotland, B. N. Peach and J. Horne, 1947.

Guide to the Geological Model of the Assynt Mountains, B. N. Peach and J. Horne, 1914.

The Old Statistical Account of Scotland (1791–99), giving accounts by Parishes written by the Parish Ministers.

The New Statistical Account of Scotland (1845), also by Parishes.

Scottish Mountaineering Trust

The Northern Highlands District Guide (2nd Edition), 1936 – W. N. Ling and J. Rooke Corbett.

The Northern Highlands District Guide (3rd Edition), 1953 – E. W. Hodge.

Munro's Tables and other Tables of Lesser Heights – Revised Edition, 1969 – J. L. Donaldson and W. L. Coats.

Northern Highlands Rock Guide (6 volumes), 1969–72.

Scottish Mountaineering Club Journals, Vols. XXIV (1948) – *Vol. XXIX* (1968).

APPENDIX IV

Estates

The following list indicates the principal landowners within the area of the text and where possible the name and address of the estate factor is given in the hope that it may prove of assistance.

CHAPTER 1
APPLECROSS – Wills' Estate
Factor: Bingham, Hughes & Macpherson, 6 Queensgate, Inverness.
Estate Office – Applecross 209.
SHIELDAIG – A. C. Greg (*Tel. No.* Kinloch 221)
Factors: Anderson, Shaw & Gilbert, Inverness.
COULDORAN – The Misses J. & S. Huntsman, Couldoron, Strathcarron (*Tel. No.* Kishorn 227)
Enquiries direct.

CHAPTER 2
SHIELDAIG – A. C. Greg (*Tel. No.* Kinloch 221)
Factors: Anderson, Shaw & Gilbert, Inverness.
NEW KELSO – Bruce Reid
Factor: Angus Macdonald, Conon Bank.
BEN DAMPH – Torridon Hotel (*Tel. No.* Torridon 242)
Enquiries direct.
ACHNASHELLACH – Forestry Commission and Wills' Estate
COULIN – Wills' Estate
LEDGOWAN – G. E. Ruggles Brise (*Tel. No.* Achnasheen 205)
Factor: Bingham, Hughes & Macpherson, 6 Queensgate, Inverness.

CHAPTER 3
Nature Conservancy, 12 Hope Terrace, Edinburgh.

The National Trust for Scotland, 5 Charlotte Square, Edinburgh, 2.
GAIRLOCH and CONON ESTATE – Flowerdale
    Factor: J. A. McIntyre, Fairburn Estate Office, Muir of Ord
    (*Tel. No.* Urray 203)

CHAPTER 4
FISHERFIELD and LETTEREWE – Col. Whitbread, Kin-
lochewe Lodge (*Tel. No.* Kinlochewe 200)
    Manager's House – Kinlochewe 217
    Factors: Bingham, Hughes & Macpherson, 6 Queensgate,
    Inverness.
STRATHNASHELLAG – The Lady McCorquodale, Cotswold
Park, Cirencester, Glos.
    Manager's House – Gruinard Laide (*Tel. No.* Aultbea 240)

CHAPTER 5
FANNICH – T. W. Sandeman, Fannich Lodge, Lochluichart
(*Tel. No.* Garve 227)
    Factors: Bingham, Hughes & Macpherson, 6 Queensgate,
    Inverness.
LOCHLUICHART – The Rt Hon. Spencer, Loch Aultdearg
House, Lochluichart
    Manager's Residence – Forest Hill, Lochluichart (*Tel. No.*
    Garve 228)

CHAPTER 6
LOWER WYVIS ESTATE – Col. Vickers
    Factors: Duncan & Duncan, Solicitors, Inverness.
WYVIS ESTATE – The Rt Hon. Viscount Mountgarret
    Factor: at Estate Office, Nidd.
KILDERMORIE ESTATE – Lt-Col. D. Hignett, Kildermorie
Lodge (*Tel. No.* Alness 240)
or East Langton Grange, Market Harborough, Leics.
GLENCALVIE – Mr Hickley, The Craigs, by Ardgay (*Tel. No.*
The Craigs 323)

CHAPTER 7
STRATH VAICH and STRATH RANNOCH – R. Williams, Strathvaich House, Garve (*Tel. No.* Aultguish 226)

BRAEMORE – Lt-Col. P. C. Mitford, Entrance Lodge, Braemore (*Tel. No.* Lochbroom 222)

FAICH – Col. St George, Faich Lodge, Ullapool (*Tel. No.* Lochbroom 203)

LOCH BROOM – L. W. Rolson, 4 Cofthall Avenue, London, S.E.2

EAST RHIDDOROCH – Van Veen, Rekhemseng 129 Doetuichem, Holland. Rhiddoroch Old Lodge (*Tel. No.* Ullapool 65)

WEST RHIDDOROCH – Major I. Scobie, Coulmore Estate Office, North Kessock (*Tel. No.* Kessock 212)

BEN MORE ESTATES – Miss Godman
    Factor: Mr N. Graham Campbell, Estate Office, Ardgay (*Tel. No.* Ardgay 366)

LANGWELL ESTATE – A. W. Fenwick, Langwell Lodge, Ullapool (*Tel. No.* Strathkanaird 201)

CHAPTER 8
STRATHKANAIRD – Commander C. G. Vyner, Keanchulish, Ullapool (*Tel. No.* Ullapool 100)

ASSYNT ESTATE – Mr E. H. Vestey, Estate Office, Lochinver (*Tel. No.* Lochinver 203)

CHAPTER 9
ASSYNT ESTATE – Mr E. H. Vestey, Estate Office, Lochinver
BEN MORE ESTATES – Miss Godman
    Factor: Mr N. Graham Campbell, Estate Office, Ardgay.

LOCH ASSYNT (QUINAG) – W. P. Philmore Sankey
    Enquiries direct to Loch Assynt Lodge.

CHAPTER 10
SCOURIE ESTATE – Mr & Mrs J. C. Balfour
    Factor: Bell, Strutt & Parker, Elgin

KYLESTROME – Lady Mary Grosvenor
    Factored by Westminster Estate Office, Achfary (*Tel. No.* Lochmore 201)

WESTMINSTER ESTATE – Duchess of Westminster

Tel. Nos.

Estate Office	(Lochmore 201)
Factor's House	(Scourie 212)
Keeper's House Ardchuillen (Mr Scobie)	(Lochmore 203)
Head Stalker	(Lochmore 209)
Gobernuisgach Lodge	(Altnaharra 247)

GUALIN ESTATE – Mrs Ferguson
Factor: Renton, Finlayson & Co., Aberfeldy.

MERKLAND ESTATES – Mrs Garton, Merkland Lodge
Factor: W. Urquhart, Solicitor, Golspie (*Tel. No.* Golspie 214)

ERRIBOL ESTATE – Trustees of late John Elliot
Factor: Shepherd & Wedderburn, W.S., 16 Charlotte Square, Edinburgh, 2.

CHAPTER 11

TONGUE ESTATE – Lt-Col. Moncrieff, Kinloch Lodge
Factors: Condie, Mackay & Co., Perth
or Enquiries direct to Minmonth, Rhynd, Perthshire.

CHAPTER 12

ACHINTOUL and BERRIEDALE – Duke of Portland
Factor: M. R. M. Leslie, Portland Estate Office, Berriedale, Caithness.

BEN ARMINE ESTATE – Countess of Sutherland
Factor: J. L. Scott, Estate Office, Golspie (*Tel. No.* Golspie 265)

SUTHERLAND ESTATES – Countess of Sutherland
Factor: J. L. Scott, Estate Office, Golspie (*Tel. No.* Golspie 265)

KLIBRECK ESTATE – Captain M. R. Kimball, M.P., Altnaharra Lodge
Factor: W. M. Urquhart, Solicitor, Golspie (*Tel. No.* Golspie 214)

FORESTRY COMMISSION –
Conservancy Office, 60 Church Street, Inverness (*Tel. No.* Inverness 32811)
Achnashellach Forest (*Tel. No.* Achnashellach 273)
Lael Forest (*Tel. No.* Lochbroom 206)
Oykel Forest (*Tel. No.* Rosehall 236)
Shin Forest (*Tel. No.* Lairg 75)
Slattadale Forest (*Tel. No.* Loch Maree 203)

INDEX